ACROSS THE WORLDS OF ISLAM

ACROSS THE WORLDS OF ISLAM

MUSLIM IDENTITIES, BELIEFS, AND PRACTICES FROM ASIA TO AMERICA

EDITED BY

EDWARD E. CURTIS IV

Columbia University Press *New York*

Columbia University Press
Publishers Since 1893
New York   Chichester, West Sussex
cup.columbia.edu
Copyright © 2023 Columbia University Press
All rights reserved

Library of Congress Cataloging-in-Publication Data
Names: Curtis, Edward E., IV, 1970– editor.
Title: Across the worlds of Islam : Muslim identities, beliefs,
and practices from Asia to America / Edward E. Curtis IV, editor.
Description: New York : Columbia University Press, 2023. |
Includes bibliographical references and index.
Identifiers: LCCN 2022050919 (print) | LCCN 2022050920 (ebook) |
ISBN 9780231210645 (hardback) | ISBN 9780231210652 (trade paperback) |
ISBN 9780231558525 (ebook)
Subjects: LCSH: Islamic sociology. | Islamic sects. | Minorities—Islamic
countries—Social conditions. | Minorities—Religious aspects—Islam.
Classification: LCC BP173.25 .A338 2023 (print) | LCC BP173.25 (ebook) |
DDC 297.8—dc23/eng/20221027
LC record available at https://lccn.loc.gov/2022050919
LC ebook record available at https://lccn.loc.gov/2022050920

Cover image: Topkapi Palace Museum, Istanbul,
Turkey / Bridgeman Images

CONTENTS

Introduction 1
EDWARD E. CURTIS IV

1 Islam and Its Others: Ambivalent Orientations
Toward the Margins of Islam 15
FARAH BAKAARI

2 Rethinking the Center: Margins and
Multiplicity in Hadith Texts 45
MICHAEL MUHAMMAD KNIGHT

3 Islamic Tattooing: Embodying Healing, Materializing
Relationships, and Mediating Tradition 67
MAX JOHNSON DUGAN

4 Lover's Words Are Eternal: Alevi Ashik Poetry
Beyond the Margins 99
TESS M. WAGGONER

5 On the Margins of Islamic Doctrine, at the Heart
of Islamic Ethics: Elijah Muhammad's Nation of
Islam and Black Liberation 135
EDWARD E. CURTIS IV

6 Love and Care at the Margins of Future Generations 161
HOLLY DONAHUE SINGH

7 Writing Mongol History on the Margins: Sufi and Kinship Connectivity in the *Tarikh-i Rashidi* 193
HENRY D. BRILL

8 Journey to the Teaching of Islam 223
KATHRYN D. BLANCHARD

Conclusion: Let the Margins Be the Center 249
VERNON JAMES SCHUBEL

Contributors 285
Acknowledgments 287
Index 289

ACROSS
THE WORLDS OF
ISLAM

INTRODUCTION

EDWARD E. CURTIS IV

What happens if we put Muslims who are socially, culturally, theologically, and politically marginalized at the center of our understanding of Islam and Muslim communities? Instead of thinking of the marginalized as a problem, what if we unapologetically embrace them? This edited volume of essays explores Islamic religion and Muslim life by focusing our attention on Islamic practices and ideas as well as Muslim groups that are sometimes seen to be questionable—or just plain wrong—by some other Muslims and non-Muslims, too. The book does not favor the margins over the center, although there is a lot of solidarity expressed in its pages for those Muslims who have been marginalized. Instead, it insists that by paying attention to the margins of Islam, we learn a much more inclusive and accurate version of the religion and its many interrelated communities. This book also does more than defend Muslims against Islamophobia or gesture toward theological, social, and political inclusivity. In our rendering, the margin of Islam disappears as we begin to see values, stories, and aesthetics that characterize Muslim life across sectarian and other forms of division.

Written with students and general readers in mind, this book offers an alternative to most introductions to Islamic religion and Muslim people. On the Internet, and in many media outlets and college textbooks, Islam is often summed up in a nutshell, a digestible sound bite—what some have called "pamphlet Islam." Sidebars on the "five pillars of Islam" boil down the essence of Islam to Muslim beliefs in God and the prophecy of Muhammad, daily prayer, pilgrimage to Mecca, fasting during the month of Ramadan, and alms for the poor. Unsuspecting consumers of such media may not be aware that some Muslim groups have more than five pillars, or that, for many Muslims, the five pillars (*arkan al-islam*) are not actually the heart of Islam.

But we also recognize that beginners have to start somewhere. It is generally necessary to construct before we complicate or deconstruct. Human beings often yearn for clarity and concision. The problem with the five pillars approach is not primarily its brevity; it is that the thumbnail takes sides in long-running Islamic theological and legal debates and, in so doing, falsely summarizes what Islam represents to all Muslims. There is nothing wrong with generalizing; the challenge occurs when we fail to do so accurately and imaginatively. What we argue instead is that there are ways to talk about shared traditions in Islam that are more inclusive *and* more accurate at the same time. Drawing boundaries around what is and what is not Muslim becomes less important than searching for elements that, no matter their differences, Muslim embrace or argue over. In these pages, for example, it is clear that the Qur'an, the Word of God, may not always be understood, studied, used, symbolized, and copied in the same way, but it is hard to find Muslim communities where the Qur'an is irrelevant or unimportant. The same goes for the Prophet Muhammad.

The dogged persistence held by some that theology—people's beliefs about God—is the first and last thing that one should learn about a religion can be too costly. It deprives us of too much knowledge, understanding, and empathy. It stigmatizes those who may share a deep history with the community, but occupy a more marginalized theological position. In this volume, there is instead an emphasis on humanistic Islamic values that are shared by Muslim communities who may disagree with one another about doctrine. For example, for many Muslims, they can't be Muslim unless they love justice and beauty; since God is both just and beautiful, all of God's creation should embody and mirror justice and beauty. In this volume we see how Islamic values materialize in Muslim rituals, communal gatherings, life passages, poetry, soundscapes, diet, and fashion; there is a special focus on how Muslim express their religious identities in the way they care for, train, and beautify their own bodies. Rather than focus only on bookish theology, this book considers a wider range of human activity as worthy of our study.

There is, we admit, a danger in our focus on margins. By calling out some people, ideas, rituals, and practices as "marginal," we might add to their marginalization. "See," a critic might say, "even their supporters call them marginal to Islam." There is a beautiful discomfort expressed in some of this book's pages with the whole idea of identifying some Muslims as marginal or marginalized. Making room for our own ambivalence and hesitation—even at the risk of confusing the reader, or making ourselves vulnerable to accusations of inconsistency—has been an important act of embracing the very diversity of thought that we advocate. Though concerned about the potential downsides of our approach, we believe, on the whole, that it is important to identify the marginalization that some Muslim communities and individuals face from non-Muslims and other Muslims. Only if we name their oppression can we hope to transcend or address it in in our understanding of what it means to be Muslim. Ignoring such marginalization makes us complicit with the oppression that sometimes accompanies it.

Our point, to be clear, is not to condemn the whole idea of doctrinal disagreements. It is normal and expected that people who are part of a religious community will disagree with one another about important questions like the nature of the universe, the supernatural, and the meaning of life. Debate is often part of the vitality of any community. But it is another thing to hurt those with whom you disagree because of their cosmological or theological orientations. When doctrine or ideology enters public life in this way, it can have terrible consequences for human solidarity and social cohesion. Excluding a rival religious group from a community—whether done in the name of God or not—means that certain groups no longer have equal status in a community; they become strangers, outcasts, heretics, cultists, and so on. Our understanding of Islam and Muslims instead reflects the fact that there are contests among Muslims about Islamic beliefs and practices, but is clear in its hope that doctrinal and other disagreements do not lead to prejudice and violence.

Loving the Margins of Islam explores the geographic, social, political, cultural, and doctrinal margins of the world of Islam. By seeing Muslim identity and practice from the perspective of the marginalized, readers come to understand how regions beyond the Middle East, including Central Asia, South Asia, and North America, are central to the past, present, and future of Islamic religion and Muslim people. Including Muslim communities, practices, and people beyond the doctrinal boundaries of modern Sunni Islam—sometimes called "orthodox" Islam—as part of our vision renders a more encompassing and accurate view of what Islam is and what Muslims do. We also consider the role of non-Muslims in furthering and challenging the marginalization of minoritized Muslims. Finally, we signal the linguistic diversity of Muslims by using a number of foreign words, not just from Arabic, but from Turkish, Persian, and Urdu as well. Certain Islamic terms are shared by Muslims, but such terms are not always spelled in in the same way. What's important is that reader understands the basic meaning of a term, and so, in each chapter, we offer translations of these words, unless they have become common in English—like the word "Qur'an." Overall, the volume gives readers the chance to think about controversial topics in Islam without having to side either with anti-Muslim critics or academic apologists for a singular vision of Islam. Instead, one is able to develop a view of Islam and Muslims in which commonalities across opposing viewpoints can be discovered and even embraced as an example of human solidarity.

THE SCHOLARLY BACKGROUND

Nonacademic and student readers are sometimes less interested in the scholarly debates that undergird a book's purposes than professional scholars, but it is important for us to name the reasons why we believe loving the margins of Islam is important. The fact that certain Islamic ideas, figures, and texts are studied more often than others is not only a product of an individual scholar's preferences but also a consequence of our historical moment. In the wake of 9/11, the resources available for the professional study of Islam and Muslims, especially in the United States, dramatically increased. The number of academic positions, books and journals, foundation and government grants, and undergraduate enrollments changed the nature of the study of Islam and Muslims in the Anglophone world; the demand for scholars of Islam actually outpaced the supply of those in the graduate school pipeline.[1] This new popularity of the academic study of Islam and Muslims had profound consequences for the direction of the field. As university administrators, funders, and scholars unfamiliar with Islam became decision makers about hiring and grant-making, stereotypes about Islam long abandoned by the relatively smaller number of specialists in Islam and Muslim studies became regnant again.

Take, for example, the centrality of the Arabic language to the study of Islam and Muslims. During the second half of the twentieth century, scholars of Islam and Muslims challenged their own Orientalist roots and went beyond them. Instead of focusing solely on Arabic texts, they conducted pioneering ethnographic and philological research that centered the experiences and significance of non-Arab Muslims. This reorientation reflected the fact that, despite the importance of Arabic, the vast majority of Muslims do not read or speak Arabic as a native language, and Muslim cultures have used other languages in Islamic scholarship and Muslim culture-making. Studies in Persian language, which became a dominant literary and court language during the Middle Ages, proliferated, and many scholars wrote about Sufism rather than focusing on Islamic scriptures or Islamic law and ethics, all written in Arabic.[2] In the field of cultural anthropology, scholars such as Clifford Geertz and then later Talal Asad and Saba Mahmoud not only contributed to the study of Islam but were also deeply influential in the social sciences and humanities more generally.[3] A critique of Orientalism, or the study of Islamic texts, generally in Arabic, was made famous in the 1970s by literary scholar Edward Said, but, long before, there were towering figures in the field of Islamic studies, including the Islamicist Marshall Hodgson at the University of Chicago, who had already gone beyond the centrality of Arabic texts to understand the history of Muslims. The generation of scholars who were training graduate students and influencing the field in 1990s—among them Carl Ernst, Bruce Lawrence, and Marilyn Waldman Robinson—insisted that philology was not a sufficient method for Islamic studies; they demanded that colleagues incorporate history, comparative religion, literary theory, social theory, and other disciplinary perspectives in their approaches.

However, after 9/11, scholarly attention to Islamic texts written in Arabic came roaring back.[4] It was animated by the assumption of many higher education administrators and hiring committees that the heart of Islam and of Muslim experience could be found in reading the Qur'an, the hadith (the reports of the sayings and deeds the Prophet Muhammad and his companions), and scholarly interpretations of both. Without a doubt, this belief was a tenable intellectual position, especially if one adopted a modern, scriptural approach to religion. Many Muslim scholars of Islam, especially those who chose to focus on the Qur'an and sharia, or law and ethics, maintained the position that they were studying the norms set out in the Islamic tradition itself. Moreover, some of the scholarship produced in this resurgent era for Orientalism—that is, the study of sacred texts and their interpretation—was diverse, vibrant, and original. Some of these approaches insisted on readings of texts that challenged homophobia, sexism, racism, and other forms of oppression.[5]

But, as a consequence of this renaissance for Orientalism, both popular and scholarly interpretations of Islam reflected older, more textual—one might even say more Protestant— understandings of Islam. Scholars of Arabic were often the ones who benefited from the new jobs, although this factor alone did not explain the feelings of marginalization increasingly felt by scholars who did not focus on the Qur'an, Islamic law, or Arabic. The new Orientalism was also accompanied in some places (for example, in the American Academy of Religion) by an emphasis on normative Islamic practice. The reaction to the rise of normativity as a subject for scholarly inquiry had a number of repercussions. Some scholars left the AAR for the Middle East Studies Association, where they felt they could adopt a more critical stance toward Islamic traditions. Other scholars embraced the study of doctrinal heterodoxy as a form of protest or sought to defend those Muslims accused of heresy against limited and limiting visions of Islam.[6]

There was also an approach that stubbornly refused to cede the intellectual territory of normativity to Orientalists who wrote about the Qur'an, the Sunna, and Islamic jurisprudence. Its dominant idea was that there were and are (contested) norms and ideals in Islam, but these existed as much in Muslim material cultures, practice, rituals, vernacular poetry, institutions, social structures, experience, and feelings as in sacred texts. For these scholars, to become an expert on Islam meant much more than becoming a scholar of the Qur'an and hadith or Islamic theology and law. One also had to become a student of Muslim cultures so that, as Shahab Ahmed argued in *What Is Islam?*, a scholar could analyze Islamic contexts and pretexts as much as texts.[7] Once a scholar's perspective shifts from observing Islam mainly from the perspective of theological, doctrinal, and legal discourses of a certain class of Islamic scholars to those of the lived realities of all Muslims, whether scholars or not, one can then identify norms and ideals that, sometimes contrary to doctrine, cut across binaries such as Sunni/Shi'a, poor/rich, men/women, orthodox/heretic. Examples of this approach could be found in the scholarship of Vernon Schubel, whose work has influenced many of this volume's contributors. Schubel has revealed that in the cases of Pakistani Twelver Shiʻa Muslims and Turkish Alevis, both communities engaged many of the same figures, stories, themes, and emotions at the heart of the same Islamic tradition claimed by advocates of Sunni Muslim normativity. His research demonstrates that there were shared elements that went far beyond the pillars of Islamic practice and faith, including humanistic values such as compassion, justice, and wonder.[8]

THE CHAPTERS

Similarly, this book approaches Islam from the perspective that its traditions, texts included, can never be divorced from the people who produce, interpret, use, and value them. Taking this idea as our point of entry, this volume begins with an autobiographical account of Muslim marginalization. Farah Bakaari's prolegomenon asks an essential question about the nature of our collective intellectual pursuit. Speaking directly from her experience as a Black, African, and Muslim woman, Bakaari questions whether and to what extent it is possible to think and write about Islam beyond the constraints of Islamophobia and the other prejudices that have defined her life as both a Muslim and a scholar. Using the theories of Franz Fanon, Edward Said, amina wadud, and others, she narrates her quest to avoid imagining herself through the mirror of the non-Muslim who dislikes her, is afraid of her, or wants to save her. Will her own naming of Muslims marginalized by other Muslims be used to further oppress Muslim communities, she asks? The chapter makes us pause to consider how the political marginalization of both Islam and Muslims shapes the possibility of what and how we know anything about our subject matter.

If Bakaari's chapter meditates on the pressures of neocolonialism and imperial knowledge on the Muslim subject, chapter 2 by Michael Muhammad Knight tackles a different form of marginalizing hegemony. His analysis of hadith, Islam's "second" holy scripture, reveals how the most reliable, authoritative, and important reports about the sayings and deeds of Muhammad express substantively divergent views of the Messenger of God. He argues that diverse but still authoritative voices have been canonized in Islam (i.e., they are part and parcel of the tradition) and that this fact demands a humbler approach toward the diversity of interpretation and practice among Muslims. The chapter is a rejoinder to those who claim that the hadith produce a singular, coherent narrative of the Prophet Muhammad's life. Instead, we see how the possibility of the margin—namely, a view of the Prophet that diverges from the majority—is "baked in" to Islam's scriptures.

In chapter 3, Max Johnson Dugan explores some of the consequences of a singular reading of Islamic scriptures by taking up the phenomenon of Muslim tattooing. As Dugan points out, authoritative interpretations of Islam's scriptures have determined that tattoos are un-Islamic. And yet tattooing has been and continues to be an important cultural, and sometimes religious, practice among Muslims. Focusing on contemporary Muslims who see tattoos as an expression of their Islamic identity, this chapter explores bodily practices that are on the margins of Islam. Dugan shows how contemporary practices of tattooing resonate with the Islamic past while challenging or transforming some traditional prohibitions against tattoos in Islam. Rather than explicating Islamic tattooing in terms of Islamic law, Dugan shows that this aesthetic practice is not only a form of power-making that Muslims assert over their own bodies but is also art: the making of a Muslim body that projects meaning concerning the person's gender and other identities.

Chapter 4 by Tess M. Waggoner analyzes an entire Muslim community whose beliefs and practices are often seen as misguided, if not heretical, by many other Muslims. Her account of Alevi Muslim ashiks, or teacher-poets, in contemporary Turkey tracks the way Turkish nationalism and the state's support of one authoritative interpretation of Sunni Islam has marginalized Alevi Muslims. Waggoner reveals the categories of marginalization that were sometimes adopted and adapted by Alevi themselves, while charting how Alevi insist that they occupy the heart of the Islamic tradition. Challenging ideas about the decline of Alevi Islam, she explores how poetry and its performance in multiple venues keeps the tradition of the ashik alive. Waggoner concludes with original translations of poems to show how Alevi Muslims resist state repression and vigilante violence and claim the mantle of the Prophet Muhammad and his family for the Alevi.

Edward Curtis's analysis of Elijah Muhammad's Nation of Islam in chapter 5 examines a Muslim community whose doctrines have similarly been rejected by other Muslims as un-Islamic. Curtis outlines some of the differences between most Muslim traditions and the theologies, doctrines, and mythologies of the Nation of Islam, explaining their meaning and significance in the context of twentieth-century U.S. Black history. Curtis emphasizes how Nation of Islam members embraced their status on the margins of Islamic doctrine while supporting an Islamic ethos that characterized most of African American Islam. Whether African American Muslims identified as "orthodox" or not, most shared the belief that, at its heart, Islam was a religious tradition of Black liberation. In the second half of the chapter, Curtis shows how the embodied rituals and practices of the Nation of Islam, like the practices of tattooing that Max Johnson Dugan examines, actualizes the belief that Muslim bodies are beautiful, and, in the case of the Nation of Islam, strong and free.

In chapter 6, Holly Donahue Singh explores the embodied marginalization of Muslim people, but does so from the perspective of an anthropologist who conducts ethnographic research with Muslim women in India. She focuses on their decision-making about reproduction. Her chapter is not a liberal attempt to save Muslim women from a lack of reproductive choices—a theme that Bakaari introduces in the first chapter of the book—but is an account, like Bakaari's, of how the minoritization of Muslims affects the possibility of Muslim flourishing. For Indian Muslims, the very act of giving birth in a country where having *Muslim* children is stigmatized raises life and death questions about the future of Muslim well-being. Singh shows how the political and social marginalization of reproduction among minoritized populations constrains and challenges a vision for shared global futures both in India and beyond.

In chapter 7, Henry D. Brill, too, casts a light on a form of political marginalization among Muslim communities. He focuses on an individual: taking us to sixteenth-century Central Asia, he unearths the story of Moghul historian Mirza Muhammad Haydar Dughlat (d.1551). Showing how and why Dughlat was exiled from court, Brill analyzes how the historian's attempts to write himself and his family back into power. This history of the Turko-Mongols emphasized his own connections to Sufism and the importance of his Muslim kinship networks. Dughlat thus used appeals to spiritual and genealogical authority to restore his rightful place at the center of Muslim power.

Chapters 1 through 7 consider the margins of Islamic religion and the marginalization of Muslims in both the past and present. Chapter 8 by Kathryn D. Blanchard considers a different marginal position: that of a non-Muslim teaching about Islam and Muslims. Blanchard offers a memoir of how the study of Islam affected her as an evangelical Christian undergraduate and challenged her further to consider a question of pedagogical, ethical, and epistemological importance when she became a religion professor: How was she supposed to teach about Islam as an outsider? Blanchard reflects on her attempts to teach diverse Muslim voices in ways that resonate with her largely white, Christian students at a Midwestern liberal arts college, and she trumpets the importance of humility and honesty about one's own social position and baggage when teaching about any religion, including Islam. As an anonymous reviewer of this book pointed out, Blanchard "demonstrates the dynamic nature of marginal identities, and who and what is marginal is contextual."

Responding to each of the chapters in the volume, Vernon Schubel's conclusion outlines an approach to teaching about Islam that eliminates the dichotomy between the center and margin. He first traces his own intellectual genealogy from Oklahoma and Virginia to South Asia and Central Asia, crediting the influence of his teachers, most of whom were neither Arab nor Sunni, in leading him to see an Islam beyond the orthodoxy/heterodoxy binary. Alluding to his decades of classroom experience as well as the insights of this volume's chapters, Schubel explains the importance of understanding Islam and Muslims from the perspective of a student of the humanities rather than exclusively as an Islamic studies specialist. As a teacher of the liberal arts, Schubel models a pedagogy of inclusion that relies on multiple humanistic traditions and theories to show how Islam is part of a shared global heritage.

NOTES

1. Edward E. Curtis IV, "The Perils of Public Scholarship About Islam," *Practical Matters*, no. 5 (August 2012): 5–7.
2. Rosemary R. Hicks, "Comparative Religion and the Cold War Transformation of Indo-Persian 'Mysticism' Into Liberal Islamic Modernity," in *Secularism and Religion-Making*, ed. Markus Dressler and Arvind-Pal S. Mandair (New York: Oxford University Press, 2011), 141–68.
3. Clifford Geertz, *The Interpretation of Cultures* (New York: Basic Books, 1973); Talal Asad, *Genealogies of Religion: Discipline and Reasons of Power in Christianity and Islam* (Baltimore: Johns Hopkins University Press, 1993); Saba Mahmoud, *The Politics of Piety: The Islamic Revival and the Feminist Subject* (Princeton, N.J.: Princeton University Press, 2011).
4. Ilyse Morgenstein Fuerst, "Job Ads Don't Add Up: Arabic + Middle East + Texts ≠ Islam," *Journal of the American Academy of Religion* 88, no. 4 (December 2020): 915–46.
5. See, for example, Kecia Ali, *Sexual Ethics and Islam* (Oxford: Oneworld, 2006).
6. My book, *Black Muslim Religion in the Nation of Islam, 1960–1975* (Chapel Hill: University of North Carolina Press, 2006), utilized newer theories of Islamization to explain how it was fruitful to analyze Black Muslims as "real" Muslims.
7. Shahab Ahmed, *What Is Islam? The Importance of Being Islamic* (Princeton, N.J.: Princeton University Press, 2015).
8. Vernon Schubel, *Religious Performance in Contemporary Islam: Shi'i Devotional Rituals in South Asia* (Columbia: University of South Carolina Press, 1993), Vernon Schubel, "When the Prophet Went on the *Mirac* He Saw a Lion On the Road: The *Mirac* in the Alevi-Bektaşi Tradition," in *The Prophet Muhammad's Ascension: New Cross-Cultural Encounters*, ed. Frederick Colby and Christiane Gruber (Bloomington: Indiana University Press, 2010), 330–43.

1

ISLAM AND ITS OTHERS

Ambivalent Orientations Toward

the Margins of Islam

FARAH BAKAARI

In *Black Skin, White Masks*, Frantz Fanon meditates on the alienating effects of the white gaze. "Look, a Negro!" yells the white child to his mother, frightened and amused, the child only vocalizing the already ongoing racial scenario in which the Black person finds himself.[1] Fanon sees himself become a body, a Black body, a public body. This gaze of the Other, this Othering gaze, threatens to fracture him, reduce him to a mere representation, a form. "It was a question of being aware of my body," he laments, "no longer in the third person but in triple."[2] Fanon's explanation of the "triple person" reminds us of W. E. B. Du Bois's double consciousness, which he defined as "the sense of always looking at one's self through the eyes of others, of measuring one's soul by the tape of a world that looks on in amused contempt and pity."[3] I first came to Fanon's lived experience of the Black man, or "fact of blackness," as it sometimes translated—not as a Black person (though I would soon come to appreciate it as such), but as a Muslim woman, living, working, and being educated in predominately white secular institutions. I could sense, on a daily basis, how others saw and digested me, not as an individual but as a version of an idea, as an archive, to borrow Edward Said's characterization of Orientalism.[4] But what does it mean to encounter oneself as an idea, an image constructed from this archive? For years, this question—or, rather, the task inscribed within it—paralyzed me. And so, terrified to disintegrate in front of it, I vowed to outrun it.

One of the primary ways I tried to outrun this deidealizing image was by working diligently, though not always consciously or successfully, to never take up Islam in my intellectual and public life. For instance, I went through college without taking a single religious studies course, despite reading fervently on the subject and later working as a research assistant on a project about Muslim American public life. I wore the hijab back then and had a smashing accent; I simply couldn't bring myself to be present while others intellectually processed an imaginative rendering of me, a representation to which, by virtue of my presence, I would be frequently compared. So, the occasional acquiescence notwithstanding (I agreed to appear on a community panel and published a brief reflection on the Muslim ban as well as colead the effort to restore the praying space for Muslim students on my college campus), I declined to write about, publicly reflect on, or "speak to" the contested condition of "being Muslim"—or, worse, "Muslim woman." Said describes his groundbreaking text *Orientalism* as "an attempt to inventory the traces upon me, the Oriental subject, of the culture whose domination has been so powerful a factor in the life of all Orientals."[5] I knew that writing about Islam and what it means to be a Muslim in the West would induce a similar kind of reckoning and prompt me to take inventory of my own traces. I would need to account for the profound hold the gaze of the Other, the specter of the archive, has had on my psyche. I would need to name the various intellectual chokeholds they impose and face the dwarfing of my own imagination.

In what follows I meditate on what it means to be on the religio-cultural margins of U.S. society and the struggle to ethically respond to such marginalization without being limited by it. More specifically, I ask: How does awareness of the marginality of one's community affect how one recognizes and relates to the margins within that community? What happens when one can only articulate life from the margins? I will argue that the acute awareness of the prolific deidealized images about Muslims and their communities makes it virtually impossible—or, at least, undesirable—for individual Muslims, especially those residing in the West, to stake a claim or champion the margins of Islam. The imperative of always speaking to the non-Muslim in an Islamophobic society disciplines our imagination in a way that prevents us from acknowledging and embracing the margins of and in Muslim communities.

Shortly after I began working on my contribution to this volume, I called a friend who is an Islamic studies scholar to brainstorm possible directions the chapter could take and strategize ways to manage my anxieties and reservations around writing about Islam. "I will not write about women, the hijab, terrorism, or Islamophobia," I declared firmly, then laughed out loud at myself. It is this lifelong, albeit unsuccessful, commitment to not publicly engage Islam as an object of study, this prohibitive punitive command to myself, in which I delineate the margins to my own thinking that I hope to interrogate in this chapter. What precisely—what haunting image and narrative—have I been fearing? And what, if anything, does this fear tell us about the struggle to attempt intellectual labor in the shadow of religious, racial, and ethnic Othering?

Accounting for the image that does not account for you is terrifying. But there is no running away from it, for it concerns, at its core, one's own community. Fanon understood how, in encounters with the white gaze, he ceased to be an individual and instead became a stand-in for the Black race. "I was responsible not only for my body," he writes, "but also for my race and my ancestors."[6] It is a twisted responsibility, less beholden to the Black community than to the white archive on Blackness. And in that dissociative triple person he becomes an ethnographer of a constructed ethnography.

I do not often think about Islam or what it means to be Muslim, and I rarely reflect on the strength or the absence of my faith—that is, until I encounter myself (or a version of myself) in a text and am jolted by the act of being interpellated by it. I recently visited a class on the politics of dress at my alma mater. The instructor, a white woman member of the theater department, invited me after she came across a piece I wrote on Somali theater traditions. A day before my visit, my host shared with me the planned readings for the day so I could get a sense of what else the students had read for the unit. They included a book chapter on the evolution of Somali women's dress written by a North American white woman academic. The chapter, despite being well intentioned and well researched, played on tired Orientalist tropes of shell-shocked Somali women discovering Western dress. In my view, it obscured if not entirely disregarded Somali women's rich, paradoxical, and evolving relationship to dress and to tradition.

I read the chapter on the morning of my visit, after I had already prepared my presentation for the class. I now needed to decide how, if at all, I was going to address the chapter whose pages depicted me without necessarily accounting either for my presence or for my response. It felt irresponsible to ignore the chapter, but then addressing it would mean dramatically restructuring my own prepared remarks. In the end, I abandoned my lecture on the resilience and innovation of Somali theater and spent the morning making a new presentation, one that I hoped depicted more accurately the rich material culture of Somali women. The students were engaged and welcomed my interventions, and the session went relatively well. However, I left the session feeling deflated and defeated. My visit amounted to just that, I thought: *a response*. I presented no independent thought of my own. The experience crystallized for me both the desire to correct the incomplete rendering of me and my community, and the fear that doing so would mean living, writing, and dreaming within the confines of someone else's imagination. And yet, time and time again, we respond. We risk being engulfed by the Others' archives because we recognize the real-life consequences of *not* responding—because we know sometimes it is a matter of life and death.

TO ENGAGE, OR NOT TO ENGAGE, THAT IS NOT THE QUESTION

Muslims everywhere are haunted by the figure of the alien, unassimilable Muslim. They are frightened of this received idea of themselves, because they know it to be ripe with violent, at times fatal, potential. For years I worked on the research team of Caleb Elfenbein's Mapping Islamophobia Project. My primary task was building and maintaining a dataset on Muslim American efforts to curb anti-Muslim hostility in their communities. These included open mosque and "Ask a Muslim" events, interfaith dialogues, and public presentations on Islam. Each event was held with the explicit goal of educating the public about the peacefulness of Islam. For instance, in the fall of 2011, volunteers for the Muslims Against Hunger Project in New York City partnered with Rutgers Shalom-Salaam and the Foundation for Ethnic Understanding to prepare and deliver hundreds of meals to the homeless. President of the mosque Iqbal Jafri stated that, in addition to fighting hunger in the city, the event was intended to highlight the Muslim community's investment in the welfare of their neighbors.[7] In 2016, in response to heightened anti-Muslim sentiment in several of that year's presidential campaigns, the Islamic Circle of North America, one of the largest Muslim organizations in North America, placed 135 billboards on U.S. highways advertising "Why Islam?" hotlines. The campaign encouraged callers to inquire about Islam, the Qur'anic recognition of Jesus, women's rights, and the reason mainstream Muslims do not denounce terrorist attacks committed in the name of their religion.[8] A few months later, members of the Ahmadiyya Muslim Youth Association spent several Saturdays on street corners of downtown Tempe, Arizona, holding signs that read "I am a Muslim. Ask me anything." The volunteers cited a Pew Research Poll that claimed 62 percent of Americans have not met a Muslim as the motivation for their work.[9] These are just a few of the thousands of data points I had collected for the project. Having spent several years on the Mapping Islamophobia team—even conducting some fieldwork where I attended events in person and interviewed the organizers and attendees—three things became clear.

First, for many Muslims, engaging in outreach efforts, such as helping the poor and being a welcoming neighbor as Islamic acts of worship, come second to exonerating their communities from public suspicion. In other words, Muslim Americans sometimes emphasize the feeding of the poor or welcoming the stranger not merely or even mostly as an act of worship—an *ibada*—as an antidiscrimination strategy. Fighting for public respect and recognition of one's basic humanity consumes much, if not most, of the Muslim community's time; it is as if practicing Islam has become first and foremost about responding to stereotypes rather than praying or fasting. I understand that this finding may surprise and even disturb some readers, who might think that being religious is mainly about one's belief in God or ritual acts like prayer, but this observation speaks to the heart of this chapter's main point: it underscores Muslims' acute awareness of themselves through the eyes of the Other so much so that it reshapes the public expression of their faith, including the privileging of outward-facing charity over personal *ijtihad*, or religious questioning, and quiet *taqwa*, or God consciousness, and personal piety. I am not trying to suggest that one is better than the other, but instead illustrate how the violence of being interpellated as a certain kind of a Muslim alters Muslim Americans relationship to each other and to the tenets of their faith. What metamorphosis might the practice of a surveilled faith by a surveilled people suffer?

Second, because these public discussions are intended to dispel myths and demystify Islam and therefore are always already a reaction to an existing image, there can be no room for nuances, resulting in what is now known as "pamphlet Islam." Most events in the dataset—whether organized by large Islamic organizations, local mosques, student groups, or just everyday people enlisting themselves as ambassadors—would almost always include a few stable ingredients: a discussion on women's rights in Islam (there are plenty; let go of your obsession with the hijab), terrorism (we don't condone it, because Islam is a peaceful religion), Abrahamic religions (do you know we also recognize and love Jesus?), and, finally, we can be your fun neighbor (do you want a henna tattoo?). Thus a fourteen-hundred-year-old religion practiced by over one-quarter of the world's population becomes tragically but understandably reduced to digestible bites and aphoristic slogans printed on colorful pamphlets. The reductive structure of these events, as well as the immense labor involved in their production, made me uncomfortable, sometimes angry, but always grateful, which brings me to my third observation.

Although it took me a while to come to terms with this, the Mapping Islamophobia Project attests to the ways in which sometimes one does not have a choice in recognizing and engaging with the received images of oneself and one's community, especially when the danger of not engaging outweighs one's intellectual reservations. No matter what one's philosophical objections or existential anxieties about outreach might be, the fact remains that Muslims in this country and in most other Western nations are thought of as monolithic, closed-minded, violent people who are guilty until proven innocent. In *Presumed Guilty*, scholar Todd Green describes this presumption of guilt as tied to deep-seated anti-Muslim sentiments.[10] He explains how the logic behind the impulse to hold all Muslims accountable for the violence of the few is predicated on the assumption that "Muslims as a whole are presumed guilty because they have failed to reform an inherently violent religion, to atone for the sins of their co-religionists, and to come to terms with their religion's unique history of horrific violence."[11] This presumption of guilt has resulted in the increased harassment, discrimination, and violence against Muslims in the two decades since 9/11. In fact, in his study of the effect of Islamophobia on the health of public life, Caleb Elfenbein establishes a clear link between the two phenomena with sharp increases in both anti-Muslim activities and Muslim outreach whenever a terrorist attack by Islamic militants/extremists/activists (or some other word than "fundamentalist," please!) occurs or local and national leaders engage in hateful speech.[12] In his words, "The way that people think about and talk about Islam and Muslims in public settings, play out in people's lives in very real ways."[13]

Apprehending this daunting reality explains why, despite my skepticism and long-standing commitment to never be a spokesperson for Islam, I suddenly found myself engaged in humanizing efforts in my own community. In the winter of 2018, I organized an Islamic Awareness Week on behalf of the Muslim Student Association of Grinnell College, of which I was the president at the time. The week-long programming included, among other events, a lecture by a leading woman scholar on the intricacies of Muslim marriage, a conversation with a councilwoman who was the first Muslim woman and immigrant to serve in that city's council, a presentation from the Mapping Islamophobia research team, and a henna/calligraphy social hour. I found it disturbing, even comical, that, despite my enduring skepticism of these kinds of humanizing work, I went ahead and replicated it in my own life. Was my decision to resist my profound aversion to talking about Islam in public in part a concession to the enduring power of the image that haunted me all these years—a recognition that outrunning it was simply not possible, maybe even irresponsible?

As much as I was frightened to enter the textual and lived scenarios of others' fictions about me, I became even more afraid of how such images translated and manifested in the real world. I had in front of me thousands of pieces of data documenting what happens when a perverse idea of you runs amok. I had in mind the Somali cab driver who in 2017 was beaten to death in Pittsburgh, Pennsylvania.[14] I thought about the members of the Islamic Community of Bryan-College Station, Texas, the morning they found bullets lodged in the walls of their mosque.[15] It took no effort to imagine the humiliation and the fear felt by the mayor of Prospect Park, New Jersey, when he was detained and questioned by U.S. Customs and Border Protection for hours without a cause.[16] These and the thousands of other incidents confirm that the real-world consequences of received ideas about Muslims are too colossal to ignore. My willingness to perform this labor in spite of my misgivings allowed me to better understand the individuals whose frequent and persistent labor I have tracked and documented over the years. Maybe they, too, were conflicted about and wrestled with the paradoxical nature of humanizing work; maybe they, too, were enraged and amused by the need to repackage the rich and complicated traditions and ethics that guided their lives into catchy sound bites, aware all along that nuance is something only true citizens enjoy, and that true citizenship remains unavailable to Muslim Americans.

Muslim outreach efforts reveal the rigid margins to Muslim public life. The Mapping Islamophobia Project captures not only the desire and the obligation Muslims feel to correct the incomplete representation of their communities but also the intellectually and politically paralyzing effect of public engagement on someone else's terms. What happens when outreach becomes the primary and, in many cases, the only role Muslims are allowed to play in public life? This question is at the heart of Elfenbein's study of the repercussions of anti-Muslim sentiments on Muslim public life, including how "the increasing acceptability of anti-Muslim hostility led to an unprecedented policing of Muslims in public space and public life more generally."[17] Put differently, the demand for Muslims to respond and combat the worsening conditions of public life meant that, for the two-plus decades since 9/11, it had become virtually impossible for Muslim Americans to engage in other forms of public life.

Elfenbein offers the fast disappearance of Muslims from American local and state politics since 2002 as one chilling and compelling example. He finds that, while at least seven hundred Muslims ran for a public office in the year 2000, only seventy ran in 2002—a precipitous decline that would persist for the next decade.[18] Outreach efforts have dwarfed Muslim Americans' capacity to participate fully in political life so significantly that, even when they do, they are still expected to engage in some form of humanizing work. Frequently, Muslim candidates running for local offices face global questions about foreign policy and Middle Eastern geopolitics in an effort to test their loyalty to the United States and prove they are don't have a "Muslim agenda."[19] In fact, Elfenbein's findings corroborate my own observations of the treatment of Muslims in U.S. political life. A few years ago, I interviewed a young Somali American man and former city council candidate for a mid-sized Midwestern city who recalled, with alarmed amusement, the (inter)national attention and coverage his local campaign received. "Some even came from Canada," he exclaimed while discussing the thousands of death threats he received while campaigning. His experiences, which are fairly typical of Muslim candidates, throw into relief the overdetermined nature of the received script about Muslims, the necessity as well as the futility of engaging with it, and, ultimately, the severe limitations of conducting public life in the specter of violence.

LOCATING THE MANY MARGINS OF ISLAM

Usually, and often rightly, when we discuss the margins in relations to Islam, we mean the systematic and violent marginalization of Muslims worldwide. Islamophobia is and continues to be a global project. Just in the last few years, we have witnessed the ethnic cleansing and expulsion of Rohingya Muslims from Myanmar; the systematic targeting and persecution of Uyghurs in China; the continued dispossessions of the Palestinian people living under the apartheid state of Israel; and the intensifying violence and discrimination faced by Indian Muslims, the largest Muslim-minority population in the world. These campaigns of anti-Muslim discrimination also include the numerous attempts to regulate the daily lives of Muslims, including the Muslim ban in the United States, the hijab regulation in France, the longer screenings at airports, the numerous legislations to ban Muslim cemeteries, and the slurs hurled at the supermarket.

The focus of this volume is different. It recognizes that, although Muslims are marginalized by anti-Muslim discrimination, margins also exist within Muslim communities. Simply put, there is, as one would expect, discrimination against Muslims by other Muslims. Scholars of Islam recognize these margins, and some of them produce scholarship that resists, questions, or critiques intra-Muslim marginalization. Among the most consequential and sustained engagement of this kind has come from feminist interventions into Islamic scholarship, among them Asma Barlas's and amina wadud's feminist exegeses of the Qur'an, Kecia Ali's careful reexamination of premodern Islamic jurisprudence, and Denise Spellberg's study of the gendered historiography of early and contemporary Islam.[20] Other crucial explorations of the margins of Islam include critical scholarships on queer Muslims,[21] as well as the exclusions of ethnic and racial groups outside mainstream Sunni Islam.[22] Su'ad Abdul Khabeer's tour de force ethnography of young multiethnic U.S. Muslims challenges the binary of "Black" and "Muslim" by showcasing how both Black and non-Black Muslims engage with Black cultural and artistic traditions in the formation of their Muslim identities.²³ In this volume, for instance, Edward Curtis explores Black Muslim practices and the Nation of Islam's cultivation of an ethics of Black liberation rooted in Islamic traditions. This is part and parcel of this volume's contribution: to render a deeper and more encompassing view of what Islam is and what Muslims do by centering those who occupy the geographic, pedagogical, social, political, queered, embodied, reproductive, and doctrinal margins of the world of Islam.

It is in the spirit of this radical act of scholarly curiosity and solidarity that I want to explore a different, more popular, and more insidious investment in the margins of Islam that positions itself as an interest in the diversity of modern Muslim life but in effect cements the tired trope of Islam as the alien Other. I want to speculate about the near impossibility of claiming a space on the margins of Islam while living with the epistemic violence of racialized hostile perception (and consumption) of Muslim public life. My contention is not that the margins of Islam do not exist (they do and there are plenty), but that it becomes increasingly harder to claim it once one recognizes the ease with which her own marginality can be appropriated and deployed for anti-Muslim proposes.

The experience of my personal encounter with amina wadud's groundbreaking work *Woman and the Qur'an: Rereading the Sacred Text from a Woman's Perspective* illustrates my point that it may be impossible in this historical moment to uplift the marginalized in Islam without also, inadvertently, encouraging those who want to marginalize Muslims in general. The first time I read this book, I was fifteen years old.²⁴ In many ways, wadud's innovative and scathing text marks a crucial turn in feminist interventions of modern Qur'anic exegesis as it brilliantly challenges the centuries-long male-centered, male-dominated interpretations of the Qur'an. As a young person, I had studied the Qur'an extensively, even memorized half of it (the longer half!). I remain grateful that this kind of education was made available to me in addition to my regular education, even though my family was not particularly religious, even as I was keenly aware, then and now, of the conservative spirit of my religious education.[25] For instance, for Muslims worldwide, public recitations of the Qur'an are considered a tremendous intellectual and spiritual feat, a divine performance. So, when, despite my debilitating shyness, I professed my desire to memorize the Qur'an so I could compete in these public performances, my teacher advised me against it, telling me of a young woman he knew who went mad after she herself tried. And when, a couple years later, I wanted to study *tafsir*, or traditional Qur'anic commentary, another teacher cautioned me that women ought not to attempt tafsir in case they might go mad. There was always talk of madness those days, and, in a sense, they were speaking the truth: knowing can be maddening, especially if one is not a man. So it is no surprise that wadud's book remains one of the most formative reading experiences of my life. In it I had observed her reclaim not just the holy scripture but the divine pursuit of knowledge—it was madness sanctified.

This experience was made more complex, however, by the fact that wadud's book was a gift from a white non-Muslim male teacher who equally unexpectedly and inexplicably lent me a copy of ex-Muslim activist Ayaan Hirsi Ali's controversial memoir, *Infidel*.[26] The two books could not be more different: one finds refuge in and seeks to excavate the progressive teachings of the Qur'an while the other sees no salvation in what she considers to be barbaric, violent teachings of Islam. What they share, however, is their emphatic marginality to mainstream Islam and Islamic scholarship, a marginality my teacher had imagined I shared as well. As much as I had enjoyed reading the two extremes, it was disorienting to be forced to think of myself as occupying the margins of my own community and therefore more alienated, or, worse, more enlightened. In fact, I am certain my teacher thought of these texts less as two opposing extremes and more as testaments and attempts to break free from the repressive, prohibitive spirit of mainstream Islam—a desire he imagined I, too, must have had, given my commitment to feminist politics. And, of course, I reside on the margins: I am a woman and a feminist and, therefore, conscious of the ways in which I am not treated like a full citizen, not fully entitled to public spaces, not encouraged to follow certain intellectual and spiritual paths. Some of these experiences are blatant, like being harassed on the street on semidaily basis, some subtle, like being discouraged from pursuing certain kinds of knowledge, but none are unique to the condition of being Muslim. Therefore, my aim here is not to contest my own marginality but, rather, investigate the Other's desire for it.

The investment in a certain kind of marginal Muslim stems from the fact that Islam as a religious category is perceived primarily through its prohibitions and supposed resistance to modernity. A few years ago, I attended a literary event in which half a dozen writers from around the world gave readings first in the original languages of their works then in translation, followed by a moderated discussion. Among the distinguished guests was a German writer of Turkish descent who was asked a vague question about writing and representation. In her answer she spoke of her understandable frustrations at being branded as "a Muslim writer" with special access to the desires and trepidations of Muslim immigrants in Germany. Then, as if to underscore her nonauthority on "Muslim issues," she added, "I drink. I enjoy sausages. Obviously, I'm not the best person to speak for Islam." A joke, clearly, but instructive, nonetheless. Her tongue and cheek comment puzzled me. Is that what Islam is, I wondered? A list of prohibitions? A religion encapsulated in its practitioner's inability to indulge in a glass of wine and cured meats? I thought about my own list of firm and bruised prohibitions: I enjoy wine, I don't eat pork, I give to charity but have not gotten around to figuring out my *zakka* (sometimes called alms or the "poor tax"), I fast during Ramadan (OK, I fast on most days of Ramadan), I do not pray but say *alhamdulillah* (praise be to God) whenever I sneeze and make *du'a* (supplicatory prayer) during a thunderstorm, and not only do I lack *taqwa* (consciousness of God) but I am also not even certain of the existence of a one supreme God. None of these makes me a Muslim or non-Muslim. Instead, it is the combination, the particular constellation of them, that amounts to a "form of life," to borrow Ludwig Wittgenstein's phrase, that is recognizable as—or at least disproportionally inspired by—a particular tradition.[27] Talal Asad, building on Wittgenstein's philosophy of ritual and practice, reminds us that "when we tend to practices that are mastered what emerges is neither the origin of belief nor what truly validates it. What emerges is simply the formation of the ability to live a distinctive form of life."[28] Take the literal translation of sharia, sometimes called Islamic law. It actually means "a street," "a way": sharia as a divine offering, a vision for a way of life.

Many religious communities, of course, observe prohibitive prescriptions. Orthodox Jews cannot eat shellfish and are forbidden from mixing dairy and poultry. Bible-believing Christians are not supposed to take God's name in vain or engage in secular labor on the Sabbath. Hindus cannot consume the flesh of the cow. Sunni and Shi'a Muslims are not supposed to consume pork, drink alcohol, or practice usury. All Abrahamic religions prohibit premarital sex and adultery. In other words, in most religious teachings, prohibition on certain acts remains integral to how they order life. As these teachings evolve over time, some are deemed archaic and left behind, like the prohibition against wearing a garment of mixed fabric, while others are brought forth to be negotiated by current and future generations, like the hijab or sexual ethics. In almost each case, these negotiations are at once communal and deeply personal. Thus, when we speak of Islam primarily through its prohibitions, we deny the elasticity of its traditions, and it becomes instead a static thing stuck in the seventh century and therefore unadaptable to modern life. Talal Asad even goes so far as to claim that the investment in excavating the Judeo-Christian roots of secularism serves to enunciate the "grammatical exclusion of Muslims" from modernity.[29] So, while the Muslim can acquire what Asad describes as the modern sensibility of secularism, Islam itself is closed to reform.

THE MELANCHOLIC MUSLIM AND THE PURSUIT OF MODERNITY

When my teacher gave me a copy of both *Infidel* and *Qur'an and Woman*, it felt like being told that, in order to become modern and liberated, I would have to leave behind my association with "traditional" Islam. This is why, as I have stated, those who claim the margins of Islam or are labeled as such by scholars, may, in effect, reify the stereotype that Muslims and Islam are, by definition, alien to both the West and to the modern age. In the following section, I want to illustrate this idea by exploring how American popular culture, including Muslim American popular culture, identifies backward, oppressive prohibitions at the core of Muslims' supposed problems with modernity, and how, in turn, feminist scholars of Islam have attempted to reclaim different interpretations of Islam from inside rather than outside Islamic tradition.

The assumed confrontation between a static monolithic Islam and modernity can be seen in many places, but none more powerfully than in the West's affection for the figure of melancholic Muslim caught up between the restrictive demands of Islam and the liberal freedoms of the West.[30] An excellent representation of the melancholic Muslim can be found in the award-winning Hulu original series *Ramy*, which chronicles the quotidian struggles of a twenty-something second-generation Egyptian American Muslim in New Jersey. The show, which is cowritten, codirected, and starred in by Egyptian American comedian and actor Ramy Youssef, aims to highlight the spiritual and philosophical challenges that animate Muslim American life but spectacularly falls short, not only because of the damaging binaries through which it frames Islam and the West but also for its failure to break free from the Other's imaging of itself.

One of the ways the show reinforces the supposed ontological incompatibility between Islam and the West is by depicting Islam prohibitively. The first episode begins with a scene at the mosque. Ramy is performing ablutions when an elderly member of the mosque interrupts him and asks, in Arabic, "Do you want to live a sinful life or a halal life? What you are doing is wrong. Before you pray, you must wash up properly." Ramy, who appears confused, tells the man that he is clean, that he showered just that morning. But the elderly man won't have it; he insists that Ramy wash his toes and eventually proceeds to wash his toes for him.[31] The scene is set up in such a way that Ramy is both a translator and a stand-in for the audience. The puzzled contours of his face, the earnestness of his questions, the deadpan tone with which he delivers them are all intended to mirror the audience's reactions and elicit its sympathies. We are equally baffled by the rigid and esoteric demands of mainstream Islamic tradition exhibited by the elderly man; we are on Ramy's side. At the end of the first episode, after several failed romantic attempts with women, Ramy once more runs into the elderly man from the mosque and delivers, unprompted, the following monologue: "Yes, I have sex even though I am not married, and I'm probably gonna try mushrooms one day. So what? That means I am not a good Muslim. Like, I can't do it because I don't follow all the rules and the fucking judgments that are always put on us?" The monologue sets the stage for the show's central conflict, which propels the narrative forward: the struggle to participate in modern life while adhering to the prohibitive demands of Islam.

In the show, Islam is represented by what it asks its practitioners to give up, while the West is represented by the liberal freedoms it offers—a binary tension for which sex stands in. Rebellion against, negotiations with, and devotions to Islam are all principally measured by a character's attitude toward sex. It is through sex, moreover, that the show emphasizes Islam's regulatory streak and dramatizes any detour from this restrictive understanding of Islam as an existential catastrophe. In episode 3, Ramy finds himself in the mosque after doing drugs for the first time and strikes up a conversation with a white male convert cleaning the mosque.[32] Sensing Ramy's existential anguish, the convert shares the moment he achieved spiritual clarity: "I was staring at the most perfect ass that I have ever seen. I mean bare naked, in my face, and there was a line of beautiful snow-white coke on there. I snorted the coke, and she was, like, 'You can have this, you can have this ass.' And I was, like, 'I don't want it.' And that is when I knew I was ready to follow the path of the Prophet P.B.U.H." The demonstrated restraint and discipline stuns Ramy, who keeps exclaiming, "You, you didn't want that ass?" Ramy is envious, in awe. The message: true Muslimhood necessitates complete surrender, a relinquishing of all desire, that successfully frames Islam as that which stands in the way of modern living.

The personal and messy struggle to strike a balance between the ethics of an ancient scripture and the stresses of modern life are timeless and universal. However, when Muslims engage in this struggle and deviate from stereotypical scripts, it often does little to disrupt the rigid Orientalist ideas about Muslims; rather, it merely celebrates the rebellious individuals whom it imagines found (or at least desired) modernity *in spite* of Islam. American spectators adore characters like Ramy at least in part because of their collective disdain for Islam, a contempt rooted in profound misunderstanding of it as an arrested, and therefore arresting, tradition. Islam is what needs to be accommodated and wrestled with because it does not allow itself to be easily translated, hence the persistent obsession and admiration for the marginal melancholic Muslim, who is suspended between modernity and tradition. When my teacher gave me those radical books, I believe that he fancied me a rebel on the periphery of mainstream Islam. He was pointing out to me what he saw as the cultural and intellectual deficiencies of my own community simply because I was vocal about my commitments to radical politics—a celebration of difference imagined only because Islam is imagined otherwise, as an entity devoid of imagination.

We can only conceive of an individual's small deviations from traditional understanding of Islam as rebellious acts rather than as signs of the banal and profound ways in which humans reform and reimagine their lives if we believe Islam to be incapable of changing. In this logic, individual Muslims can be rehabilitated, rewarded for their modern impulses and desires, but the source of this disposition can never be found in Islam itself. In fact, those on the margins of Islam can sometimes be deployed to reinforce harmful Orientalist images of themselves. But, of course, despite the political machines that engineer and sustain this misunderstanding, Muslims, like all humans, participate in discursive practices and innovative readings that challenge old covenants and forge new paths.

Framing the layered, complex traditions of a people's faith through a set of predetermined prohibitions erases centuries-long traditions of interpretations, contestations, and negotiations. Take the West's favorite scary term, "sharia." Generally assumed to be a set of unchanging laws that include terrible punishments for theft and adultery, the term "sharia" ("way" or "path") refers to a system of law and ethics developed in the Middle Ages by both Sunni and Shi'a scholars. Based on the Qur'an, the Sunna (or sayings and deeds of the Prophet Muhammad), and, for Shi'a Muslims, the teachings of their Imams, this system theoretically categorized all human behavior into five categories: required, recommended, neutral, discouraged, and prohibited. But the "law" produced by these scholars was different from the government law (*qanun*) and customary practices (*'urf*) that often governed criminal matters and social life—that is, it existed alongside other systems of law and was not necessarily enforced by the state. Moreover, scholars never claimed that their rulings were the same as God's commandments, so they made a distinction between the sharia, which was God's path, and their interpretation of it, which they called *fiqh*, or jurisprudence. This law was never codified; it did not exist in any one set of books. There were and are several schools of both Sunni and Shi'a fiqh, and these schools often disagreed with one another. These were branches of interpretation extending from the same Islamic roots, they said, making it an inherently pluralistic endeavor. This means that, while there may be a prevailing interpretation of sharia in a specific time and place, there is not and can never be a definitive Islamic law to which all Muslims refer and follow. Instead, we are left with a rich and sometimes vexing tradition in which learned but fallible humans read and interpret what they believe to be the infallible word of God. And, even then, ordinary Muslims must make sense of the guidelines of the religious scholars in the context of their own lives.

An excellent example of this constitutive constant contestation of Islamic tradition both at the scholarly and the individual level is marriage. Many progressive Muslims struggle with the basic structure of the Muslim marriage contract, which, as developed by early Sunni jurists, follows a logic of ownership, where the wife's sexual availability is granted in exchange for the husband's full financial support.[33] This structure results in a profound inequality between the spouses, with the husband holding not only an exclusive right to sex but also (with few exceptions) an exclusive access to divorce. Many Muslims find this arrangement simply unpalatable, and while some Muslims turn to secular models for their marriages, others make sure to amend their individual marriage contracts to enshrine their own progressive values. Scholar Kecia Ali, responding to these feminist reimagining of the marriage contract, however, cautions us against conceding the primacy of the current contract model, which she argues was a product of its time.[34]

Ali demonstrates how the prevalence of slavery and concubinage in the pre-modern period affected the early jurists' thinking about marriage, with the jurists establishing parallels between the institutions of marriage and slavery, even going so far as employing the language of commerce to discuss marriage contracts.[35] It is no surprise, then, that a framework modeled after deeply unequal institutions would yield unequal arrangements. Thus, efforts at reform must begin with an understanding that the model we have inherited "is not God-given but rather was developed by men working at a particular time and place, governed by certain assumptions."[36] As Ali herself stresses, the troubling roots of this jurisprudence need neither paralyze us nor convince us it is God's plan for us; instead, they must serve as a stark reminder that imperfect humans render imperfect readings to devise imperfect rules. It will take another group of imperfect humans, equally engaged in ijtihad and committed to the common good, to reimagine those rules and arrive at new methods of analysis.

It is precisely because Islamic jurisprudence is, at its core, a process born out of ijtihad, or reasoning, of learned individuals that reform is always possible, even if at times improbable. For instance, responding to Ali's call to feminist reformers to seriously contend with the model of commerce on which Islamic marriage contract is predicated, Asifa Quraishi-Landes has proposed modeling marriage contracts on partnership contracts. Islamic jurisprudence recognizes numerous types of partnership contracts with each "[depending] on all the parties' continuous concurrent consent, in both the continuation of partnership and the terms imposed on each party."[37] The partnership contracts are customizable and can be terminated at will by either party and, therefore, have the potential to effectively eliminate the unilateral right to divorce granted to the male spouse by the early jurists. And, finally, Quraishi-Landes argues, the partnership model could imagine a new role for the *mahr*, or dower. Although mandated in scripture, the purpose of mahr is never made clear; the narrative that the mahr is what makes the marriage licit is only one possible conjecture offered by the early jurists. A renewed ijtihad, suggests Quraishi-Landes, could reimagine the mahr so that it allows the woman to access monetary protection if she desires, but can also take on other meaningful significations.[38]

I have observed Quraishi-Landes's legal theorizing in my own family. When my eldest sister got married, she insisted that her mahr be symbolic, a gesture that would honor her devoutness and reflect the pious marriage that she hoped to build with her spouse. Thus, she and her husband decided her mahr would be a pilgrimage the two of them would make to Mecca. But when my other, less religious, sister got married, she negotiated her mahr to be a monetary gift that her husband paid a few years into their marriage; my sister, aware of the financial vulnerabilities women face in our unequal world, bought a piece of land in her daughter's name, to help my niece feel financially secure in the future. This is to say that these new articulations and renegotiations of tradition by people for whom tradition matters a great deal attest to the ways in which Islam is a living, breathing organism constantly being reimagined at personal, familial, and scholarly levels. Oftentimes these challenges to tradition are rooted not necessarily in secular values but in Islamic teachings, like the child's divine right to education or recognition of women's property rights.

People are sophisticated readers of their own lives and the contradictory traditions and desires that guide them. Consider, for instance, how Ali herself officiated a Muslim marriage ceremony in 2004 at the request of a Muslim American bride in Florida.[39] Together, the bride, Ali, and the guests interrupted the unofficial but long-standing tradition of only men presiding over Muslim marriages. The part of the story I find most compelling is how Ali and the bride navigated the sticky issue of witnesses. Muslim marriage ceremonies ask for two male witnesses or two women and one man, which many Muslims understandably find disconcerting. But when Ali suggested the popular remedy of having two men and two women as witnesses, the bride refused, "rightly noting that it attempts to create the illusion of parity where it does not exist; the female witnesses are, in such a case, redundant."⁴⁰ In the end, Ali invited all of the attendees to serve as one collective witness.⁴¹ I find this moment so moving because it shows the creative spirit of a religious life: reading scripture as an imaginative act, interpreting fiqh (or jurisprudence) as an imaginative endeavor, of exegesis as a process steeped in imaginative leaps. I dwell on these examples because they elucidate what we miss when we center prohibitions as a convenient stand-in for Islam. Just like everyone else, Muslims lead complex, messy lives guided by a set of ethics that are not settled or static but continuously and vigorously contested. It is clear that no one owns modernity or has an exclusive right to dictate the terms of its evolution or violation.

Yet the kind of reinterpretations performed by Kecia Ali, Asifa Quraishi-Landes, and my sisters—some of which are radical, some of which are modest—are so often interpreted by non-Muslims and Muslims alike as an abandonment of the Islamic tradition in favor of a secular modernity or the "American way of life." In this chapter, I have tried to ask whether it is possible for us to embrace this kind of Muslim margin without reaffirming the claims of anti-Muslim critics that if we are true Muslims, then we are also Other. I have tried to meditate on what it means, as a member of a racialized religious minority, to encounter an incomplete image, an overdetermined idea of oneself. What does it take—what does it take from us—to survive the violence of being interpellated by a text or a scene that cannot account for our full humanity? I wanted to interrogate how the fear of this limited and limiting image (and the desire to flee it) operates as an intellectual chokehold and makes it impossible to nurture the margins of one's own community. How devastatingly comical, for instance, that I vowed to never write about Muslim women, given that I am one, that I was raised by and alongside a legion of Muslim women who could not be more different from one another and in whose lives I am profoundly and unapologetically invested. I realize that this is rather an uninteresting, unsurprising conclusion: prejudice, hate, violence, and unbalanced power dynamics limit us. So, what is to be done?

I have neither a bold vision nor grand solutions; none are apparent to me. Instead, I offer this: I engage. In these brief pages, I dared to engage, to look back at the haunting script from which I spent years running and to assess its hold over me. And, in taking inventory, I came to appreciate how those two early, parallel, and persistent prescriptions—to not go mad and to be modern— became the pillars of my intellectual and spiritual pursuits. I have also come to recognize that "modern," "marginal," "moderate," and "mainstream" are frequently synonyms for "disciplined." And I am no longer interested in being disciplined, which is to say I am no longer invested in evidencing just how modern I am. Maybe then I can begin to fully embrace the fact that many of us reside on the margins of our own communities—a lonely place sometimes, but one filled with the potential to engender reflection and reform. Yes, life conducted in response bores at best, but so does one of unfulfilled curiosities.

NOTES

1. Frantz Fanon, *Black Skin, White Masks*, trans. Richard Philcox (New York: Grove, 2008), 91.
2. Fanon, *Black Skin, White Masks*, 112.
3. W. E. B. Du Bois, *The Souls of Black Folk* (Chicago: A. C. McClurg, 1904), 3.
4. Edward W. Said, *Orientalism*, 25th ed. (New York: Vintage, 1994).
5. Said, *Orientalism*, 25.
6. Fanon, *Black Skin, White Masks*, 112.

7. Cheryl Makin, "Serving Up the Peace," *Home News Tribune*, November 24, 2011, B1–B2.
8. Katie Mettler, "Billboards Aim to Spread Understanding of Islam," *Tampa Bay Times*, January 6, 2016, https://www.tampabay.com/news/religion/billboards-aim-to-spread-understanding-of-islam/2260209/.
9. Garrett Mitchell, "Do You Know a Muslim? No? Group Hopes to Change That," *Republic*, March 11, 2017, https://www.azcentral.com/story/news/local/tempe/2017/03/11/do-you-know-muslim-no-group-hopes-change/99050998/.
10. Todd H. Green, *Presumed Guilty: Why We Shouldn't Ask Muslims to Condemn Terrorism* (Minneapolis: Fortress, 2018).
11. Green, *Presumed Guilty*, xxv.
12. Caleb Iyer Elfenbein, *Fear in Our Hearts: What Islamophobia Tells Us about America* (New York: New York University Press, 2021).
13. Elfenbein, *Fear in Our Hearts*, 48.
14. Paula Reed Ward, "Trial Opens for Man Accused in Beating Death of Somali Cab Driver," *Pittsburgh Post-Gazette*, November 12, 2019, https://www.post-gazette.com/news/crime-courts/2019/11/12/Ramadhan-Mohamed-cab-driver-Somali-homicide-Daniel-Russell-trial-opens/stories/201911120102.
15. Amanda Brandt and Jake Walker, "Gunshots Hit Islamic Center; CS Police and FBI Investigating," *Eagle*, July 7, 2016, https://theeagle.com/news/local/gunshots-hit-islamic-center-cs-police-and-fbi-investigating/article_e3ca0570-4450-11e6-8519-0b1f66f94c08.html.
16. Antonia Noori Farzan, "'Just Flat-out Profiling': Muslim Mayor Says He Was Detained at Airport and Asked Whether He Knew Terrorists," *Washington Post*, September 16, 2019, https://www.washingtonpost.com/nation/2019/09/16/new-jersey-muslim-mayor-detained-jfk-terrorists.
17. Elfenbein, *Fear in Our Hearts*, 56.
18. Elfenbein, 139–141.
19. Elfenbein, 142.
20. Asma Barlas, *"Believing Women" in Islam: Unreading Patriarchal Interpretations of the Qur'ān* (Austin: University of Texas Press, 2002); amina wadud, *Qur'an and Woman: Rereading the Sacred Text* (New York: Oxford University Press, 1999); Kecia Ali, *Marriage and Slavery in*

Early Islam (Cambridge, Mass.: Harvard University Press, 2010); Denise A. Spellberg, *Politics, Gender, and the Islamic Past: The Legacy of 'A'isha Bint Abi Bakr* (New York: Columbia University Press, 1994).

21. See Scott Siraj al-Haqq Kugle, *Homosexuality in Islam: Critical Reflection on Gay, Lesbian, and Transgender Muslims* (Oxford: Oneworld, 2010).

22. See Edward E. Curtis IV, *The Call of Bilal: Islam in the African Diaspora* (Chapel Hill: University of North Carolina Press, 2014); and Sylvia Chan-Malik, *Being Muslim: A Cultural History of Women of Color in American Islam* (New York: New York University Press, 2018).

23. Su'ad Abdul Khabeer, *Muslim Cool: Race, Religion, and Hip-Hop in the United States* (New York: New York University Press, 2016).

24. wadud, *Qur'an and Woman.*

25. In the aftermath of the Somaliland civil war, which decimated most of the country's infrastructure, including public education, a thriving private education sector emerged. In the early 2000s, these private, predominantly religious schools were schools often funded and supported by religious charity organizations abroad, including in Saudi Arabia and, later, Turkey. As such, they have introduced and fiercely promoted Salafism, the revivalist orthodox movement in Sunni Islam, that is dominant in countries like Saudi Arabia and other Gulf states.

26. Ayaan Hirsi Ali, *Infidel* (New York: Free Press, 2007).

27. Ludwig Wittgenstein, *Philosophische Untersuchungen*, trans. G. E. M. Anscombe, P. M. S. Hacker, and Joachim Schulte, 4th ed. (Oxford: Wiley-Blackwell, 2009); quoted in Talal Asad, "Thinking About Religion Through Wittgenstein," *Critical Times* 3, no. 3 (December 2020): 405.

28. Asad, "Thinking About Religion Through Wittgenstein," 404.

29. Talal Asad, *Secular Translations: Nation-State, Modern Self, and Calculative Reason* (New York: Columbia University Press, 2018), 15.

30. My reading of the melancholic Muslim is greatly inspired by Sara Ahmad's brilliant interrogation of the figure of the melancholic migrant in her 2010 monograph, *The Promise of Happiness*. Ahmad deploys the term to think about the figure who embodies or makes apparent the injuries of racism and migration and who is, therefore, seen as a threat to national happiness. Here, I want to consider a kind

of melancholy that, while still highlighting a difference (a difference held on to), is in fact desired and celebrated by the white majority.

31. *Ramy*, "Between the Toes," season 1, episode 1, directed by Harry Bradbeer, aired April 19, 2019, on Hulu.
32. *Ramy*, "Black Spot on the Heart," season 1, episode 3, directed by Christopher Storer, aired April 19, 2019, on Hulu.
33. Ali, *Marriage and Slavery in Early Islam*.
34. Kecia Ali, "Progressive Muslims and Islamic Jurisprudence: The Necessity for Critical Engagement with Marriage and Divorce Law," in *Half of Faith: American Muslim Marriage and Divorce in the Twenty-First Century*, ed. Kecia Ali (Boston: Open BU, 2021), 34–51.
35. Ali, "Progressive Muslims and Islamic Jurisprudence," 34–51. See also Leila Aḥmed, *Women and Gender in Islam: Historical Roots of a Modern Debate* (New Haven, Conn.: Yale University Press, 1992).
36. Ali, "Progressive Muslims and Islamic Jurisprudence," 36.
37. Asifa Quraishi-Landes, "A Meditation on Mahr, Modernity, and Muslim Marriage Contract Law," in *Half of Faith: American Muslim Marriage and Divorce in the Twenty-First Century*, ed. Kecia Ali (Boston: Open BU, 2021), 62.
38. Quraishi-Landes, "Meditation on Mahr," 64.
39. Kecia Ali, "Acting on a Frontier of Religious Ceremony," in *Half of Faith: American Muslim Marriage and Divorce in the Twenty-First Century*, ed. Kecia Ali (Boston: Open BU, 2021), 17–21.
40. Ali, "Acting on a Frontier," 19.
41. Ali, 19.

2

RETHINKING THE CENTER

Margins and Multiplicity in Hadith Texts

MICHAEL MUHAMMAD KNIGHT

Long before I earned a PhD in Islamic studies, I was a creative writer. My writing involved some ethnographic work, though I initially envisioned this more as "gonzo" journalism in the vein of Hunter S. Thompson than as scholarship. The Islamic community in which I conducted much of my earlier research—the Five Percenters, a heterodox African American movement with roots in the Nation of Islam, whose adherents delved into an esoteric alphanumeric language and self-identified as gods—had me feeling at odds with mainstream Islamic studies, since my work was bound to be too marginal and weird for scholars to whom "Islamic studies" meant Qur'an commentary, classical thinkers such as al-Ghazali, and Muslim jurisprudence. As normative Islamic studies prioritized its center as Arabic translation and elite intellectual traditions, could the field have a place for communities such as the Five Percenters?

Eventually, I began to rethink the possibilities for Islamic studies; it was, or could be, so much more than the privileged topics and textual canon. There must be spaces in the field for the noncanonical, the heterodox, and the marginal, and the edge was as Islamic as the center, wherever the actual "center" might be. Islamic studies had no intrinsic center on geographic, linguistic, or sectarian terms—or, rather, possessed a multiplicity of possible centers. Islam was always local, and the mainstream was never as mainstream as widely imagined.

As someone who works with/on marginalized traditions and noncanonical or even anticanonical sources, it seems odd that in this chapter I turn away from the margins and head straight to the most institutionally supported and advantaged center: the hadith corpus, the reported teachings and practices of Muhammad. At first glance, this could look like a midnight conversion–like turn away from my previous work: I'm engaging the canonical texts, seemingly enforcing the model of real Islamic studies as Arabic translation and classical sources. Instead, I want to affirm the importance of thinking about Islam beyond orthodoxy and canon, but to do so by diving into the supreme orthodoxy-making canon machines. In the discussion that follows, I try to speak to the real-world issues of Muslim contests over authenticity (i.e., who possesses "correct" knowledge of Islam) and authority (i.e., who possesses the qualifications to represent this "correct" Islam) as they manifest in canonical Sunni hadith sources. I have heard it said that scholars work on hadiths either because they love hadiths or want to deconstruct them; I hope that the two are not mutually exclusive.

In recent decades, transnational media has often reported on Islamic revivalist forces, acting both within recognized state power (such as the kingdom of Saudi Arabia) and outside it (as in al-Qaeda and ISIS), bulldozing, bombing, or otherwise demolishing shrines and tombs dedicated to Muslim figures. The destroyers of shrines and tombs draw from a particular strand of modern Sunni thought, popularly termed "Salafism," or, pejoratively, "Wahhabism," that claims authorization from an intellectual tradition tracing back to the premodern scholars of hadith, the sayings and actions of Muhammad. These groups typically regard themselves as purging Muslim practices of unacceptable deviations and returning to a pure, original Islam within the limits prescribed by this scholarly tradition and its privileged textual canon. In their eyes, the struggle over shrines is simply one of textually authenticated, real Islam against illegitimate folk or popular practices. Not only is Islam thereby treated as a monolithic unity with a singular archive of canonical sources, but these texts themselves are imagined to speak with a fundamentally singular voice.

"To my mind," Vernon Schubel writes in *Religious Performance in Contemporary Islam*, "the discipline of Islamic studies should have at its center the experience of Muslim people. That experience certainly includes classical texts . . . but it also includes the experience of ordinary Muslims."[1] Making this assertion in the early 1990s, Schubel pushed back against dominant trends in Western scholarship, informed by Orientalist textualism, in which the academic study of Islam was reduced to an archive of "Great Books" and elite intellectual histories, the marginalizing treatment of Shi'ism as a heterodox derivative from "mainstream" Sunni Islam, and studies of Shi'ism that prioritized a classical "high tradition" ("law, theology, and philosophy") over less valid folk or popular expressions.[2] As a corrective intervention, Schubel's work has called for engagements of Islam as not only a universal tradition spanning across continents but also a multiplicity of local traditions without an organic and self-evident center of gravity. Schubel's critique, made nearly thirty years ago, remains salient in contemporary Islamic studies, which has faced controversy between hostile camps over issues such as the necessity of training in Arabic and the priority of philological approaches; the relevance of critical theory lenses such as academic studies of race and gender, as well as the analytical frameworks of religious studies as a discipline; and the ways in which Islam's boundaries as a field of study become narrowed or expanded between textualist and ethnographic work. The problems that Schubel highlighted in 1993—and has continued to challenge in the years since—have not gone away.

Schubel's decentering of Islam can move in two directions: first, it makes an argument for the inclusion of numerous marginalized communities, traditions, and Muslim experiences as authentically Islamic. Second, it calls for us to consider the hidden multiplicities and heterogeneities *inside* what some Muslims and non-Muslims alike would take for granted as a universal orthodox Islam and its canonical sources. While modern Islamic revivalists issue calls for a pure return to "what the texts say" and imagine an early golden age in which the original Muslim community collectively achieved perfect unity and coherence, the Sunni hadith corpus reveals a surprising diversity of opinions and worldviews. Hadith (pl. *ahadith*), the collected reports of Muhammad's precedents, are sometimes called "the second holy scripture of Islam," used to determine what Muhammad said and did; it is this life example that most observant Muslims have sought to follow in their own lives. Muhammad's Sunna (literally "custom" or "precedent"), his precedent-setting habits and behavior, have been articulated as a divine revelation. Early scholars thought of Muhammad's Sunna in multiple ways: the foundational jurist Malik ibn Anas (d. 795 CE) regarded the true source of Sunna as the collective precedent of the community that Muhammad founded in Medina, though his student al-Shafi'i (d. 820 CE) argued for hadith reports as the most authoritative source of Sunna. Al-Shafi'i's argument won, as hadith collections with the most highly regarded scholarly vetting became crucial sources for Islamic knowledge. Though Sunni and Shi'i Muslims developed separate methodologies for assessing a hadith's authenticity and application (and thus produced separate hadith collections and ideas of textual canon), hadiths appear in both traditions as essential to determining Islamic theology, practice, and ethics.

The hadith corpus might look like a natural center, but Muslim scholars have historically disagreed with each other over how to determine the most reliable hadiths and their precise significance. Even within the specific hadith canon of Sunni Muslims, the body of hadiths privileged as authentic or sound do not present a unified, monolithic portrait of what Muhammad and his companions said and did. This diversity undermines the image of a universal Islam among Muhammad's companions and their students, and it also challenges the binary opposition pitting canonical, textual, and universal Islam against popular, folk, and local Islam. Put another way, even if scholars rely exclusively on canonical texts, rather than lived experience, to determine "what Islam teaches," it becomes impossible to render a singular view. As Schubel implies, it is human beings, living in specific contexts, who determine authoritative, hegemonic readings. In this chapter, I examine the Sunni hadith corpus to consider the multiplicity of Muslim experiences at work *within* the texts. In the Sunni hadith canon, we find various networks speaking from the subjectivities of the sources that they deemed authoritative, disagreeing with each other and attempting to disseminate distinct views of Muhammad.

THE MAKING OF HADITHS

It's easy to imagine the hadith corpus as a singular, self-contained text, analogous to the Qur'an, through which we access the consistent voice of a single author—in the case of the hadith corpus, the voice of Muhammad. We often see these reports referred to collectively as "the Hadith," as though they all sit in the same codified book. The resources through which we engage the hadiths, whether encyclopedic volumes or online archives, lead us to think of the corpus as an intact whole. However, the hadiths do not exist as a textual unity, but rather appear through countless collections, many of which span dozens of volumes and contain thousands of hadiths. Some of these collections are regarded as more reliable than others in terms of vetting their material and authentically representing Muhammad's words and behavior. Sunni and Shi'i intellectual traditions have developed separate methodologies for assessing hadiths and have thus arrived at different senses of hadith canon.[3] Within Sunni tradition, scholarly authorities gradually reached a consensus on the most authoritative sources, regarding six collections as especially authentic. Within this "six books" canon, they have ranked the two *Sahih* collections of Bukhari and Muslim as the most trustworthy sources for Muhammad's sayings and actions.

A hadith consists of two parts: its *isnad*, the transmission history through which it traveled across generations of scholars to pass from an eyewitness of Muhammad to a later compiler, and its *matn*, the hadith's textual content. The isnad appears as a chain of reporters, citing the compiler's sources and establishing the matn's credentials. In Sunni hadith scholarship, the most authoritative hadiths would be those with unbroken chains that can confidently trace back to one of Muhammad's Companions (a category including those Muslims who met Muhammad, became Muslim while he was alive, and remained Muslims until their own death). Sunni hadith methodologies in Islam's early centuries developed a concept of Muhammad's Companions as, collectively, an unassailable class of reporters: if hadith scholars could confidently attribute a report about Muhammad to one of his Companions, it would be impossible to question that Companion's integrity and suggest that they were being untruthful in the report. To accuse a Companion of lying, in the view of Sunni intellectual tradition, transgressed the bounds of legitimate Islam.

This view of the Companions as an unimpeachable class with across-the-board integrity was not shared by Twelver Shi'i hadith scholars, who assessed Companions on a case-by-case basis, determined by their alignments in early Muslim power struggles either with or against 'Ali.[4] Muslims who opposed 'Ali and his family could not be treated as untouchably reliable sources for hadiths. Additionally, Shi'i hadith scholars bestowed supreme truthmaking authority on 'Ali and his descendants in the line of infallible Imams, whose reports held a transcendent gravitas. Sunni and Shi'i hadith collections are not purely isolated from one another, but exhibit a great degree of overlap: 'Ali; his wife (Muhammad's daughter) Fatima; and their sons, Hasan and Husayn, after all, were Companions themselves and thereby unassailable in Sunni hadith methodology, and their later descendants among the Imams were also hadith transmitters held in high esteem by Sunni critics. 'Ali's great-great-grandson, Ja'far as-Sadiq, to name just one example, was not only the sixth Shi'i Imam (or the fifth Imam for Nizari Isma'ili Shi'i Muslims), but claimed as an authoritative voice in Sunni traditions as well.

The Sunni doctrine of the Companions' collective authority as hadith reporters, seemingly reconstructing them as objective fact-retrieval machines, could lead us to erase their subjectivity as human beings. But, looking at the isnad, the chain of transmission that accompanies a hadith, can become helpful in analyzing the matn, its content, even at the level of the eyewitness Companion. For an example of one hadith's matn: when Muhammad's wife Aisha, who did not have children, complained that she did not have an honorific name (i.e., "Mother of _____") like his other wives, Muhammad gave her the honorific name Umm 'Abd Allah (Mother of 'Abd Allah). The hadith seemingly recognizes Aisha's nephew 'Abd Allah ibn al-Zubayr as her symbolic son. This matn may seem rather innocuous, but we must also consider the isnad: the report of Muhammad ostensibly declaring 'Abd Allah ibn al-Zubayr a virtual son of Aisha (and thereby Muhammad himself?) comes to us from Hisham ibn al-Zubayr, whose father, 'Urwa ibn al-Zubayr, was an immeasurably important scholar among the earliest Muslims and a major source for reports from his aunt Aisha, and 'Urwa's brother was 'Abd Allah ibn al-Zubayr himself. Similarly, hadiths with matns praising al-Zubayr, the father of 'Abd Allah and 'Urwa, also appear frequently as transmissions from 'Urwa to his son Hisham. When we examine the chains of transmission, we find that hadiths with matns attributing special significance to 'Abd Allah ibn al-Zubayr (and his father, al-Zubayr) tend to come, perhaps unsurprisingly, from Zubayrid reporters.[5] Moreover, hadiths privileging 'Abd Allah ibn al-Zubayr and his father, both opponents of 'Ali, come to us through networks of transmitters with connections to Aisha, who had been 'Ali's opponent in early power struggles that led to them meeting each other on the battlefield.[6] At the same time, while Sunnism and Shi'ism have developed as generally distinct intellectual traditions with separate textual canons, a close look at Sunni hadith transmission chains points to the ways that these sectarian formations have not been clearly defined in every context. Again, if we look at Sunni isnads—the chains of transmitters that Sunni hadith scholars regarded as trustworthy authorities—we find leading figures in Shi'i tradition, including the infallible Shi'i Imams and their prominent students.

Therefore, while the matn of a hadith could appear as straightforward, empirically observed facts about Muhammad's life, the hadith's isnad highlights the subjectivity of our reporters, causing us to consider their personal relationships to Muhammad and positions within later communal strife and political power struggles, as well as the various networks that would adopt a particular Companion's voice as their own. This subjectivity appears at every level of the isnad, from the original eyewitness to Muhammad to their students, on to the master scholars who compiled massive collections of hadiths and were themselves capable of exercising some editorial sovereignty over the material they collected.

Between the original Muslim community of the seventh century CE and the generation of the master canonical compilers in the ninth century, the hadith corpus emerges not as one prophetic figure producing content for a passive audience, nor a united coterie of his Companions working in collaboration or a coherent network of scholars within a specific institution, but, rather, thousands of actors occupying varieties of geographic, sectarian, methodological, ethnic, and gendered positions. Taking these identities into account as we survey the isnads, the hadith corpus becomes not only a site of proliferating multiplicities but also a site of power struggle in which the gradual crystallization of the corpus and its established class of professional experts accompanied a suppression of diversity.

Many projects researching isnads have exposed the ways in which hadith scholarship as a professional field narrowed by the ninth century CE. Searching for records in the isnads of women as hadith transmitters, Asma Sayeed has shown that women appear at the earliest level of the isnads (Muhammad's eyewitness reporters) but disappear almost entirely in successive generations, in part as a growing professionalization of hadith scholarship valorized travel and face-to-face interaction that effectively pushed women out.[7] Christopher Melchert tracks the inclusion of hadith reporters within the six books canon who had been affiliated with groups branded as "heterodox" and "heretical," finding that the sectarian minorities were increasingly excluded from hadith scholarship over time.[8] Lyall R. Armstrong has looked at popular storytellers *(qussas)*, who were largely deemed acceptable as hadith authorities but fell out of favor as the hadith scholar guild grew insular and more methodologically exclusive.[9] John Nawas's isnad analysis has demonstrated that while Arab reporters constituted a majority of hadith transmitters at earlier levels of the isnads, *mawali* (non-Arab) reporters became more prominent at later levels.[10] These projects would all locate their periods of transformation in roughly the same period, the eight to ninth century CE. It was during this time that the center of Islamic imperial power shifted from Damascus to the new city of Baghdad, hadith scholarship (and a rich diversity of other Muslim groups and schools of thought as well) gravitated toward Baghdad, and hadith scholars became increasingly crystallized as a unique class and even sectarian movement.

For a sense of the multiplicities that come together to form the image of a singular hadith corpus, I have looked at proto-Sunni hadith scholar Sulayman Abu Dawud al-Tayalisi (751–820) and his hadith collection, the *Musnad*, with a focus on four of the Companions who appear with greatest frequency as his sources: Anas ibn Malik, Aisha bint Abi Bakr, 'Abd Allah ibn Mas'ud, and 'Abd Allah ibn 'Abbas. Of the nearly three hundred Companions who appear in al-Tayalisi's *Musnad*, these four are named as sources in more than 25 percent of his material. Examining the isnads traced to these Companions, we don't see much evidence for a united Companion school that transmitted

Muhammad's words and actions to their students with any sense of a collaborative project. Of over two hundred transmitters at the earliest level in al-Tayalisi's material from these four Companions, not a single transmitter had reported material from all four, and fewer than twenty narrated from two or more. In other words, we don't see a developed network connecting these four major sources.

At the next layer of the isnads (students of those who had reported from Muhammad's Companions), more overlap appears with transmitters who had heard directly from one Companion but at this level rely on secondhand reports from others. Moving up another layer in the isnads, we see numerous transmitters whose archives include reports traced back to all four of these Companions. A hadith transmitter such as the Basran scholar Qatada ibn Da'ima (d. ca. 735) or Kufan scholar al-Amash (d. ca. 745–752) thus occupies a position at which separate teaching circles have converged into increasingly entangled lineages, allowing for an imaginary of the Companions as constituting a collective project and these distinct student networks as having transmitted a single body of knowledge.[11] With these local lines coming together in a larger corpus of traditions and a concept of the Companions as a universally authoritative class, it becomes easy to forget the diverse subjectivities existing within the hadith corpus, imagining this literature as instead constituting a monolithic Islamic scripture that can offer a singular Sunni conception of Muhammad.

What happens when we take two of the figures—the "two 'Abd Allahs" (Ibn 'Abbas and Ibn Mas'ud)—and survey their massive bodies of hadiths? Does it give us a sense of them both speaking on behalf of a collective Companion school? It must first be noted that, though they are both regarded as members of the original Muslim community, Ibn 'Abbas and Ibn Mas'ud would later speak from different contexts. Significantly younger than Ibn Mas'ud, Ibn 'Abbas lived through the waves of political discord and factional strife that troubled the Muslim community after Muhammad's death; he even actively participated in these power struggles, leading troops for his cousin 'Ali's army against Aisha and later fought the forces of the Umayyad caliphate's founder, Mu'awiyya, on 'Ali's behalf. Ibn 'Abbas's circle of students were prominently associated with Shi'ism and often experienced conflict with and persecution by the ruling powers. In contrast, Ibn Mas'ud, one of the earliest converts to Islam, died before 'Uthman's assassination, and therefore did not witness or take a side in the turmoil that followed 'Ali's reign as caliph. Ibn 'Abbas and Ibn Mas'ud (and the circles reporting from their authority) occupied different historical moments and represented different locales among the garrison towns of Iraq: Ibn 'Abbas's circle was centered in Basra, while Ibn Mas'ud became the revered sage of Kufa. Reading the two bodies of reports in Ibn Hanbal's (d.855 CE) massive *Musnad* alongside each other, we see different sets of values and priorities. Different themes appear frequently between the two; a topic that appears to be of no importance to one might read as of urgent concern to the other. And, sometimes, these Companions disagree with each other. Beyond the subjectivities of Ibn 'Abbas and Ibn Mas'ud, we must also consider their respective networks of students, who come to them from different backgrounds and ask different questions. At this early stage in the chains of transmission, it becomes difficult to imagine a universal blueprint for naming Islam's top concerns and how to fulfill them.

Ibn 'Abbas's corpus exhibits an abundance of narrations on the topic of Muslims performing pilgrimage or other good deeds to benefit their relatives who died before performing the acts themselves, or were unable to due to disability or old age. Ibn

'Abbas's reports also treat regulations regarding the buying and selling of foodstuffs as a matter of importance. Meanwhile, Ibn Mas'ud's hadiths display a major concern with tattooing (a topic covered extensively in this volume by Max Johnson Dugan), eyebrow plucking, wearing hair extensions, filing teeth, and reading bird omens, often clustered in various combinations together as a single topic, though none of these issues appear in Ibn 'Abbas's reports.

Surveying Ibn 'Abbas's hadiths, his most obvious priority appears to have been correct praxis regarding the Mecca-centered pilgrimages, hajj and *umra*, especially questions of what a pilgrim can do while in ihram, the special status of ritual purity. Generally speaking, it is understood that, after entering into ihram, pilgrims do not have sexual intercourse or kill animals until they exit ihram status. It appears that Ibn 'Abbas's students asked him about other activities, such as fasting, cupping, and contracting (not consummating) a marriage while in the state of ihram.[12] Ibn 'Abbas also speaks as a source on Muhammad's nighttime prayers, which Ibn 'Abbas witnessed at the home of his aunt Maymuna (whom Muhammad had married while in ihram).[13] Another major theme of Ibn 'Abbas's narrations concerns the permissibility of earthenware jars. Though this question's relevance might not be obvious to all modern readers, it related to the condition of *nabidh*, an alcoholic beverage that caused early Muslims some anxiety: Was nabidh in the same category as *khamr* (wine made from grapes), which the Qur'an expressly prohibited? As Muslims argued over nabidh's legal status, they circulated narrations attributed to Ibn 'Abbas that supported both sides. In hadiths in which Ibn 'Abbas presents nabidh as a permissible drink, and one consumed even by Muhammad, he gives disclaimers: Muhammad drank from a leather skin, not an earthenware jar; he did not drink nabidh that had been prepared two days ago; and he did not drink enough to quench his thirst. All of these points help to establish that Muhammad did not drink nabidh as an intoxicant; Ibn ʿAbbas's anti-nabidh hadiths tend to connect the issue to questions of permissible jars.

In dramatic contrast to the silence in Ibn Masʿud's material, Ibn ʿAbbas hadiths repeatedly speak on prophetic sex laws: punishments or curses for transgressions such as bestiality, anal sex between men, lesbian sex, adultery, and men having sex with their wives during menstruation, as well as a policing of gender binaries. Did Muhammad himself prescribe the punishments and condemnations attributed to him? We could ask why Ibn ʿAbbas speaks as such a prolific source, while other major transmitters among the Companions have less (or nothing) to say on sex laws. The question "What does Islam say about homosexuality?" has an answer if we read Ibn ʿAbbas in the *Musnad*, but not if we read Ibn Masʿud. While considering Ibn ʿAbbas as such a prominent reporter on sex laws, we could take our inquiry one step further and ask why, among Ibn ʿAbbas's students, his former slave ʿIkrima dominates these topics to a near-absolute exclusion of Ibn ʿAbbas's other transmitters. ʿIkrima, incidentally, was a controversial transmitter deemed unreliable and dishonest in the eyes of many classical hadith scholars, not to mention ʿIkrima's peers in the Ibn ʿAbbas network. In his examination of hadiths that criminalize homosexuality, Scott Kugle calls attention to ʿIkrima as the most prominent source for these narrations and asks that we give consideration to ʿIkrima's particular subjectivity.[14] Hadiths are never only a question of "Did Muhammad say that?," but forever require that we think about the generations of reporters who mediate his presence.

What does the future look like? In Ibn Masʿud's hadiths, we find a recurring theme of dystopian futures and an Islam that becomes degraded and even extinguished over time. Ibn Masʿud speaks repeatedly of a future in which Muslims fight other Muslims, rulers deviate from the precedents set forth by Muhammad,[15] and the "millstone of Islam" comes to an end within seventy years.[16] Ibn Mas'ud also provides the hadith made famous by modern Salafi networks, in which Muhammad promises that his own generation is the greatest, followed by the next generation, and then the next one in turn, after which Muslims continue to decline through the generations until the end of time.[17] Ibn Mas'ud's interest in a future of decline and deviation connects to another major theme of his hadith narrations, the issue of illegitimately delaying prayers, which was controversial in his immediate setting, apparently the practice of Kufa governor al-Walid ibn 'Uqba.[18]

Beyond these topics in which one Companion offers a wealth of material and the other says little or nothing, we see points on which Ibn 'Abbas and Ibn Mas'ud disagree. One such question concerns the Qur'an's seventy-second sura, which refers to an assembly of jinns (beings created from smokeless fire, from which the English "genie" derives) who hear the Qur'an and recognize it as divinely revealed. Ibn 'Abbas and Ibn Mas'ud (or their networks of students) were both asked if Muhammad personally recited the Qur'an to the jinns, as opposed to them overhearing it, and whether he saw these jinns with his own eyes. In Ibn Hanbal's *Musnad*, Ibn 'Abbas emphatically states that Muhammad neither recited to jinns nor saw them. But Ibn Mas'ud narrates his own experience of the "night of the jinn," which he spent in terror that Muhammad had been killed by the jinns. Muhammad describes the jinns' visual appearance as resembling the people of al-Zutt, and it appears to be possible but not exactly confirmed that Ibn Mas'ud himself saw the jinns.[19] In Ibn Mas'ud's accounts, Muhammad's interactions with the jinns sometimes relate to a question of praxis, as in the detail that, afterward, Muhammad had no water to restore his ritual purity, so he washed with nabidh (establishing that this was a legitimate practice).[20] Additionally, he gave Ibn Mas'ud instructions to never use bones or dung for hygenic purposes (as the jinns rely on bones and dung for their food).[21]

Relatively early in Islamic history, hadith collections shifted from the *musnad* format seen with al-Tayalisi and Ibn Hanbal, in which hadiths were organized by reporter, to the *musannaf* format, in which hadiths were organized by topic. This change reflects a growing sense of the Companions as a united block of authoritative content: rather than look to the teachings of a specific Companion, one would look to the Companions as a collective for what they could say on your question. But, even with the appearance of a monolithic textual canon, multiplicity persists. In the exploration that follows, I move from musnad to musannaf, asking about what many would consider a natural center for Islam: Muhammad. Specifically, I look to Muhammad's body, a natural center of Islam in its own right, asking how Companions experienced and reported Muhammad's body to later generations of Muslims that could not have seen or touched Muhammad themselves.

BODIES AND BARAKA

Asking a question of the Sunni hadith corpus, it can become clear that the Companions (or the networks reporting in their names) did not exist as a singularity of early, pure, original Islam, as though Islam and Muhammad could have meant the same things for everyone who experienced them. The Sunni hadith corpus does not even offer a consistent narrative of what Muhammad looked like, differing in accounts of details such as his skin color and the Seal, either an organic birthmark or literal sealing on his back. Transmissions linked to 'Ali generally describe Muhammad's complexion as white and red, while reports from Anas often report his complexion as medium (along with Muhammad having a medium height and medium hair texture); Anas also narrates that Muhammad's hands were softer than silk and his bodily fragrance was superior to perfume. While a variety of reports from Companions provide details of Muhammad's body, Aisha notably remains all but silent on her husband's appearance.[22]

Different investments in Muhammad's body find expression throughout the hadith corpus. Traditions proliferate in which Muhammad's saliva heals injuries, Companions bottle his sweat for the baraka that it contains, water pours forth from his fingers in times of need, and even his blood and urine offer medicinal and soteriological benefits to those who consume them.[23] These various narrations differ from each other in their relative canonical privilege and the sources to whom they are attributed, but Aisha consistently speaks about Muhammad's bodily fluids and disjecta without an interest in their special properties, though she would have had more access to them than anyone. Aisha speaks of Muhammad's semen, for example, as nothing more than a problem of ritual purity, explaining how she cleaned his clothes. Though the sheer vastness of the hadith corpus and the thousands of transmitters who contributed to it enable some outlier accounts (which are likely outliers not only in their matns but also their isnads), Aisha consistently downplays the powers of her husband's body. Her reports reflect no clearly stated interest in his bodily by-products as modes of connection to flows of baraka. In contrast to narrations from Companions such as Anas that Muhammad's sweat smelled better than perfume, Aisha implies an unpleasant odor when Muhammad sweated heavily while wearing a black wool cloak, and she even suggests that Muhammad has bad breath after he visits her cowife.[24] Regarding the controversy of Muhammad seeing God, whether with his physical eyes or "the eyes of his heart," Aisha stands as the most vehement denier of the vision, insisting that Muhammad only witnessed the angel Gabriel and opposing Companions such as Ibn 'Abbas who believed that Muhammad indeed saw his lord.[25] Finally, the hadith corpus contains reports of Companions preserving traces of Muhammad's body after his death, such as his hair, fingernails, bottled sweat, and objects that he had touched, and using these objects for healing, but Aisha does not appear as a practitioner, reporter, or advocate of these traditions.[26]

These multiplicities, while obscured in treatments of the Companions as a collective class transmitting a singular vision of Islam, become increasingly visible in hadith collections devoted to specific topics concerning Muhammad. Bayhaqi's *Hayat al-Anbiya' fi Quburihim* (Lives of the Prophets in their graves), for example, provides hadiths as evidence that prophets are physically alive, sentient, and peforming prayer in their graves. The hadiths' isnads trace them back to Companions such as Anas, Abu Hurayra, Ibn 'Abbas, and Ibn Mas'ud. Aisha, however, does not appear as a source for this concept of the postmortem prophetic body.[27] Likewise, chapters and subsections within specific hadith collections privilege some Companions over others or otherwise point to a divergence between their experiences of Muhammad. In Ibn Sa'd's *Tabaqat*, for example, a section devoted to Muhammad's *khalq*, his nature, offers a wealth of narrations from various Companions on the transcendent beauty and special qualities of Muhammad's body (*khalq* in this context signifying his physical form) while Aisha only produces a pair of reports about how he moved or positioned his body when turning or praying. Aisha's remark that Muhammad's khalq was the Qur'an itself—reinscribing the matter of Muhammad's khalq as not his body, but his innate disposition and character—appears elsewhere in the collection.[28]

Consistently, Aisha (or the network reporting in her name) presents Muhammad's body as mundane and unexceptional, in marked contrast from other reporters and networks that report a miraculous and perfect prophetic corporeality. Some of these, such as the reports attributed to Ibn 'Abbas, represent pro-'Alid or proto-Shi'i forces, politically opposed to the Aisha network. Hadiths in which Muhammad is said to have descended from the best of God's creation, for example, can be found in Sunni sources with isnads that include Ja'far as-Sadiq, the Shi'i imam, reporting from his father, al-Baqir.[29] Interestingly, the only hadith that I could find in which Aisha provides a "checklist" account of her husband's physical appearance bears an isnad that includes a reputed Shi'i transmitter.[30] While allowing for exceptions and outliers, it would be a thinkable project to identify multiple networks of transmitters in these hadith sources with diverse prophetologies.

The hadith corpus might give the appearance of a natural center in Islam, but is of course a contested terrain. The possibilities for rethinking centers and margins in Islam could not only include movement away from hadith texts but also look at the ways that hadiths factor into ongoing struggles and constructions of "orthodoxy" and "heterodoxy." Contrary to popular imagination, for example, the Nation of Islam has made extensive use of hadith sources, most prominently in Wesley Muhammad's scholarship, which I term a "Nation Salafism" for its work of locating Nation theology among the Salaf, the first three generations of Muslims.[31]

Complicating the binary opposition of textual versus folk Islam in terms of practices related to baraka and bodies is the reality that the hadith corpus, a sacred textual source in Islam second only to the Qur'an in universal acceptance, does not speak with a consistent and singular voice—even if we were to limit the hadith corpus to Sunni sources and neglect Shi'i hadith texts, and then further limit the Sunni hadith corpus to only its most canonical books. Moreover, the Sunni hadith corpus isn't even absolutely Sunni, or at least it challenges popular notions of Sunni-Shi'i boundaries, given the significant presence of Shi'i (or proto-Shi'i) hadith reporters, as well as the ways in which they preserve Shi'i visions of Muhammad's prophetic ontology and Islamic history within the Sunni canon.

While ostensibly a central rather than marginal Islamic source, and a textual body often vested in the modern world with supreme orthodoxy-making power and privilege, the Sunni hadith archive's appearance of monolithic unity betrays a radical diversity. Though Sunni intellectual tradition *eventually* established the concept of the Companions' collective probity as trustworthy reporters of Muhammad's words and actions, is it clear that the Companions themselves did not regard each other in this way, or even share a collective definition of what it meant to be a Companion. The figures retroactively categorized by later scholars as Companions disagreed and even fought with each other in battle. The hadith corpus offers the presentation of a united Companion voice speaking for a united Islam, but the multiplicity of views and concepts found in hadith literature and the transmission histories evidenced in their isnads betray the notion of a singular original, authentic Islam that could be recovered from the text.

Returning to one of the central ideas of this volume—namely, that Islamic studies should center the "experience of Muslim people," specifically "the experience of ordinary Muslims," rather than only prioritize the classical texts—I acknowledge that my focus on hadith might appear to be moving in the opposite direction. I am trying, however, to inject this approach *into* the hadiths. At one time in history, Muhammad's Companions were Muslims (whether ordinary or not is beyond my scope here) who narrated their lived experiences. Obviously, we can question whether the hadith corpus accurately represents their accounts; the academic debate on that question is not closed. But there are reasons to consider that we can confidently encounter the diverse individual subjectivities that went into this material. As we look into the multiplicity among the Companions themselves that only gradually, over the course of generations, assembles into something that *looks* like a united singular body, we could find generative new openings in the canonical texts. The result could look like a deconstruction of the hadith corpus, the Sunna, and perhaps Muhammad himself, but it could also reflect a deconstruction that enables creative new reassemblies.

NOTES

1. Vernon Schubel, *Religious Performance in Contemporary Islam: Shi'i Devotional Rituals in South Asia* (Columbia: University of South Carolina Press, 1993), 160.
2. Schubel, *Religious Performance in Contemporary Islam*, xi.
3. Etan Kohlberg, "Shī'ī Ḥadīth," in *The Cambridge History of Arabic Literature, Vol. 1: Arabic Literature Until the End of the Umayyad Period*, ed. A. F. L. Beeston (Cambridge: Cambridge University Press, 1983), 299–307.
4. It is worth noting here that my observations on Shi'i hadith scholars focus on Twelver Shi'a rather than on Isma'ili or Zaydi Shi'a, whose collections of hadith "operate under district methodologies," as an anonymous reviewer of this book helpfully pointed out.
5. Michael Muhammad Knight, *Muhammad's Body: Baraka Networks and the Prophetic Assemblage* (Chapel Hill: University of North Carolina Press, 2020), 100–101.

6. Knight, *Muhammad's Body*, 100–1.
7. Asma Sayeed, *Women and the Transmission of Religious Knowledge in Islam* (Cambridge: Cambridge University Press, 2013).
8. Christopher Melchert, "Sectaries in the Six Books: Evidence for Their Exclusion from the Sunni Community," *Muslim World* 82 (1992): 287–95.
9. Lyall R. Armstrong, *The Qussas of Early Islam* (Leiden: Brill, 2016).
10. John Nawas, "The Contribution of the Mawali to the Six Sunnite Canonical Hadith Collections," in *Ideas, Images, and Methods of Portrayal: Insights into Classical Arabic Literature and Islam,* ed. Sebastian Gunther (Leiden: Brill, 2005),141–51.
11. Abu Dawud al-Tayalisi, *al-Musnad* (Beirut: Dar Ibn Hazm, 2013).
12. Ahmad Ibn Hanbal, *Musnad al-Imam Ahmad ibn Hanbal* (Beirut: 'Alam al-Kutub, 1998), #2890, #3109.
13. Ibn Hanbal, *Musnad al-Imam Ahmad*, #2164, #2196, #2559, #2567, #3194, #3372.
14. Scott Kugle, *Homosexuality in Islam* (Oxford: Oxford University Press, 2015), 102–7.
15. Ibn Hanbal, *al-Musnad,* #4363, #4402.
16. Ibn Hanbal, #4315.
17. Ibn Hanbal, #3594.
18. Ibn Hanbal, #4298.
19. Ibn Hanbal, #4353.
20. Ibn Hanbal, #3781, #3810, #4301, #4343.
21. Ibn Hanbal, #4375.
22. Knight, *Muhammad's Body*, 39–42.
23. Knight, 71–102.
24. Knight, 83–84.
25. Melchert, "The Early Controversy Over Whether the Prophet Saw God," *Arabica* 62 (2015): 459–76.
26. Knight, *Muhammad's Body*, 82, 84–87.
27. Knight, 143.
28. Knight, 43–48.
29. Knight, 32.
30. Knight, 47.
31. Wesley Williams, "Tajalli wa-Ru'ya: A Study of Anthropomorphic Theophany and Visio Dei in the Hebrew Bible, the Qur'an and Early Sunni Islam" (PhD diss., University of Michigan, 2008).

3

ISLAMIC TATTOOING

Embodying Healing, Materializing Relationships, and Mediating Tradition

MAX JOHNSON DUGAN

> Living as we did—on the edge—we developed a particular way of seeing reality. We looked both from the outside and from the inside out. We focused our attention on the center as well as on the margin. We understood both. This mode of seeing reminded us of the existence of a whole universe, a main body made up of both margin and center. Our survival depended on an ongoing public awareness of the separation between margin and center and an ongoing private acknowledgement that we were a necessary, vital part of that whole.
>
> —bell hooks

On December 16, 2019, the Associated Press published an article about the struggles faced by a tattoo artist in Kabul, Afghanistan. The headline, "A Tattoo at a Time, Afghan Woman Takes on Society's Taboos," gestured to the main themes of the piece: patriarchal Islam, conflict, the long shadow cast by the Taliban, and widespread social conservatism in Afghanistan.[1] Packed between these harrowing anecdotes of oppressive, patriarchal applications of Islamic tradition and death threats were several nuanced representations of Suraya Shaheedi's experience as a Muslim woman living in Kabul. In the article, Shaheedi explains that her first tattoo "symbolizes overcoming adversity," and the author of the piece also depicts a network of supporters, from parents to social media users, who encourage Shaheedi and other tattoo artists in Afghanistan to continue their work. But these momentary humanistic representations of an Afghan woman tattoo artist were drowned out by an overarching message of conflict and hazard. In 2021, following the tragically mishandled withdrawal of U.S. troops from Afghanistan, many of the dangers—the Taliban's takeover and the imminent threat posed to many segments of the nation, especially women—seem justified. Yet, in 2019, the themes of this article echo an old narrative of a struggle between a peaceful, modern, and Western-compatible Islam, and a conservative, reactionary, Middle Eastern Islam. In this Orientalist narrative, tattoos are merely a vehicle for recycling a harmful depiction of the good West struggling with the soul of a dangerous Islamic East.

Three years earlier, on August 27, 2016, a piece written by author and poet Fariha Róisín about her tattoos in a conversation format with writer Jenna Wortham appeared in the less widely circulated *Flare* magazine.[2] Themes like taboo and struggle are present, but do not drown out the humanistic description of what tattoos have done for Róisín as a Muslim woman of color. For her, the tattoos materialize personal history, especially relationships with other people, and they rekindled her embodied sense of self, especially during deeply stressful transitions or challenges. It should come as no surprise, then, that Róisín's first tattoo was *La ilaha illAllah*, or "There is no god but God, the first part of the Shahadah, or

Muslim profession of faith." In Róisín's account, while Islamic tattoos may involve struggle and conflict, like most lived experiences do, they are far more than that. In accounts like hers, Islamic tattoos might also allow one to reclaim one's body, commemorate a friendship, or deepen a relationship with and commitment to God. Essays from the perspective of tattooed Muslims also offer a view from "the edge": what Farah Bakaari writes about in the first chapter of this volume as the margins of and in Islamic tradition. This chapter focuses on a recent wave of articles about Islamic tattooing in order to understand what tattoos do for Muslims and what we might learn about Islamic embodiment by prioritizing marginalized perspectives. Conceptualizing Islamic tattooing as marginal—as opposed to conflicting or exterior—clarifies that Islamic tattooing is not necessarily a break with or exit from tradition, but, rather, an embodied enactment of Islamic tradition. Islamic tattooing may be in tension with some aspects of that tradition, such as certain restrictions around permanently marking the skin, but it also emerges from other parts of Islamic tradition, such as Islamic aesthetic motifs or exterior demonstrations of piety.[3] Ultimately, Islamic tattooing shows the ways in which Muslims engage their bodies as means of healing, mediating Islamic tradition, and materializing relationships.

To illustrate this, I focus primarily on several recent articles written by Muslim women about their tattoos and tattoos of other Muslims, mostly women. I provide background about tattooing generally, media coverage of Islamic tattooing, and tattooing in Islamic tradition, focusing on Sunni Islamic tradition. This background will show, first, that tattooing has been marginalized in Western European representations that cast it as exotic, primitive, and depraved, or popular discourse that has repackaged Orientalist tropes: a conflict between East and West, or the essential backwardness and patriarchy of Islam. Second, it will demonstrate that tattooing has been marginalized in Sunni Islamic tradition despite the fact that—as my brief survey of foundational Islamic sources shows—its condemnation may lie more in its function in the early Islamic context than in tattoos themselves. Finally, I turn to the main focus of the chapter: recently published articles and photo-essays about Islamic tattooing. The sources place the margins at the center of the analysis, in turn elucidating the healing, mediating, and materializing power of Islamic tattooing. The voices contained within these essays show how struggle conjoins to peace, how difficulty coexists with relief. These tattooed, marginalized bodies point to opportunities for a more just world while materializing devotion in the present.

WHY TATTOOS?

I first noticed the complexity of Islamic tattooing after a conversation with a parent at an afterschool program in North Philadelphia. I managed the program and handled pickups, which meant that I frequently caught up with parents while their children prepared to leave. This parent and I were both converts to Islam, and we quickly moved on from discussing the weather and other pleasantries to talking about *deen*.[4] One day, he arrived distraught. Influential members of the nearby mosque, he informed me, had told him he could not pray there unless he wore long sleeves and gloves that covered up his tattooed forearms and hands. No one had explained to him the reasoning behind this new requirement or the sources it was based upon. He felt that leaders in the community were holding his past life against him and pushing him out. Already on the margins at this particular mosque, he worried that his tattoos would lead to his final exit.

Rather than accept its abnormality, this chapter centers Islamic tattooing by learning about it on its own terms. People acquire tattoos for all kinds of reasons. A tattoo might commemorate an event like qualifying for the Olympics or carrying a four-ton giglio through Brooklyn.[5] A tattoo might protect its wearer,[6] or control "contagious sacredness."[7] Tattoos may also heal by resignifying traumatic scars from a double mastectomy,[8] or help one embody their own agency and self-determination.[9] For all of these intentional and serious tattoos, many others are spontaneous and light hearted—for instance, the tongue-in-cheek "I am 25" written in sans serif font on my twin brother's forearm. This is to say nothing of the aesthetics or the sensations of tattooing. Just like any art form, tattoos are visually appealing in ways that some appreciate and others do not. And, like any embodied act, the feeling of being tattooed or having tattoos may compel or repulse.

Western writing about tattoos has long marginalized communities and individuals who have them. Examples of tattooing, or inserting long-lasting pigments into deeper layers of skin, are found widely across human societies for thousands of years. The oldest known tattooed body dates between 3100 and 3700 BCE and was found in the Ötztal Alps in Italy. Other ancient tattooed bodies have been found in areas as disparate as Greenland, Western China, Siberia, the Philippines, Africa, Europe, Mexico, and the Andes.[10] Yet the dominant narratives originate tattooing in the South Pacific Islands ("tattoo" likely derives from the Polynesian *tatau*), and, more recently, Native American communities on the frontiers of settler colonial expansion—two communities that have been misrepresented as essentially primitive or especially barbaric.[11] Even though its practice continued in East Africa, South Asia and the Mediterranean, early origin stories have relegated tattooing to the literal margins of a Eurocentric world.[12]

When Europeans began grappling with tattooing, they associated it with criminality. This is best exemplified in the work of Cesare Lombroso (d. 1909). Opposed to the notion that criminality was an inherited trait, Lombroso relied heavily on physiognomy, or the study of character based on outward appearance, as a predictive method. Physiognomy was often used for transparently racist ends—for example, the likening of people of African descent to apes to imply their less-evolved state—while having a more complicated history.[13] In Lombroso's scheme, tattoos were strong indicators of a criminal nature.[14] Influential in criminology, sociology, and psychology, Lombroso's ideas circulated throughout academic spaces and, via popular works like *Sherlock Holmes*, the general public.[15] These representations acknowledged the presence of tattooing in European society while placing it on the fringes of civility, always in jeopardy of falling outside the norm.

In many ways, the history of tattooing is one of shifting margins and centers. Colonial narratives located it on the geographic peripheries of Western Europe. In the mid-nineteenth century, racially charged writing about criminals represented tattooing as a sign of criminality, a habit limited to those on the margins of European society. As it moved from so-called circus freak shows (a nomenclature rooted in ableism and racism) to the outskirts and underbellies of navy towns to, currently, the mainstream of American culture, tattooing relied on adapting margins.[16] Some of this is visible on the body, as tattoos have migrated from covered body parts (back, biceps, and thighs) to coverable spots (lower back, forearms, and chest), to unavoidable locations (face and neck). But this is also a matter of social, political, and religious marginalization. When we look at the coverage of Islamic tattooing, we see that Muslims are one of the groups that is now marginalized in discussions about tattooing.

THE MARGINALIZATION OF ISLAMIC TATTOOING IN THE MEDIA

Portrayals of Islamic tattooing in newspapers, television shows, and new media formats often place it on the margins in a problematic manner. English-language media frequently thematizes conflict in its coverage of Islamic tattooing, with the implication that "Western" tattooing is incompatible with "Oriental" Islam. Ultimately, this approach prevents us from learning about Islamic tattooing from those involved in it. Notably absent in this coverage are Muslims who are Black and tattooed. This likely stems from the association of Islam with Arabs and, to a lesser extent, South Asia—Black Muslims with tattoos fall outside of the Orientalist conflict narrative and thus lack the coverage of Arab or South Asian Muslims with tattoos. Even if they continue to focus on Muslims of Arab or South Asian descent, the recent publications I examine later in the chapter offer new perspectives on tattooing that show how tattoos can heal bodies, mediate Islamic tradition, and materialize relationships. The current ways of writing about Islamic tattooing fall short. Centering Islamic tattooing opens up new ways of conceptualizing Islam, Muslim bodies, and tattooing.

The limited coverage of Islamic tattooing in English-language media centers around conflict. Coverage of Kendyl Noor Aurora (or the "Tattooed Hijabi") focused overwhelmingly on the dissonance between her tattoos (which symbolized her Western life) and her conversion to Islam.[17] The Associated Press's coverage of Suraya Shaheedi's work as a tattoo artist in Afghanistan nestled details of her father's support of her work in a story about the death threats she receives from conservative Muslims and her fear of what will happen if the Taliban were to take control of Kabul.[18] Similarly, Sonny Bill Williams, a former New Zealand rugby star who converted to Islam, garnered more coverage when a small group of Muslims on social media criticized his tattoos than for his good public acts since converting.[19] The *Daily Mail* in Australia even published an inaccurate representation of Muslim opposition to Islamic tattooing, mentioning Williams when the Muslim leader criticized neither tattooing nor Williams.[20] And when Ira Khan, the daughter of Bollywood superstar Aamir Khan, became interested in tattooing, many outlets framed the story around the limited pushback she received online from social media users.[21]

These representations of tattooing reek of Orientalism, or the representation of Muslims and the East as essentially incompatible with the West. In these representations, tattooing evokes the West and a range of concepts and values, such as "freedom" (especially of women), "development," and "creativity." Islam and the East are defined in contradistinction. So, the implicit logic of Orientalism goes: if tattooing is Western, and thus free and creative, then Islam must be restrictive and stagnant. As Edward Said's *Orientalism* demonstrates, these representations are far from innocent accidents or objective representations of reality.[22] On the contrary, they originated during colonialism (or were recirculated during colonialism) and perpetuated through scholarship that harms Muslims.[23] A particularly stark example of this violence is the reliance of the George W. Bush White House on the scholarship of Samuel P. Huntington—who asserted the inevitability of a "clash of civilizations" between Islam and the West because of their essentially different values—in their decision to wage war on Afghanistan and Iraq following September 11.[24] Similarly, these representations superimpose "Islam" and "the West" on any struggles faced by tattooed Muslims. In the process, the complex perspective of those tattooed Muslims is muted by a familiar, pernicious cacophony of Orientalism.

Recent scholarship by Alyssa Maldonado-Estrada on tattoos and Catholic masculinity offers a better approach for understanding what tattoos do for those who get them. In Maldonado-Estrada's research on Catholic masculinity in a Brooklyn parish, she found that tattoos materialized and deepened relationships between male parishioners.[25] Elsewhere, Maldonado-Estrada has written about the way these tattoos serve as religious sacraments insofar as they have a purpose for those who have them.[26] This mode of analysis focuses on what tattoos do for bodies rather than their weighty cosmological or theological implications. Theology, religious ethics, and protection from supernatural forces are no doubt important to many, but the material, local, and social dimensions of religious tattoos are often more salient for everyday people. Like a close friendship with a fellow worshipper or a charitable act for a stranger, the relationships materialized in a religious tattoo are often more integral than doctrine to devotion or religious feelings.

Additionally, Tamara Santibañez's writing and activism has framed tattooing as "liberation work."[27] Santibañez's experience shows how tattooing—its ritual aspects, the relationship between the tattooer and the tattooed, its imagery, and its placement on the body—can heal trauma and subvert oppression. In this respect, Santibañez takes the observation that tattoos can provide comfort to those recovering from, for instance, a mastectomy,[28] and extends it to traumas rooted in structural violence.[29] For example, Santibañez upends the all-too-common narrative that prison tattoos are inextricably gang related, arguing instead that tattooing intervenes in the traumatizing expropriation of embodied agency experienced by incarcerated peoples.[30] She also clarifies that tattooing facilitates healing and recovery for other traumas, be they related to gender-based violence, intergenerational trauma, or body dysmorphia. If one's body and the traumas it experiences are political, then so, too, are the processes that repair those bodies political. While Santibañez does not write specifically about Islamic tattooing, her work extends to and illuminates the healing that Muslims with tattoos write about.

If we look at the discourse about Islamic tattooing from the marginalized perspective of tattooed Muslims, the Orientalism that fuels it becomes apparent. In this way, we follow bell hooks's observation that marginalized groups—such as many tattooed Muslims—have "a special vantage point" of oppressive centers, since they experience both the margin and the center. hooks's *Feminist Theory* (1981) contends that the double marginalization of Black women by patriarchy and racism, and the anger it has engendered in Black women toward that oppression, generated a uniquely clear perspective from which to build a feminist movement.[31] In this way, hooks contends that marginalized positions provide a sounder basis for understanding inequity, as well as creating more just systems. Although this chapter focuses on what tattoos do for tattooed Muslims, it is important to look, as hooks writes, "on the center as well as on the margin." In this case, tattooed Muslims confront several "centers," one of which is popular media discourse about Islamic tattooing. In the following section, I look at another center: Islamic tradition.

TATTOOING IN SUNNI ISLAMIC TRADITION

Looking from the margins means that we should understand more about the sources that justified the stigmatization of my friend in that Philadelphia mosque and that continue to obfuscate the effects of Islamic tattooing for tattooed Muslims. This section begins with a brief review of tattooing in the early Islamic period, starting with the meaning of "tattoo," or *al-washm*, in this social context. Then I look closely at several hadith—prophetic traditions, mainly of the sayings and actions of Muhammad, but sometimes his companions, as well as sayings of God—that contain the prohibition of tattooing. At the core of the following analysis is the question: Are the tattoos adorning his hands the same thing that is forbidden in the sources of Islamic tradition?[32] Ultimately, this section shows that the tattooing that has been marginalized in Islamic tradition may be substantially different than the contemporary practice.

Although the foundational texts of Islamic tradition provide the basis for prohibition of tattoos, what "tattoo" meant in the early Islamic milieu is less certain. For one, the term used in these foundational texts is not "tattoo" but *al-washm*. Looking at sources about *al-washm*, we find that the feelings it evoked and the meaning it communicated differed from "tattoo." In poetic sources from the early Islamic period, for example, *al-washm* gave the sense of a mark of longing or nostalgia, mixed with affiliation, beautification, and particular body parts, especially the hands and mouth. Two of the Suspended Odes (*al-muʿallaqāt*), or prototypical Arabic poems from around the early Islamic period, include words related to "tattoo."[33] In both cases, tattoos evoke things of the past whose memory and appearance fade with time. Additionally, tattooing likely communicated a recommitment to a tribe.[34]

Other Islamic scholarly sources indicate that *al-washm* was often a mark on or around the hands, mouth, and lips that connoted the beautification of women or tribal affiliation. Many prominent Arabic lexicographies,[35] or compilations of other Arabic dictionary entries, emphasize the importance of beautification and femininity in their depiction of tattooing.[36] Ibn Shumayl, as related by Ibn Manẓūr, also connects *al-wushūm* (pl. *al-washm*) to *al-wusūm*, meaning "brands, tribal marks, marks."[37] This implies that tattoos symbolized things, likely Arab tribal affiliations. Regarding placement on the body, the overwhelming number of sources cited by Ibn Manẓūr identify the hand as the site of the tattoo.[38] Although not lexicographic, al-Zawzanī defines tattooing as "pricking the back of the hand and other things."[39] At least one other lexicography mentions the mouth and lips as the site of tattooing.[40] What kind of sense, then, do we get of the function of tattoos in the early Islamic milieu? What kind of practices might Muhammad have opposed when he, as we will see, cursed the tattooer?

One possible explanation is that tattooing, or *al-washm*, was associated with slavery and enslavement. The sense that tattoos would have been used to mark enslaved bodies as property or affiliated is supported by the considerable history of visibly marking enslaved people in the ancient Near East.[41] The Hammurabi Code mentions slave marks in three paragraphs (146, 226, and 227) and specifies the punishment for those who unlawfully aid a slave in removing their mark of enslavement (*abbuttu*, which was possibly a clay or metal tablet worn around the neck, or a hot iron brand).[42] Scholars have demonstrated the continued practice of marking slaves with clay or metal tablets in early Islamic communities over two millennia later.[43] In her research on Jewish bodily practices, Sandra Jacobs found that ancient Jewish communities also employed several body modification practices to communicate property ownership.[44] These examples indicate that bodily marking may well have signaled ownership of a body to the early Muslim community.

Hadith that address tattoos and tattooers do so in a condemnatory, prohibitive manner.[45] In a few brief hadith, Muhammed curses the tattooer and the seeker of a tattoo. Far more often, however, tattoos (or words derived from *w-sh-m*) are listed along with a set of parallel prohibited practices or cursed actors. One hadith included by Al-Bukhāri in the chapter on hair removers (*bāb al-mutanammiṣāt*) contains one of the more frequently transmitted accounts about tattooing. The text (*matn*) of the hadith is: "Abd-Allah [Muhammad] cursed the tattooers, hair-removers, and teeth-spacers for the beautification that changes the creation of God."[46] Other hadith forbade commercial transactions involving tattooing (mentioned alongside usury, dogs, and picture-makers) and using tattoos to ward off the evil eye.[47] Contemporary opinions against tattooing have relied on these hadith in their prohibitions, explaining that tattooing illicitly and unnecessarily changes the creation of God (*khalq Allah*).[48]

These seemingly straightforward condemnations become more nuanced when we account for the different meanings and functions of *al-washm* in the early Islamic milieu. In the case of beautification practices, Al-'Asqalānī's commentary on the hadith clarifies that the concern is not simply body modification, but beautification that leads to illicit sex.[49] The key difference is the husband's permission for the licit beautification, implying that illicit beauty is that which leads to illicit sex—that is, outside of marriage, or concubinage.[50] Al-'Asqalānī's commentary on another hadith included in *Ṣaḥīḥ Bukhārī* clarifies that it is the act of tattooing, not the tattoo itself, that is prohibited.[51]

Again, considering the association of tattooing with enslavement, this would indicate that the tattooer, and not the enslaved person, would be at fault for the tattoos. And yet another hadith condemning tattooing focuses especially on the prohibited use of tattooing as a protection from the evil eye.[52]

The web of meaning, function, and practice around the prohibition of tattooing is a tangled one. Early Islamic sources and commentaries on those sources support a prohibition of *al-washm*, but there is more to *al-washm* than the straightforward translation of "tattooing." For one, there is substantial evidence that tattooing would have evoked enslavement and sex work. Other commentaries on hadith about tattooing add that *al-washm* may have been used as an apotropaic device, or protection against harmful supernatural forces. The opinion that tattooing changes creation in a manner that should be prohibited connects neatly with contemporary justifications for the impermissibility of tattooing. But even that justification is tied up with the notion that the change brought on by tattooing signals illicit sex. In other words, the marginalization of Islamic tattooing in Islamic tradition does not rest on univocal condemnation of tattooing as such. The next section centers the experiences of tattooed Muslims to recover something thus far absent from this discussion: the impetuses for and benefits of Islamic tattooing in the present.

ISLAMIC TATTOOING IN PRACTICE

Centering Islamic tattooing reveals that this practice helps Muslims heal, mediate tradition, and materialize relationships. Tattooing may be condemned in Sunni discursive tradition, but it also emerges from Islamic tradition more generally, drawing on its aesthetics, valorized relationships, and the impetus to care for oneself and oppose injustice. Regarding embodiment, tattoos often redress trauma and the structures that traumatize. In particular, tattooed Muslims frequently assert control over their body in the face of encroachments upon it. Aesthetically, tattoos mediate Islamic tradition in their frequent merging of styles or motifs prevalent in contemporary tattoo culture with Islamic ones. Islamic tattoos also make material the relationships they signify, not only symbolizing friends or family members but also inscribing those relationships into the skin. Centering the perspectives of tattooed Muslims elucidates the work that tattoos do for their wearers, while demonstrating the animating force of healing, renewing, and relating.

Healing

To understand how Islamic tattooing can heal bodies, I center the perspective of Fariha Róisín, a queer South Asian Muslim poet and writer.[53] Specifically, I focus on an interview between Róisín and Jenna Wortham, a writer for the *New York Times Magazine*, that includes commentary and photographs by Róisín. The conversation transitions from their early experiences with and reasons for tattooing to discussion of their specific tattoos and the tattoo community in general. Healing takes many forms. Róisín specifically describes how tattoos have reinvigorated her body and notions of self, as well as the way that tattoos can protect the body through marking the skin. In an era when notions of identity and self are increasingly in flux, tattoos have been, for Róisín, an instrument of self-identification and identity-marking. She writes: "Tattooing became a way to claim my body, or a space for my body, especially during moments when my body didn't feel like mine anymore. I got my first tattoo around the time I got pregnant; I needed to remind myself of who I was: a Muslim, at a time when I felt so far from God, my faith, and mostly myself. Marking my skin felt like a conscious act of control. It was as if I could relearn who I was through the ink."

In this description, Róisín makes clear the connection between a destabilization of her Muslim identity and a sense of distance from components of her religious identity. The aesthetics and backstories of Róisín's over thiry tattoos are quite varied. One of these clearly relates to reengagement with her Muslimness: a tattoo of the Kalimah (*la ilaha illAllah*, Arabic for "There is no god but God"), which is one part of the Shahadah, or profession of faith. Róisín describes this Kalimah tattoo as, for her, a "spiritual oath to Allah." Róisín describes how tattoos like this one enabled her to "relearn" her identity. This description of "relearn" indicates an engagement with one's past self that, like reading a nostalgic children's book in adulthood, incorporates new experiences and perspectives.

Elsewhere in the interview, Róisín discusses the protective aspects of tattoos. Róisín writes that "friends that wear the hijab have claimed the veil as a shield; my very own sister has described it as a second layer of skin. For me, that's the intuitive teleology of a tattoo." Here, Róisín explicates the protective aspect of her tattoos by using the unmistakably Muslim hijab as a reference. This immediately demonstrates that Róisín frames her tattoos as analogous to Islamic practice. But, as we consider this in the context of healing, we can also see how tattooing can be a kind of preventative care, like getting a flu shot or regularly exercising to preempt unwellness. The protective dimension of tattooing expands notions of healing while echoing Islamic practices like wearing the hijab or adorning oneself with a khamsa or Hand of Fatima.

The kind of healing that Róisín describes here exceeds a dominant understanding of "treatment." The trauma Róisín describes lies in the loss of agency and disruption of identity that stem from structural oppression. This oppression is enmeshed with patriarchy and the vestiges of colonialism, especially in the reduction of "Muslim" to adherence to a set of jurisprudential norms. Róisín describes in profound, evocative terms the harmful embodied effects of these structures—a disconnection from one's body and from God. Tattooing was the intervention; tattooing treated this disconnection. Furthermore, tattooing provides a kind of protection as a persistent second skin. As Santibañez observes and Róisín exemplifies, the healing of one's body with permanent ink challenges oppressive power structures. Rather than understanding it as an exclusively individual act, we should approach tattooing as a confrontation with larger societal forces that alienate people from their bodies and relegate them to the fringes.

Mediating Islamic Tradition

To understand how tattoos mediate Islamic tradition, I turn to the article "Challenging Taboos: Muslim and Tattooed," which appeared in *Brown Girl Magazine* (henceforth *BG*) in May 2017.[54] The article, written by Elizabeth Jaikaran,[55] consists of profiles of eight Muslims—all of Arab or South Asian descent, with the lone exception being Kendyl Noor Aurora, who is white—with tattoos and describes two larger Muslim tattoo phenomena (Twelver Shi'a tattooing and Algerian Berber tattooing).[56] The article succinctly introduces many notable themes in Islamic tattooing, such as the tension between lived Islam and Islamic tradition. But I invoke it here because of the way the Muslim interviewees mediate Islamic tradition in their tattoos. I describe this process as "mediation" to point to the way tattoos structure and transform the messages or images that constitute them. A tattoo not only communicates an image; it also embodies and transforms the contents of that image for viewers. In the examples I will give, Islamic tattoos mediate Islamic tradition by pulling together Islamic aesthetics, Islamic texts and myth, personal experiences, and popular tattoo styles.

An observant South Asian Muslim, Jamin began acquiring tattoos when she was sixteen years old as a coping mechanism and means of self-expression.[57] Jamin considered the tattoos a way to "honor" her journey through life by representing significant relationships and aspects of her identity. Jamin notes that her tattoos distinguish her as the "rebel" among her South Asian friends. Jamin has two large, vibrantly colored pieces. The shoulder piece—a collection of lilies and orchids that represent different family members and Jamin's South Asian roots—would only be apparent as religious after explanation. By contrast, her pastiche of crescent moon, lote tree, and lotus flower clearly merges Islamic aesthetics with South Asian and popular tattoo styles. The lote tree, which in Islamic mythology exists at the end of the seventh heaven, and the lotus flower are not obviously Islamic prior to explanation, but the crescent moon is clear enough to index "Muslim" to a knowledgeable viewer. These tattoos ground personal experience and South Asian identity in a vibrantly colored scheme of pinks, greens, and oranges. They also mediate Islamic tradition, bringing these different familial, regional, and Islamic aesthetics into conversation with one another.

Employing substantially different aesthetics and cultural allusions, Azam acquired a full back tattoo to honor his Muslim grandfather. After his grandfather passed away in 2011, Azam sought a way to honor him, especially his guidance through Azam's troubled youth. The tattoo covers his back, the center consisting of an English translation excerpt of Surat al-Baqrah that reads: "In Loving Memory: Who when a misfortune overtakes them say surely we belong to God and to Him we shall return."[58] The words are embedded in clouds alongside Gaelic faerie-style angels praying adjacent to and beneath the text. This synthesis of Islamic content with Christian visual motifs offers another example of the way Islamic tattooing draws on Islamic tradition while remixing it aesthetically. Moreover, the Christian appearance of the tattoo shields Azam from Islamophobia he might encounter; though the chronology is unclear, Azam implies that he obtained the tattoo while serving in the U.S. Army. Azam also mentions that his tattoo materializes his aspiration to "live up to the man he [his grandfather] wanted me to be." Thus, this mediation interweaves ideas of normative masculinity into Islamic tradition and popular Christian tattoo aesthetics.

Many of Suraiya's tattoos symbolize aspects of her Muslim identity, but in ways that would be difficult for outsiders to discern. Take, for example, the breaking chains inscribed on her forearm, or the noose on the right side of her torso. Growing up in the United States, I immediately associate those images with slavery and anti-Black racism: the chains with emancipation, the civil rights movement, and ongoing activism; and the noose with lynching and structural violence against Black people. For Suraiya, however, these symbols relate to the chains that Twelver Shi'a Muslims use to flagellate themselves during Ashura—an embodied commemoration of the murder of Imam Husayn, members of his family, and close supporters at Karbala, which more generally symbolizes worldly injustice and occurs on the tenth (*'ashura*) day of the month of Muharram—and the noose with which Mansur Al-Hallaj was hung.[59] Here, Suraiya materializes Muslim belonging and mystical affinity in minimalist blackwork that resonates with U.S. history, Sufism, and Shiʻi mythology. What's even more remarkable about this tattoo is the fact that Suraiya is an Ismaʻili rather than a Twelver Shiʻi Muslim. As one of the anonymous reviewers of this book observes, the martyrdom of Husayn at Karbala resonates differently in many Ismaʻili traditions that it does in many Twelver Shiʻi communities.

Materializing Relationships

In addition to their healing and mediating capacities, tattoos also materialize relationships. The relationship between tattooer and tattooed is always present in the ink. Yet Islamic tattooing frequently captures other relationships that are familial, social, or devotional. We have already encountered examples of these, such as the floral representations of Jamin's family or Azam's tribute to his grandfather in the ink on his back. Additionally, I turn to a photo-essay by Yasmin Bendaas, published in *Al Jazeera* in 2013, about Algerian Berber women's tattooing. This piece offers a third kind of relationship: the fading intracommunal bonds in the context of colonialism and increasingly jurisprudential-minded Islamic tradition. This materialization merges the three themes explored in this section by showing how relationships, the mediation of tradition, and healing dovetail in Islamic tattooing. These echo Holly Donahue Singh's argument in chapter 6 of this volume that relationships are vital, as well as the power granted by authoring new relationships. Islamic tattooing can create new bonds, reinscribe old ones, and, when loss of authorship occurs, break the links between generations.

Róisín and Wortham discuss at length the importance of community and relationship-formation for tattoos. Tattooing is almost always a social activity. Róisín and Wortham point out that the interactions that happen around and through tattooing remain in the ink long after the skin has healed. Outside of instances when one tattoos oneeself alone, tattooing always involves a second individual and usually occurs in the company of others. The particular social setting infuses itself into the tattoo. In this way, Róisín and Wortham echo scholars of material religion who have argued that the environment surrounding religious acts suffuses religion.[60] Some elements, like the tattoo ink and the kind of instrument, are apparent in the tattoo, whereas others, such as the ambience or decor of the shop, are invisible. In her essay, Róisín draws our attention to the way another invisible condition of the tattoo, the relationships surrounding it, persist in the tattoo.

Tattoos also materialize and signify significant bonds between family, friends, and mentors. Azam's back tattoo represented his relationship with grandfather; similarly, the ink on Jamin's shoulder symbolized kin. Rather than signify individual family members, the chains on Suraiya's forearm connect her to her Shi'i relatives and Shi'i communities more generally. This kind of materialization resembles the observations of Alyssa Maldonado-Estrada in her research on Catholic tattoos: they materialize significant bonds between family, friends, and mentors in religiously significant ways. And, like those observed by Maldonado-Estrada, many of these tattoos prominently inscribe gendered notions of self. The clearest example comes in Azam's tribute to his grandfather, which not only honored him but also reminded Azam of the kind of man he aspired to be and certified that ideal with a passage from the Qur'an. In these we see how bodies, social dynamics, and ink merge in religious acts that persist in the tattooed skin itself.

Yasmin Bendaas's photo-essay shows how tattoos can also materialize relationships with one's community across time, especially in response to colonialism and the dominance of more jurisprudentially minded enactments of Islamic tradition. Bendaas writes specifically about Chaouia tattooing among older women in and around Chemora, a small town in the Aures Mountains in Algeria.[61] The article, entitled "Algeria's Tattoos: Myths and Truths," details how this older generation used tattoos for beautification and protection as well as the gradual disappearance of this practice, as the younger generations choose to not acquire tattoos.[62] Bendaas's conversation with women in their eighth and ninth decades indicated that tattooing persisted in the region despite French admonition of the practice—though not, as sometimes was stated, as a protection against French soldiers—and began to fade with rising literacy rates and growing awareness of the prohibitions of tattooing in Islamic sources. Bendaas does not account for the importance of interpretation of those sources or the role of institutions in the decline of tattooing. Still, her photo-essay offers an example of the bonds that tattooing forms across generations. Yet this example is an unfortunate one, evidencing the importance of embodied practices in their fading because of prohibiting forces.

Islamic tattooing does things for Muslims that exceed its marginalization. The case studies I have mentioned show how Islamic tattooing can heal bodies, in turn challenging the structural forces that induce trauma. It can also mediate tradition by merging the mythology and aesthetics of Islamic tradition with contemporary tattoo styles and gendered embodiment, and it can materialize relationships, familial, communal, or cultural. Learning about the complexities of Muslim life means attending to Islamic jurisprudence, as well as the way that Muslims reproduce Islamic tradition with their bodies. While contradictions and dissonances emerge in this analysis, so, too, do opportunities for better ways of living and relating to others; forms of life that may be "profoundly important for understanding one's own."[63]

This analysis also points to the need to trouble the very notion of the margins. Like any concept that presupposes boundaries, borders, and centers, margins may benefit and harm. Used carefully, the term "margin" can help scholars and communities understand how power works and rectify oppressive relationships. But, carelessly applied, a term like "marginalized" may reinforce the inequitable power distributions it seeks to expose by uncritically affirming the power of the center, or, as in Bakaari's critique in chapter 1 of this book of the orientation of Islamic studies to the white non-Muslim gaze, preventing acknowledgment of simultaneous marginalization of and within Muslim communities. This is especially the case with religious traditions, wherein describing a practice as "central" or "marginal" can variously affirm or deny its religious authenticity.[64] This chapter attempted to follow bell hooks's womanist theory and Vernon Schubel's margin-centering scholarship to the extent of disrupting the binary or margins and centers altogether.

Whatever contributions this chapter made regarding Islamic tattooing and Islamic embodiment, it also created new margins that require future scholarship. One pressing absence in this chapter is discussion of tattoos among Black Muslims, the result being a dearth of analysis of tensions regarding race and ethnicity in Muslim communities. This chapter also lacks an extended discussion of Shi'i tattooing, especially the Twelver aesthetics found in Lebanon.⁶⁵ Yet another omission is discourse on social media regarding Islamic tattooing—Instagram, as well as, to a lesser extent, Twitter, contain robust exhibition and discussion about the aesthetics and propriety of Islamic tattooing. The examples discussed do not exhaustively represent Islamic tattooing; rather, they demonstrate the need for more scholarly attention to this mode of Islamic embodiment and, more generally, the productivity of reconsidering centers and margins. Like the other chapters in this collection, this kind of knowledge production demonstrates the vibrancy, the complexity, and the vitality of Islamic tradition, as well as the joys, struggles, and devotions of lived Muslim practice.

NOTES

Epigraph: bell hooks, *Feminist Theory: From Margin to Center*, 2nd ed. (Cambridge, Mass.: South End, 2000), xvi.

1. Tameem Akhgar, "A Tattoo at a Time, Afghan Woman Takes on Society's Taboos," Associated Press, December 16, 2019, https://apnews.com/article/asia-pacific-ap-top-news-international-news-afghanistan-tattoos-5db1f8c874fd5aca5038ca2ed91d404f.

2. Fariha Róisín, "Young, Muslim and Tattooed: How I Stayed True to Myself," *Flare*, August 27, 2016, https://www.flare.com/identity/muslim-tattoo.

3. As SherAli Tareen and Zareena Grewal have elucidated, this dynamic and embodied argument about the withins and the withouts of Islamic tradition animates it. See SherAli Tareen, *Defending Muhammad in Modernity* (Notre Dame, Ind.: University of Notre Dame Press, 2020), 11–15; and Zareena Grewal, *Islam Is a Foreign Country: American Muslims and the Global Crisis of Authority* (New York: New York University Press, 2014), 37–38.

4. Deen or *dīn* is an Arabic term with various potential translations—"religion" and "law" are common translations, like "judgment," as in *yom al-dīn* (Judgment Day)—but many Muslims today use it in the

sense of "religion," especially in contrast to worldly affairs (as in the juxtaposition of *dīn wa dunya*).

5. Alyssa Maldonado-Estrada, *Lifeblood of the Parish: Men and Catholic Devotion in Williamsburg, Brooklyn* (New York: New York University Press, 2020).
6. For example, Justin McDaniel, *The Lovelorn Ghost and the Magical Monk: Practicing Buddhism in Modern Thailand* (New York: Columbia University Press, 2011), 72–119, 173, 195, 227.
7. Alfred Gell, *Wrapping in Images: Tattooing in Polynesia* (New York: Oxford University Press, 1993), 171–76. The term that Gell translates as "contagious sacredness" is *tapu*.
8. David Allen, "Moving the Needle on Recovery from Breast Cancer: The Healing Role of Postmastectomy Tattoos," *JAMA* 317, no. 7 (2017): 672–74.
9. Tamara Santibañez, *Could This Be Magic? Tattooing as Liberation Work* (New York: Afterlife, 2021).
10. Aaron Deter-Wolf, Benoît Robitaille, Lars Krutak, and Sébastien Galliot, "The World's Oldest Tattoos," *Journal of Archaeological Science: Reports* 5 (2016): 19–24.
11. For a prominent example of the misrepresentation of South Pacific Islander communities, see Emile Durkheim's *The Elementary Forms of Religious Life*, trans. Karen E. Fields (New York: Free Press, 1995), 216–31. For the Native American origin of tattooing, see Anna Felicity Friedman Herlihy, "Tattooed Transculturites: Western Expatriates Among Amerindian and Pacific Islander Societies, 1500–1900" (PhD diss., University of Chicago, 2012).
12. Sinah Theres Kloß, *Tattoo Histories: Transcultural Perspectives on the Narratives, Practices, and Representations of Tattooing* (New York: Routledge, 2020).
13. For the translations of physiognomy from ancient to medieval cultures, see Simon Swain, *Seeing the Face, Seeing the Soul: Polemon's Physiognomy from Classical Antiquity to Medieval Islam* (Oxford: Oxford University Press, 2007); and, for premodern Islamic uses of physiognomy (*firāsat* in Persian), see, for example, Shahzad Bashir, *Sufi Bodies: Religion and Society in Medieval Islam* (New York: Columbia University Press, 2011), 45–47.
14. Gell, *Wrapping in Images*, 12.

15. Gell, 12.
16. For more on the colonialism and violence of freak shows, see Robert Bogdan, *Freak Show: Presenting Human Oddities for Amusement and Profit* (Chicago: University of Chicago Press, 1988).
17. *True Life*, "I'm Fighting my Faith," season 19, episode 3, aired February 8, 2016, on Paramount+. This episode focused on the stigma of Aurora's tattoos in the Muslim context, and the internal struggle of a young gay Black Christian male.
18. Akhgar, "Tattoo at a Time."
19. The numerically insignificant criticism of Williams for displaying his tattoos while on Umrah, a pilgrimage to Mecca distinct from Hajj, was fanned in articles like Soha Naveed, "Muslim Convert Sonny Bill Williams Went For Umrah And Muslims Focused More On His Tattoos," *Parhlo*, January 19, 2018, https://www.parhlo.com/muslim-convert-sonny-bill-williams-went-for-umrah/.
20. Stephen Johnson, "'Your Sins Are Exposed': Islamic Preacher Slams Muslims Who Show Their Tattoos—but Still Pray to Allah," *Daily Mail Australia*, August 26, 2017, https://www.dailymail.co.uk/news/article-4826824/Islamic-preacher-slams-Muslims-tattoos.html.
21. For just one example, see Garima Satija, "Aamir Khan's Daughter Ira Trolled for Turning Into a Tattoo Artist, People Say 'It's Haram,'" *India Times*, October 10, 2020, https://www.indiatimes.com/entertainment/celebs/aamir-khans-daughter-iran-khan-trolled-by-muslims-for-becoming-a-tattoo-artist-524886.html.
22. Edward Said, *Orientalism* (New York: Random House, 1978).
23. Jonathan Lyons, *Islam Through Western Eyes: From the Crusades to the War on Terrorism* (New York: Columbia University Press, 2014).
24. There are many detailed repudiations of Huntington's "The Clash of Civilizations," *Foreign Affairs* 72, no. 3 (Summer 1993): 22–49. For a compelling example that situates Huntington's writing in a larger web of Orientalism, see Adeeb Khalid, *Islam After Communism: Religion and Politics in Central Asia* (Berkeley: University of California Press, 2007), 4–8.
25. Alyssa Maldonado-Estrada, "Men, Tattoos, and Catholic Devotion in Brooklyn," *Material Religion* 16, no. 5 (May 26, 2020): 1–20; Maldonado-Estrada, *Lifeblood of the Parish*, 37–49.

26. Alyssa Maldonado-Estrada, "Tattoos as Sacramentals," *American Religion*, https://www.american-religion.org/provocations/tattoos-as-sacramentals (accessed September 3, 2019).
27. Santibañez, *Could This Be Magic?*, 15–16.
28. For example, Sali Hughes, "Why Tattoos Are More than Just Body Art," *Guardian*, October 9, 2021, https://www.theguardian.com/fashion/2021/oct/09/why-tattoos-are-more-than-just-body-art.
29. Another example of this more structurally minded approach to tattooing is Donna Torrisi and John Giugliano, *Tattoo Monologues: Indelible Marks on the Body and Soul* (Berkeley: She Writes, 2021).
30. Santibañez, *Could This Be Magic?*, 3–12.
31. Santibañez, 16–17.
32. Though in the following analysis I focus on Sunni Muslim positions on tattooing, it is worth noting here that the Shiʻi positions on tattooing are generally more sympathetic, with eminent Twelver Shiʻi leaders like Muhammad Hussein Fadlallah and Ali al-Husseini al-Sistani opining that tattoos are not prohibited so long as their intention or depictions do not violate some other Islamic notion.
33. Labīd's *muʻallaqa* includes *wāshima*, or the female tattooer, in the opening section, in comparison to the tent marks that are washed away by floods. One version of Tarafah's Ode includes *al-washm* to describe the mnemonic dimensions of the tattoo.
34. Suzanne P. Stetkevych, *Voicing the Mute Immortals* (Ithaca, N.Y.: Cornell University Press, 1993), 9.
35. Included in this study were the lexicons of Muḥammad ibn Mukarram ibn Manẓūr, *Lisān Al-ʿArab* (Beirut: Dār Iḥyāʾ al-Turāth al-ʿArabī, 1988); J. G. Hava, *Arabic English Dictionary: For Advanced Learners* (New Delhi: Goodword, 2001); Nashwān ibn Saʻīd al-Ḥimyarī, *Shams al-ʻUlūm Wa-Dawāʾ Kalām al-ʿArab Min al-Kulūm* (Beirut: Dār al-Fikr al-Muʻāṣir, 1999); Edward William Lane, *Arabic-English Lexicon* (Cambridge: Islamic Texts Society, 1984); Murtaḍá al-Zabīdī, *Tāj Al-ʿarūs Min Jawāhir al-Qāmūs* (Kuwait City: Maṭbaʻat Ḥukūmat al-Kuwayt, 1965); Francis Joseph Steingass, *English–Arabic Dictionary: For the Use of Both Travellers and Students* (New Delhi: Cosmo, 1978); Hans Wehr, *Arabic-English Dictionary: The Hans Wehr Dictionary of Modern Written Arabic*, trans. J. Milton Cowan (Urbana,

Ill.: Spoken Language Services, 1994); and Maḥmūd ibn ʿUmar al-Zamakhsharī, *Asās Al-Balāghah* (Beirut: Dār Ṣādir, 1965).

36. Albert Kazimirski de Biberstein, *Dictionnaire Arabe-Français* (Beyrouth: Librairie du Liban, 1975), 2:1544.

37. Muḥammad ibn Mukarram ibn Manẓūr, *Lisān Al-ʿArab* (Beirut: Dār Iḥyāʾ al-Turāth al-ʿArabī, 1988), 4845.

38. Ibn Manẓūr, *Lisān Al-ʿArab*, 4845.

39. Ḥusayn ibn Aḥmad al-Zawzanī, *Sharḥ al-Muʿallaqāt al-Sabʿ* (Beirut: Dār al-Thaqāfa, 1969), 53.

40. Muḥammad ibn Muḥammad Murtaḍá al-Zabīdī, *Tāj al-ʿArūs Min Jawāhir al-Qāmūs* (Kuwait City: Maṭbaʿat Ḥukūmat al-Kuwait, 1965), 50–52.

41. This should not be taken as a conflation of the ancient Near East with the early Islamic milieu but an acknowledgment that contemporaneous practices in the Near East, especially those associated with Jewish and Christian traditions, were intertwined with early Islamic communities. For more on these exchanges, see Jonathan Berkey, *The Formation of Islam: Religion and Society in the Near East, 600–1800* (New York: Cambridge University Press, 2002).

42. Isaac Mendelsohn, *Slavery in the Ancient Near East: A Comparative Study of Slavery in Babylonia, Assyria, Syria, and Palestine from the Middle of the Third Millennium to the End of the First Millennium* (New York: Oxford University Press, 1949), 42–43.

43. Chase F. Robinson, "Neck-Sealing in Early Islam," *Journal of the Economic and Social History of the Orient* 48, no. 3 (2005): 401–41.

44. Sandra Jacobs, *The Body as Property: Physical Disfigurement in Biblical Law* (New York: Bloomsbury, 2014), 190–91.

45. In the hadith identified by A. J. Wensinck in the *Concordance et Indices de la Tradition Musulmane* (London, Brill: 1969) on pages 215 and 216, tattoos are always described as prohibited.

46. "Laʿana ʿAbd-Allah al-wāshimāti wa-l-mutanammiSāti wa-l-mutafallijāti li-l-Husni khalqa Allahi."

47. Aḥmad ibn ʿAlī Ibn Ḥajar al-ʿAsqalānī, "Book of Sales," in *Fatḥ al-Bārī bi-Sharḥ Ṣaḥīḥ al-Bukhaārī* (Cairo: Maktabat al-Kullīyāt al-Azharīyah, 1978), 165; al-ʿAsqalānī, "Book of Medicine," in *Fatḥ al-Bārī bi-Sharḥ Ṣaḥīḥ al-Bukhārī*, 329.

48. In contrast to necessary medical operations that "change" a body to, for example, save an individual's life.
49. Al-'Asqalānī spends considerable time comparing illicit beautification practices with practices like "permitted hair-trimming (*al-ḥaff*), designs (*al-naqsh*), rouge (*al-taḥmīr*), and coloring the hands with dye (*al-taṭrīf*)," all of which are acceptable so long as the husband has granted permission.
50. The inclusion of concubinage here is not an endorsement, especially since contemporary Muslims have gone to great lengths to demonstrate its unacceptability. But it was the focus of robust Islamic thought, and sex within concubinage could, unfortunately, have been considered licit if it met certain criteria. For more on this topic, see Marion H. Katz, "Concubinage, in Islamic Law." in *Encyclopaedia of Islam*, 3rd ed., ed. Kate Fleet, Gudrun Krämer, Denis Matringe, John Nawas, and Everett Rowson (Leiden: Brill), https://referenceworks.brillonline.com/browse/encyclopaedia-of-islam-3 (accessed November 4, 2022).
51. The text of this hadith reads: "I saw my father buy a slave who practiced cupping (*ḥijāmh*). So, I asked him, and he said: 'The Prophet (PBUH) forbade taking a price for dogs and for blood, and he prohibited the tattooer or the one asking for a tattoo, and the one who takes [literally eats] usury and the one giving usury, and he cursed the picture-maker.'"
52. The text recorded by al-Bukhārī reads: "The evil eye is real, and tattooing is banned" *(al-'ainu haqqun wa nahā 'alā al-washm)*. Interestingly, Al-'Asqalānī's commentary focuses on the superiority of Islamic practices as a protection against the evil eye, thereby implying competition between Islamic and other kinds of protective practices. For more on competition between Islamic material culture and that of other religious traditions, see Jamal J. Elias, *Aisha's Cushion: Religious Art, Perception, and Practice in Islam* (Cambridge, Mass.: Harvard University Press, 2012), 101–7.
53. Róisín has written several books, including *How to Cure a Ghost* (2019) and *Like a Bird* (2020); published pieces in the *New York Times*, *Al Jazeera*, and the *Guardian*; edited the blog Muslim Women Speak (which promotes marginalized Muslim women's and queer issues); and currently is deputy editor of *Violet Book*. She is also an influencer, with over fifty-four thousand followers on Instagram.

54. Founded in 2008, *Brown Girl Magazine* (*BG*) targets and is produced by South Asian women, especially "millennials."
55. Elizabeth Jaikaranis a freelance writer who frequently contributes to *BG*. See Elizabeth Jaikaran, "Meet the Staff: Elizabeth Jaikaran," *Brown Girl Magazine*, March 3, 2016, https://browngirlmagazine.com/meet-staff-elizabeth-jaikaran/.
56. Elizabeth Jaikaran, "Challenging Taboos: Muslim and Tattooed," *Brown Girl Magazine*, May 9, 2017, https://browngirlmagazine.com/challenging-taboos-muslim-tattooed/.
57. Jaikaran, "Challenging Taboos."
58. From the 156th verse of Surat al-Baqarah (2:156). This particular ayah is often said upon learning that someone has died.
59. Mansur Al-Hallaj publicly exclaimed "*ana al-ḥaqq*," or "I am the Truth." For more on Al-Hallaj and the significance of this statement, see Jawid Mojaddedi, "Ḥallāj, Abu'l-Moḡit Ḥosayn," in *Encyclopaedia Iranica Online*, ed. Trustees of Columbia University in the City of New York, https://www.iranicaonline.org/articles/hallaj-1 (accessed October 24, 2022).
60. For a particularly compelling example, see Donovan Schaefer, *Religious Affects* (Durham, N.C.: Duke University Press, 2015), 61–68.
61. Bendaas clarifies her methods for collecting data about Chaouia tattooing on a blog about the journalism project. See Yasmin Bendaas, "Introduction," Chaouia Tattoos, September 29, 2013, https://chaouiatattoos.wordpress.com/category/3-introduction/.
62. Yasmin Bendaas, "Algeria's Tattoos: Myths and Truths," *Al Jazeera*, May 3, 2019, https://www.aljazeera.com/features/2013/8/11/algerias-tattoos-myths-and-truths. This piece is an odd fit with the two discussed above. It is slightly older, more a survey than a first-person account, and published in a first-tier media outlet. I include it here because it demonstrates the disjuncture that can occur when tattooing practices cease.
63. Talal Asad, "Autobiographical Reflections on Anthropology and Religion," *Religion and Society* 11, no. 1 (September 2020): 4.
64. In this respect, "margin" and "center" stand in for concepts like "orthodox" and "heterodox." For a compelling explanation of the harm done by substituting one set of concepts for a set of analogous but debunked concepts, see Talal Asad's discussion of "orthodoxy," "heterodoxy," "big

tradition," and "little tradition" in "The Idea of an Anthropology of Islam," *Qui Parle* 17, no. 2 (Spring–Summer 2009): 7–11.
65. Hassan Ammar has documented some examples. For more, see *Vice* Staff and Hassan Ammar, "Activists in Lebanon Are Using Religious Tattoos as Protest Symbols." *Vice*, April 17, 2019, https://www.vice.com/en/article/d3m9wv/activists-lebanon-religious-shia-muslim-hezbollah-tattoos.

4

LOVER'S WORDS ARE ETERNAL

Alevi Ashik Poetry Beyond the Margins

TESS M. WAGGONER

If you want to know the Truth
go beyond black and white.
—Kaygusuz Abdal

Before I could form my own sentences in Turkish, I sang in it. While teaching English through a cultural exchange program in a small industrial town just east of the Turkish capital, I joined the local university's folk music choir. This was an extracurricular student organization composed almost entirely of students studying in the school's music department. I attended weekly rehearsals and was exposed to a broad range of what was classified in that context as Turkish folk music. For a semester and a half, my repertoire slowly expanded as we practiced and perfected various pieces selected by a faculty member who also served as the choir director.

Eventually, I was able to audition and perform a solo during the choir's spring concert. I asked permission to perform "Uzun Ince Bir Yoldayim," or "I Am on a Long Thin Path." In the university's carpeted concert salon, accompanied by an entire orchestra of musicians playing traditional instruments, I stood, trembling, before the audience, my voice cracking slightly when I reached the swelling crescendo of the music in the final stanza:

> Veysel is astonished by this state
> sometimes crying, sometimes laughing
> in order to reach the place of rest
> I [keep] going, day and night

The audience was likely astonished to see an American English instructor performing a nearly canonical work of twentieth-century Turkish folk music. I wondered what they thought about me, a foreigner, performing this music, and I thought to myself that many audience members may have been even more shocked if I had told them where I first heard songs like these performed. I did not learn about this type of music from the radio or music videos on YouTube. I first encountered the lyrics from this song in a seminar room with Vernon Schubel at Kenyon College, where the topic at hand was Sufism, the mystical branch of Islamic tradition, and contemporary mystical poetry. In that class I learned that the lyrics to this and many of the songs the choir performed had meanings that went deeper than what the words said on the surface; they were full of clues, allusions, and references to other, more esoteric ideas. For those who identify as Alevi, this music is more than a Turkish cultural tradition; it is also a source of knowledge that communicates theological, doctrinal, and historic meanings that are central to their religious communities.

When I came to Turkey, I was eager to understand these lyrics in their Alevi religious context, but I was aware of just how difficult this might be. It would have been easier to adopt a one-dimensional understanding of what today is called *türkü*, Turkish folk music, which in its most general sense includes any traditional poetry set to music. But I was unsure how to do so because of the sensitivity of my questions, and, besides, it took years for me to develop the language skills to be able to ask them. Even now, I am concerned about how my arguments will land with scholars of Alevi communities and the people who comprise them, as well as Turks who may prefer that I understand the lyrics that I performed exclusively as "folk music." Still, I feel compelled to honor the creativity and resilience of the oral traditions that have informed the rich human tradition of Alevism.

This chapter contributes to the understanding of the margins of Islam by examining the role of Alevi *ashiks*—teachers, poets, bards—in transmitting and interpreting the religious beliefs, experiences, and ethics of Alevi traditions. The transmission of religious ideas from the ashik to the student and the community-at-large is central to Alevi religious practice. But, in order to explain why the song that I sang on that university stage is widely regarded as folk music rather than as the religious teachings of an ashik, I will first examine how Alevism has emerged in modern and contemporary Turkey as a minoritized and marginalized tradition. Then, I will turn to an analysis of Alevi ashik lives and their poetry in order to reveal this rich tradition's long history as a voice for the marginalized, demanding justice. I show how the Alevi ashik tradition produces poems that serve as core oral records of Alevi beliefs and experiences on their own terms, in their own words.

WHAT IS ALEVISM? THE TROUBLE WITH BOUNDARIES

There are perhaps few communities that better exemplify the potentially harmful effects of outsiders imposing categories and taxonomies on Muslims and religious people more generally than the Alevi of Anatolia. As Kathryn Blanchard points out in chapter 8 of this volume—which addresses biological taxonomies and the problems of using such categories to define religious groups—the outsider inevitably asserts power over the subject of their study, power that can impede a religious community's ability to speak for themselves. In his chapter, Max Johnson Dugan argues that the very use of the term "margin" can reify the sense that a community is indeed less than authentic or less important. This is what has happened in the case of the Alevi. Throughout their history, outsiders have determined how these communities are defined and bounded, both through the work of scholars who stand outside the community and through the influence of these scholars on how Alevi themselves debate their communal belonging, thereby impeding how Alevi religious traditions have been studied. Claims that Alevism is oral in nature and thus unknowable have been particularly harmful. But Alevi communities have persisted in developing, reexamining, and practicing their faith on their own terms. Debates among Alevis themselves about what it means to be Alevi and teach Alevi tradition are rich and ongoing. Following Dugan, reading bell hooks can help us understand how Alevi ashiks speak from the margins to envision a more just world. They have embodied the margins as a "site of resistance" through verse that speaks truth to power and offers counterhistories.[1] The works of Anatolian Alevi ashiks reflect a counterhegemonic and antiauthoritarian worldview of radical humanism and ecological harmony that speaks back to the broader tradition of Western Islamic studies that is critiqued in this volume's introduction.

Today, people belonging to ethnoreligious and/or sociopolitical communities grouped under the umbrella term "Alevi" are estimated to constitute approximately 15 to 20 percent of the population of the Republic of Turkey. It is impossible to achieve an accurate count of Alevi in the country because the state does not count them as such; their identity cards simply read "Muslim." Official statistics from the government and international bodies regularly assert that Turkey is 99 percent Muslim, ignoring the heterogenous nature of Islamic practices and beliefs in the country and its citizens who live abroad. The Alevi religious tradition in Turkey exists in several ethnic communities, including Turks, Turkmen, and both Kurmanci- and Zazaki-speaking Kurds. It wasn't until the twentieth century that "Alevi" emerged as an authoritative scholarly and communal umbrella term used to describe these historically diverse communities.[2] The groups placed under this banner formerly used self-definitions that were local, ethnic, geographic, or based on profession or occupation. Some of these terms include "Abdal," "Amucali," "Cepni," "Kocgirili," "Tahtaci," and "Zaza." Other labels for people now considered Alevi reflect historic connections to various Sufi orders or other historic antiauthority movements, like the Bektashi order, the Babai, and Bedreddini. There are also communities that are historically related to the Alevi in the Balkans, and large communities of Alevi live in Germany and other European countries. The legal distinction of the Alevi as a unique community first occurred when a 2004 European Commission report recognized them "as a non-Sunni Muslim minority." Politically speaking, such language remains extremely controversial.[3]

Before the twentieth century, the label "Alevi" mostly referred to the families of religious leaders, or *dedes*, whose lineage was linked historically to the family of the Prophet Muhammad. Generally speaking, a dede is a Sufi leader and teacher most often associated with the Alevi-Bektashi and Mevlevi Sufi orders. During the Ottoman Empire—which, at its zenith, ruled

Southeastern Europe, Anatolia, much of North Africa, and the Eastern Mediterranean—many Alevi were known as Kizilbash.[4] Kizilbash literally means "redhead" and references the red fabric worn as headgear by followers of the Safawiya Sufi order, who were regarded as followers of Shah Ismail and the Safavid Empire in the late fifteenth and sixteenth centuries. Historian Ayfer Karakaya-Stump has used lineage documents from Kizilbash Alevi dede families from Ottoman times to paint part of a much more complex picture, tracing how their social system, called *ocak*, was influenced by and in dialogue with the Vefai'i (Arabic, Rifa'i) Sufi order based in Iraq.[5]

At face value, the term "Alevi" is etymologically related to Ali, the nephew of the Prophet Muhammed, often referred to as Hazreti (a Turkish honorific designating veneration of Ali by Alevi). In truth, emphasizing this definition tells us very little about how Alevi define themselves and is often associated in Turkey with negative stereotypes that make political implications about Shi'a Muslims. For example, in the *Encyclopaedia of Islam* that is produced and maintained by the Diyanet (Ministry for Religious Affairs) in Turkey, the entry for "Alevi" reads: "A term used for various religious and political groups united in their loyalty to Ali."[6] Written by Ahmet Yasar Ocak in 1989, it states that there are two "living" forms of Alevism: the Alawaites of Syria and Hatay province in Turkey, and the Kizilbash Alevis of Anatolia, who, the entry claims, were "formed through Safavid propaganda."[7] Toward the end, the entry uses explicitly derogatory terms to describe Alevi and ignores the ways that Alevi themselves define their community.[8] The president of Turkey, Recep Tayyip Erdogan, has mirrored the encyclopedia's refusal to recognize Alevi self-definitions for decades. "If Alevism consists of love of Ali," he has said, "then I, too, am an Alevi."[9] Simply put, such nondefinitions are perceived by many Alevi to be an oversimplification that denies many aspects of Alevi worldviews as well as key elements of their historical development, on which there remains little consensus.

The emphasis on veneration of Ali at the expense of other aspects of belief and practice has many implications and effects. Foremost among these is a mode of Othering via binary juxtaposition with normative Sunni Islam (in both the Ottoman and contemporary contexts). As Islamic studies scholar Markus Dressler notes, "The modern othering of the Alevis is dialectically related to the normalization of a Sunni-Muslim identity."[10] Under the umbrella term "Alevi," these traditions already risk conflation and the erasure of localized particularity. Such attempts at definition erase and obscure other critical distinctive aspects of their traditions and foment Othering of Alevi belief and practice in polemical terms. As ethnographer of Alevi communities David Shankland states, "The boundaries of Aleviness, however, are not ultimately made up with a simple contrast between the Alevi and Sunni way of going about things."[11] Formally categorizing Alevism as a form or order of Sufism would have had significant and problematic potential outcomes in the Turkish context, in large part because such organizations were formally disbanded following the establishment of the Turkish Republic. This political reality informs the widespread resistance at present by Alevi organizations to such labels; it also has precedent in the way Alevi were studied by others historically, and the motivations that informed it.

Many scholars in the first half of the twentieth century emphasized the tribal structures and Turkic origins of Alevi, including Turkmen and those who identify with Oguz Turkic ancestry. This approach has come to be known as the "Köprülü paradigm" in Alevi studies. This term references Fuat Köprülü, one of the core architects of Turkish national history, who argued that Alevism extended from pre-Islamic Turkic traditions, mostly subsumed under the term "shamanism." It chunked the Alevi into communities of geographic bounding and tribal affiliation and lineage, while obscuring the existence of non-Turkish-speaking Alevi communities and downplaying the role of varieties of Sufism in Anatolia from at least the thirteenth century onward in the development of what is called Alevism today.[12]

The Köprülü paradigm presents Alevis as a timeless Other, said to retain an essential Turkishness via the preservation of pre-Islamic ritual practices and beliefs. By emphasizing the "folk" origins of Alevism—an outlook adopted by nationalist historians in the nineteenth and early twentieth century—the approach attempts to present the group as a primordial component of the modern nation-state of Turkey. It scrubbed Alevism of its Islamic content, reducing it to a folk tradition that informed a secular vision of Turkish-ness.

Another major consequence of the Köprülü paradigm is that scholars have used terms like "heterodoxy," "syncretism," and "heresy" to describe Alevism. Rather than provide productive indexical information, these terms instead have participated in the marginalization of Alevism vis-à-vis "Islam."[13] The first use of the term "syncretic" to describe Alevi (then under the name of Kizilbash) was by Protestant American missionaries in the second half of the nineteenth century.[14] In addition, there is an ongoing and often sensitive debate about the relationship between the Bekstashi order and Alevi Islam.[15] Markus Dressler has forcefully argued that wholesale conflation of Kizilbash Alevi and Bektashi traditions under the umbrella of Alevism feeds into a historical project whereby the homogenization of Alevi communities has been undertaken as part of a larger nationalist project.

As sociopolitical communities, Alevi and Bektashi organizations have proliferated and, in some cases, coalesced following the 1960s, with an acceleration beginning in the late 1980s, offering political representation and advocacy for Alevi issues in addition to providing programming related to ritual practice and community education. A variety of groups have come together under the Alevi umbrella in order to advocate for their rights. Alevi citizen-scholars and their interlocutors have begun to complicate the largely pejorative framings of "heterodoxy," "syncretism," and other marginalizing labels by writing their own scholarship. Intellectual and popular efforts in the wake of what is called the "Alevi awakening" have offered a wealth of primary and secondary source material about these communities. One effect of writing about the varied practices of these groups for the purposes of standardization is that it may inadvertently obscure the complexity and heterogeneity of these communities and their rituals, practices, beliefs, and identity formation processes. Such homogenization remains a core concern of scholars of Alevi practice.

The Köprülü paradigm's emphasis on Alevi as a folk tradition and the conflation of Bektashi tradition with Alevi are not the only form of scholarly erasure that Alevi have faced. While some scholars have argued that much of the Alevi tradition has literally disappeared, such wholescale claims seem to rest on binary assumptions like urban/rural, traditional/modern, and secular/religious that preclude the possibility of flexibility and adaptation. Kristina Kehl-Bodrogi's overview of the period asserts that as Alevi were incorporated into the nation-state and given equal rights and economic opportunities, their religious traditions largely went away:

The manifold transformations of republican Turkey put an end to the spatial and social marginality of the Alevis. However, their gradual integration into the majority society— migration to the towns, school attendance, state employment and the involvement in the national economy—led in the long run to a secularization of the community. As a result, the social-religious system collapsed and religion as a whole lost its previous importance. This development reached its peak in the 1970s, when the overwhelming majority of the Alevis devoted itself to leftist and universal ideologies. In this period a whole generation had grown up without being initiated into the secret doctrines and the Holy Men (*dede*) lost their function and authority. The oral transmission of knowledge was interrupted and mostly fell into oblivion.[16]

On the contrary, as I will discuss, the Alevi tradition of the teacher-poet-lover (ashik), though dynamic and changing, is alive and well; mass public gatherings, institutions, schools of music, choirs, recordings of poetry, and live performances all testify to its vitality. As David Shankland observes, "Alevi religion as a *culture*, as a collection of interlocking ideals and symbols which people may use to assert their identity survives."[17] The ashik tradition has served as a core element in that survival—in the mediation, dissemination, and consolidation of Alevi identity.

THE FIGURE OF THE ASHIK

One consequence of ignoring the religious origins, content, and context of Alevism is that ashiks, the teacher-poets of Alevism, are seen wholly as secular folk figures rather than religious masters. As mentioned earlier, the word *ashik* is most commonly rendered as "bard" or "minstrel," and ashiks have been compared to troubadour traditions in France. None of these classifications is fully satisfying, since they do not convey the significance of the ashik in historic and contemporary settings. According to the Turkish Ministry of Foreign Affairs' *Encyclopeadia of Islam*, an ashik is "a folk minstrel; the general name given to folk musicians who perform their own or others' poetry, sometimes only as poetry but usually setting it to music and with instrumental accompaniment."[18] No mention is made of the historic connection of ashiks to Alevi traditions, nor is the significance of the ashik in transmitting religious knowledge rendered. This definition thus participates in a long-standing pattern whereby Alevi religious activity is subsumed under frames that do not correspond to its own worldview, which opposes such binaries. Within the taxonomizing efforts of Republican Turkish studies, ashiks have also been called "folk/people's poets." But studying Alevi ashik practices and outputs under the banner of "folklore" denies the particularities of various localized practices through appropriation into the generalized national genre of folk music. Furthermore, it blocks us from seeing how the ashik tradition has been central to the transmission of the coherent religious and social traditions Alevism constitutes.

Vernon Schubel offers a more precise definition of the poets I consider in the rest of this chapter: "At the center of the Alevi tradition is the figure of the *ashik* (lover) who wanders composing songs of devotion for God, the Friend (*Dost*). The tradition's great pirs, such as Pir Sultan Abdal, were also *ashiks*."[19] The oral transmission of poetry by ashiks "appears to have been the main carrier of the Qizilbash-Alevi tradition, allowing for both continuity and change. While some of this poetry has been conserved in handwritten poem anthologies (cönk) and diwan works, it has mostly been transmitted via the memory of the

Qizilbash-Alevi bards."[20] Contemporary ashiks thus participate in a tradition of antinomian dissent that traces its origins to the vernacular poetry that was central to the Islamization of Anatolia.[21] The ashik improvises or performs poetic verse, most often accompanied by a *saz*, a long necked lute. There are three standard sizes: the smallest is sometimes called Dede's saz or *cura*, and medium- and long-necked versions. In poetic texts, the instrument is also sometimes referred to as *kopuz*. It can have a variety of string counts, and electronic iterations of the saz have been created and deployed in popular music beginning in the 1970s. While the ashik tradition is found in Sunni and Alevi communities, the practices and modes of performance in which they engage vary. The clearest distinguishing factor may be the vocabulary they deploy.[22]

There are two main ways that someone can become an ashik. The first way is called the master-pupil relationship (*usta-çırak*), in which they receive the necessary training from an already practicing ashik. The second is more explicitly mystical and is known as *bade içme*, literally meaning to drink the *bade*, or "illumination." The ashik is offered a goblet to drink in a dream, which contains the bade, or religious enlightenment necessary to perform ashik duties. Ethnomusicologist Ozan Aksoy adds that the relationship between father and son is the most typical chain of transmission.[23]

Ashiks often perform *zikr*. Islamic studies scholar John Renard calls zikr (in Arabic, *dhikr*) one of the three main forms of prayer in Islamic tradition, the others being *salah*, the prayers of prostration with which most non-Muslims are familiar, and *du'a*, or supplicatory prayer.[24] Throughout the history of Islam, zikr, or meditative or spiritual prayer meant to bring someone closer to God, has been a central element of Muslim religiosity.

Many observant Muslims, no matter their ethnic background, perform zikr, which can be as simple as repeating phrases such as "Allahu Akbar [God is Greater]" over and over. But from Southern Europe to Central Asia, wherever Turkic peoples have lived, it also includes the recitation of poetry and sometimes dancing accompanied by musical instruments. The *cem* are the worship ceremonies of Alevi and Bektashi communities, of various types and lengths, which include music, dance, and twelve services, including the distribution of *lokma*, or food. Cem ceremonies may utilize different genres of music and literature, and the person who performs this ritual music is called a *zakir*, related etymologically to *zikr*; they can be performed for different religious purposes, too. For example, the *nevruziyye* is held during Nevruz, the spring solstice festival, while the *mersiye* commemorates the martyrdom of Hossein, the Prophet Muhammad's grandson, at the Karbala, Iraq, in 680 CE. Dedes, zakirs, and ashiks are all distinct roles in Alevism; however, they are not necessarily mutually exclusive. Contemporary figures like Dertli Divani, who made a UNESCO list for living heritage, have served as all three at once.[25]

Though I have so far emphasized that religious content of the ashik's poetry and the religious origins of the ashiks themselves, it is also that case that the Köprülü paradigm—that is, the scholarly interpretation of Alevism as a folk tradition of Turkic origins—also plays an important role in the self-conception of some Alevi ashiks. This is an example of the way that outsiders' categories can be adopted by insiders and generate important meanings for those who identify with that tradition. An example of this phenomenon is Ruhi Su's album, *Köroğlu*, on which the artist identifies the origins of Alevism in Central Asian shamanism. I first encountered the song when I was listening to an

Internet radio program called *Şarıklarla Yürüyenler*, or "Those Who March with Song," which explores the history of leftist music both in Turkey and around the world. The album includes original works, ashik repertoire, and excerpts from oral traditions that have become classics of Turkish literature.

The first and final track on the album, "Köroğlu-Türküler-Şir," offers windows into conceptualizing the way significant texts within Turkish literature describe the oral nature of transmission in the ashik tradition. In the recording the artist reads directly from his interpretation of an old text, *The Epic of Köroğlu*: "A nomadic group's tent is gathered up, and upon setting out the bells on the animals begin to speak! The bell of the first camel, ringing out, 'My agha is rich! My agha is rich!' The bell on the second camel, crying, 'Why? Why? Why? Why?' And from the back, the last camel's bell caws, 'From here and there, from here and there and here and there and here and there.'"[26] Like many folk tales, the *Köroğlu* invites multiple interpretations. There is potential significance in the number of camels; three is an important number in Alevi cosmology and ritual practice, indicated by the common expression *Uc can bir cem* three souls, one cem—meaning that, if three souls are present, a cem ceremony may proceed.

The bell placed around the neck of the camel at the end of the caravan is the one with the answer to the question of why the agha, or leader, is rich. The answer, "From here and there," echoes the idea of both the inner and outer meanings found in Sufi teachings more broadly. It also evokes, for me, the Alevi expression *gahi saz gazi soz*, or sometimes the lute, sometimes the lyric, meaning that esoteric knowledge can be passed through verbal and nonverbal (musical) expression. In the next line, we come to understand that the riches described are not necessarily material:

This is the language of *ozan* [the ashik], truth seeing, truth speaking
Our *saz* comes from the prayers of the Shaman, to the afflicted seeking healing,
putting on a trial, the liturgy of the flowing waters of the Alaca mountain, the
Black mountain.

The agha, the leader, is actually an ashik, a teacher-poet who, by virtue of their constant search for truth and the performance of sacred dancing and other rituals, possesses the healing powers of a shaman. It seems from these verses that this ashik is a pre-Islamic figure whose power comes from the traditional homelands of Turkic peoples. The flowing streams and mountainous terrain of Central Asia root this man, who is, paradoxically, always on the move, on the road, but can call upon their power wherever he is to heal the afflicted.

But that's not where the story ends—because this shaman's power is not only associated with the topography of Central Asia but also with Allah, God. The ashik recognizes their own limitations and their dependence on God. When we first hear the ashik speak—"Let's see what he said"—we hear him supplicate, "Allah, Bismillah [In the name of God]! Oh, God, help me when misled! Oh, my *kopuz!* [*rababa*, stringed instrument used by the ashik] See true, speak true!"

This is a stunning moment in Ruhi Su's album as he both participates in and pushes against a Turkish nationalist interpretation of this canonical text. On the one hand, Ruhi Su recognizes and treasures the folkloric element of this text and its clear embrace of oral tradition from Central Asia. On the other hand, the shaman, the exemplar of pre-Islamic Turkish folklore, submits himself to the authority and power of God. This complicates the picture of folk literature as separate from the religious, as drawn by Köprülü and his students. When described as folk literature, discussion of mountain water springs is placed into a discussion of the natural world, and, therefore, the assumption goes, the pre-Islamic. But for Alevi communities who lived in mountainous regions of Anatolia, the importance of water as a miraculous life source is not taken lightly. The healing water of mountain springs are verifiable with geological maps of Anatolian hot springs in places like Tokat, which have significant Alevi communities. The ecological nature of much Alevi poetry is mistaken for being profane, or not being a religious reference. But water's sacrality in Alevism is connected to local hagiographies, as in the Munzur River in Tunceli, as well as through fasting, the ritual abstention from water called *matem orucu* to foster empathy for the thirst endured by the family of the Prophet at Karbala.

This example illustrates the vitality of Alevism in Turkish-language popular culture, showing how, at present, even radical underground online radio stations can become a vehicle for the preservation and interpretation of Alevi ideas. The advent of mass communication in the twentieth century transformed the nature of religion, and media such as radio, television, and, eventually, the Internet became central to religious missionizing and community-making. The past century has witnessed the creation of a rich archive of such materials that includes recordings from state television and radio as well as thousands of recordings produced by or with ashiks from the 1960s to the present. In this case, playing an ashik's album becomes an essential form of religious teaching in the modern and contemporary world; it is a way to pass along and speak through Alevism in public beyond the boundaries of traditional ceremonies and other forms of ritual observance.

ASHIKS' LIVES

The vitality of the ashik tradition in the past century is not confined to the mass media that popularized and extended its transmission in new spheres. Interpersonal relationships continue to play a key role in ashik development. The early lives and the work of two Alevi ashiks, Ashik Veysel and Ashik Mahzuni Serif, show how, contrary to what some scholars have said about the disappearance of Alevi tradition, teacher-student relationships have remained central to the tradition's longevity. Just like the shaman in the *Köroğlu*, their lives illustrate how itinerancy—moving constantly, to learn and to share knowledge with others—is a typical practice among ashiks. But their lives also reveal change: they show the range of influences and the polyvocality that have characterized the ashik tradition in practice.

The life story of Asik Veysel (1894–1973) offers one example of the modern master-pupil experience. Journalist and politician Mustafa Balbay describes how Veysel grew up amid Alevi traditions, which in this case are connected to the religious activities of a Bekstashi lodge: "[Veysel's] father, Karaca Ahmet, is a regular attendee" at Bektashi lodges. He "is drawn to the saz [the lute] and the words of Mustafa Abdal lodge in Örtaköy, close to Sivrialan." Balbay points out that Veysel's father welcomes ashiks into his own home, which becomes a site where their traditions are valued and learned. "Bards (ozan), masters of the saz and word not only used to go to lodges, but also to Karaca Ahmet's house," he declared. Veysel's father would invite them to share a meal, and check in with them about their lives. Then it was time for music and poetry: "The saz was filled with words, with interest, with love and affection. The poets both shared their own works and sang Yunus Emre, Pir Sultan, Dertli, Kaygusuz Abdal, Kul Himmet and Karacaoğlan."[27]

After a childhood illness left his son blind, Balbay writes, Veysel's father bought him a saz at the encouragement of those at the Sufi lodge. According to Balbay,

> he first learned how to play saz from Molla Hüseyin, who lived in Sivrialan. . . . To start, his father had him memorize Kul Abdal's poems. Even at 70, he remembered the poem he had memorized as a child. . . . This first poem that Veysel memorized, in a way, also described his future love life. Veysel suddenly found himself among dozens of sources. On the one hand, he was fed by the centuries-old accumulation of words of the poets of Anatolia; on the other hand, he was listening to the living folk poets of the Emlek region, which was what the region of Sivas was called at that time, and was nurtured by them. He wasn't just Veysel anymore. . . . He was Ashik Veysel.[28]

He continued to learn from others. Later, he worked with Ali Agha, from the Çamşıhı region of Divriği in Sivas, who reportedly taught him the poetry of Kul Abdal, Emrah, Sıtkı of Tarsus, Hüseyin of Akkaşlar, Kemter Baba from Kaleköylu, and Veli of İğdecik.[29]

This account of Veysel's multiple influences shows how Alevism was passed on in the twentieth century. In many Turkic Sufi traditions, including Bektashism, the student becomes a teacher or a master when they are recognized as such by other students. The student can trace their lineage, or *silsila*, to a connected line of teachers. In the case of Ashik Veysel, we see a more diffuse process: a young man learning from a particular master with the influence of many other ashiks from both Kizilbash and Bektashi communities in Sivas. Notably, much of that learning occurs not only in a school or a lodge but also in domestic, intimate, and informal spaces. This is not an accident;

it reflects how ritual Alevism, until quite recently, was nearly fully relegated to private spheres and marginalized from public urban space.

Ashik Mahzuni Serif (1939–2002) was a younger contemporary of Veysel known for more explicitly leftist political expression. His path to becoming an ashik sheds light on an additional thread in the Anatolian Alevi patchwork—namely, the dispersed organizational geography of the Kizilbash *ocak* system in central and eastern Anatolia. A YouTube documentary about Ashik Mahzuni's life begins with a map that traces his origins. It specifically names Hozat, a region within Dersim, today officially known as Tunceli, in the Munzur mountain range in eastern Anatolia, as the mother home (*ana yurt*) of the dede tradition. Overlaid on a rough topographical map, the audiovisual narration displays a path of migration beginning in Hozat/Tunceli, which then goes on to Malatya, passes down around Gaziantep to Hatay, then to Kahramanmaras, and, finally, to the Afsin plains (Afsin Ovasi) in today's Kahramanmaraş province. Mahzuni is said to have been born in the village of Berçenek in 1939.

It is reported that when Ashik Mahzuni Serif went to visit Ashik Veysel, Veysel stood and greeted him, defying customary practices of deference for age and authority. According to Mustafa Balbay and others, when those around him asked why he did so, Veysel said, "Comrades [*dostlar*], this one coming must be Pir Sultan." Why is such a declaration relevant to this discussion? As Schubel explains, "The tradition's great pirs (religious teachers), such as Pir Sultan Abdal, were also *ashiks*. Depicted pictorially with his baglama over his head in a defiant image of resistance, Pir Sultan Abdal is a hero not only to Alevis but also to the secular Left who see him as a defender of the poor and oppressed."[30] The way Veysel is reported to have encountered Ashik Mahzuni, in associating him with Pir Sultan Abdal, indicates a few important points about the ashik tradition more broadly. First, Veysel points to a continuity in lyric traditions to the vernacular poets of sixteenth-century Anatolia, of whom Pir Sultan Abdal is an exemplary and key source, despite little extant written sources on his life.[31] This incident also reflects the importance of the lived ethics of the ashik, which are supposed to defend the marginalized and oppressed, the poor and the hungry. That Veysel stands and proclaims Mahzuni as a key exemplar of that tradition reflects the significance of the spiritual or moral authority the ashik is seen to embody, a trait inextricably woven in the words they leave future generations.

"In the epic of the Turks," writes Balbay, "the expression 'words fly, writing lasts' has evolved to mean the following, 'Words fly, fly, and it enters into the heart and memory of another word master.'" Balbay explains that the word "lives and plays there, and from there, flies to the memory of another. In this manner, words are flying, [and] they fly such that they surpass hundreds of years, live for hundreds of years."[32]

The ashik's duty to transmit words, or knowledge, from other ashiks and to the community-at-large gains additional urgency in the face of state repression and other forms of anti-Alevi prejudice, discrimination, and violence. The marginalization Alevi face is not only experienced politically but also spiritually; it becomes a primary theme of Alevi poetry, and the recitation of that poetry becomes a way to fight the threats that Alevi face. The modern and contemporary oppression of Alevi is understood within a broader affective association with the suffering faced by members of the Prophet's family in Karbala, shared with Shi'a Muslims throughout the history of Islam. Stories about that historic oppression are a significant and meaningful archive from which ashiks draw to describe the contemporary problems of anti-Alevi violence. In the twentieth century, Ruhi Su and

Mahzuni Serif were just two among countless ashiks who were imprisoned or exiled or who faced other legal actions for expressing their Alevi and/or leftist identity publicly. While some scholars have rightly insisted that the study of Alevi must go beyond a narrative of victimhood, it remains the case that Alevi cosmology is indelibly marked by a position where martyrdom occurs as a result of the violence of the hegemonic majority against them.

The poem "Kizilbas," or "Some would damn me, some would hang me" by Mahzuni Serif presents how the marginal location of Kizilbash Alevi identity is, in bell hooks's terms, mobilized as a site of radical possibility and resistance.

> Some would damn me some would hang me
> Thanks be to The Truth I am Kızılbash
> I hate your world made up of binaries
> Thanks be to The Truth I am Kızılbash
>
> I made a promise, won't turn back
> Of these, that my name is rebellious
> Ever since I have been human
> Thanks be to The Truth I am Kizlbash
>
> God is closer than myself to me
> Every word is bismillah to me
> Evil thinking is sinful for me
> Thanks be to The Truth I am Kızılbash
>
> The start of Kizilbash is Ali
> The way of Ali is Great
> Also that of Bektash Veli
> Thanks be to The Truth I am Kızılbash

Mahzuni I flowed I cascaded
I reached The Truth step by step
I wrapped red around my head
Thanks be to The Truth I am Kızılbash[33]

In this beautiful, defiant poem, Serif recognizes how much he, like other Alevi, are oppressed by his own society, and how his life as an ashik is precarious. But he reclaims the term *Kizilbash* from those who use it an epithet and embraces a social, religious, and political position of oppugnancy and marginality. Rather than apologize for a minority status, in the last line of each stanza the ashik thanks God for making him Kızılbash, referring to Allah as Truth, *Hak*. In Alevi contexts, Hak is the primary referent for Allah, or God; it is also one of the ninety names for God in Islam. For Muslims around the world, from a variety of backgrounds, the term *Hak* (*Haqq* in Arabic) has special power and is repeated, as in this poem, over and over again during ritual remembrance (*dhikr*). The second stanza locates the ashik's devotion to the path of God from a position of defiance to authority and/or injustice.

The third stanza's line "God is closer than myself to me" could be read as a reference to the Qur'an 50:16: "Indeed, We created humankind, and We know what the human soul whispers to each person, 'God is closer to you than your jugular vein.'" Allusion to Qur'anic verse is not uncommon in ashik poetry across a variety of contextual genres. A Turkish expression, "The ashik's words are the essence of the Qur'an," indicates not only a shared metaphorical claim across Arabic to vernaculars (Turkish, Zazaki, Kurmanci) but also the belief that the lute-lyrics (*saz-soz*) performance paradigm in Alevisms has a special sacral quality, or access to Qur'anic meaning.[34]

The fourth stanza is significant because it returns us to questions raised earlier regarding the imbrication of Kizlbash and Bektashi traditions in Anatolia in the twentieth century. His inclusion of his ashik pen name, or *mahlas*, "Mahzuni," as the first word of the fourth stanza participates in a much longer border tradition in Turkish and Persian poetic forms that indicate authorship in similar ways.[35] In a litany, Mahzuni begins with Ali, the son-in-law and cousin of the Prophet Muhammad, and then recognizes the essential role of Muslim saint and teacher Haji Bektash Veli, the thirteenth-century saint from whom the Bektashi order derives its name. In my reading, this choice is significant because the poem is titled and refrains around the term *Kizilbash*. While it is clear that the Kizilbash and Bektashi orders are distinct historical communities, some scholars have portrayed an overgeneralized bifurcation of Kizilbash-Bektashi Alevi communities as being adherents of Haci Bektas Veli *or* Pir Abdal Sultan. This ultimately false binary is nonetheless clearly reflected in, for instance, the names of prominent Alevi civil society and cultural organizations today. This stanza is a reminder to the researcher that Alevism is an umbrella category that contains distinct and interacting nodes (ocaks, lodges, and lineages) with both discrete and entangled histories. Ashik poetry may prove a fertile site for further research, to unpack the role ashiks may have played in the interaction and integration of Kizilbash and Bektashi communities and systems of belief and practice, both historically and in the more recent Republican era.

If "Kizilbas" is an expression of the hopeful defiance that comes from seeking refuge in God, Ashik Mahzuni Serif's poetry is sometimes a lamentation as well. "Saying 'Allah Allah Comrade'" commemorates the violent deaths of Alevi community members who gathered on July 2, 1993, to celebrate Pir Abdal

Sultan, the sixteenth-century saint whom Alevi recognize as one of the "Seven Great Ozans," or ashiks. They were meeting at the Madimak Hotel in the city of Sivas. It was a Friday, the day of congregational prayers for observant Sunni Muslims. Allegedly incited by the presence of Salman Rushdie's translator, Aziz Nesim, who was at the meeting, a mob departed from Friday prayers. Attackers set fire to the hotel, killing thirty-seven people inside. The massacre has been commemorated each year since then and is a core event in Alevi suffering in recent history. Ashik Mazhuni Serif's poem is a wrenching expression of grief felt by Alevi both in Turkey and in the diaspora:

> Saying "Allah Allah comrade"
> We ran to the lands of Sivas
> As we sang the people's folk songs
> We lit up from the hands of Sivas
>
> Outside voices of *tekbir*
> Inside dark mourners
> Not the crime of all Sivas
> But people burned from there
>
> Lightning struck at Madımak
> Flames rose to the heavens
> at whom anger, who set alight
> we were shocked in the lands of Sivas
>
> outside voices of tekbir
> With fezzes, sticks in hand
> Is the blood of a Muslim helal?
> but people from Sivas burned

our side covered with flames
our spirits passed into Truth
Our skin burned with fire
We overflowed in your hands, Sivas

Outside voices of tekbir
Bloodied virtueless hands
Does a human sacrifice another?
Alas, burned people from Sivas

Daddy State, Daddy State
What harm did we do you to
Turning turning, burning burning
We cowered in your lands, Sivas.

Mahzuni voices of tekbir
Lives burning inside
The blood drank by the *sharia*
Is known by all people
Not the crime of all Sivas
But people from Sivas burned

We flew from Sivas to the heavens
Our hearts wishing for Truth
The Muhlises and Nesimis
Embracing the flame
Stars of the mountain, dusty smoke
Do not hold up our path

We are the last traveler on this path
Do not forget us

This way has seen many travelers
The Gültekin's the Gülsüm's

We died loving truth
What do those who don't love know
This smoke you gave us
Don't assume it chokes us
One Pir Sultan is sacrificed
One hundred thousand Mahzuni are born
One hundred thousand Mahzuni are born[36]

In this poem, Mahzuni succeeds in documenting details of the brutal attack while deploying multivalent language that subtly points to the distinct practices and vocabulary of the Alevi. The cem ritual *semah* is referenced with the line "turning, turning." Through a dual meaning, when Mahzuni references flying to the heavens, he both commemorates their passing and the ritual they were performing when they died: the Alevi *mirac story* (in Arabic, *miraj*; roughly, "the ascension"*)* as commemorated in cem ceremonies as *miraclama*.[37] The implications of heavenly ascent are manifold, depending on the perspective of the reader.

The poem also expresses incredulity over the weaponization of the Islamic tradition in order to justify the murder of other human beings. In the hands of the attackers, the sharia, the Path of God sometimes called Islamic law, becomes a vampire that drinks the blood of fellow believers not perceived as such. The attackers keep reciting the tekbir, saying "Allahu Akbar," as they make human sacrifices of others by burning them. The juxtaposition is given meaning in the implication that those outside the hotel, the ones claiming the mantle of Islamic correctness, are actually the ignorant, backward ones—those who have no knowledge of Islam. When Ashik Mahzuni uses the terms of Islamic law to demand whether human sacrifice is *helal*, or permitted by God, the question is rhetorical. Such a spectacle runs counter to what most Muslims recognize as the compassionate nature of Islamic law in contradistinction to the law of the unbeliever or the ignorant. But no event in recent memory provides a clearer example of the horrific violence Alevi have faced for being described as unbelievers. Mahzuni recognizes this as the fault of some individuals, not the entire town of Sivas. But where were his fellow citizens when he needed them? And why did the government, the Daddy State, not help them?

Moreover, how, in the face of such repression and violence, do the ashik's words fly on? In the two quatrains before the closing stanza, Ashik Mahzuni invokes the names of some of the artists, poets, and musicians who were murdered on that day: "the Muhlises and Nesimis," referencing Muhlis Akarsu and Nesimi Çimen, two among the most widely respected and prolific twentieth-century ashiks; and "the Gültekin's the Gülsüm's," referring to the stolen potential of youth, in the deaths of Hasret Gültekin, a twenty-three-year-old poet and artist, and Gülsüm Karababa, a twenty-two-year-old artist. Even in all this pain, the ashik does not give up his defiant commitment to his community. The attack may have been an attempt to put an end to the Alevi—to "choke" them— but he promises that one hundred thousand Mazhuni (the first name of the ashik-author) will be born. This evokes an echo of the popular saying, sometimes attributed to Haji Bektash and often cited by Ulas Ozdemir, *yol bir sürek binbir*, which he translates as "one path, a thousand and one practices," reflecting both the permissibility and the necessity of heterogeneity and a diversity of views and approaches within Alevism historically.[38] The light and truth of the Alevi did not go out when attacked with flames.

"By your hands, Sivas" not only documents a particular massacre that has been a cornerstone and flashpoint in contemporary Alevi struggles; it also preserves and expands on much older lyric motifs. The line "Sivas ellerinde," which is refrained by Mahzuni throughout the poem, is one that has "flown" in Balbay's terms, from the early modern world of Pir Abdal Sultan to the 1990s, by ashiks who have passed through the lands of Sivas. A famous work by Pir Adbal Sultan, "Kul Olayım Kalem Tutan Ellere," or "That I be the ink of the pen in your hands," exists in official (state) folk music archives, first recorded by Ashik Veysel. In the verses we find the line "Sivas ellerinde sazım çalınır," or "My saz plays in your hands, Sivas." But in a different textual version, the line is rendered "Sivas illerinde sazım çalınır," or "My saz plays in your lands, Sivas."[39] This faint shift in the opening letter also shifts the meaning in both the Turkish and English renderings. Thus, in my translation of the verse, I oscillate between referencing both the "hands" and "lands" of Sivas to capture these alternative translations and their possible semiotic consequences.

This is just one example of the challenges of translating works that have multiple oral iterations; another relates to the thick polyvalence certain terms can hold, which Hande Saglam calls an Alevi "lyrical code."[40] The term *dost* is a key example of this. Schubel rendered the word as "friend," the more natural and perhaps appropriate choice. For Alevi, *dost* is a polyvalent term; it also exists in the broader modern Turkish lexicon, reserved for close friends, not acquaintances. It was among those keywords signaling Alevi identity that were banned by state radio and television prior to the 1980 coup. Ashiks and other performers had to engage in strategic arrangement and lyrical revision that allowed the performance of "Alevi music" on official channels.[41] I have chosen to render *dost* as "comrade" in English, a choice both ethnographic and ideological. Using "comrade" here refracts the language used by Alevi who have found leftist politics as a space to engage their ethical worldviews while opening the poem's audience to broader potential communities of solidarity. This happened in the Alevi context from the 1960s onward, through collaboration with crossover or mainstream artists.[42] Folk-rock star Selda Bagcan, for instance, famously recorded a rearrangement of the Pir Abdal Sultan classic "Kul Olayim," swapping the first with the third stanza and putting the verse that begins with "My saz plays in your hands, Sivas" at the start of the song.

LOVER'S WORDS ARE ETERNAL

I listened to a lot of *turku* while I wrote this, eschewing more explicitly devotional music, but, really, two songs carried me. The first was "Uzun Ince Bir Yoldayim," the deeply accessible Ashik Veysel song so newly, painfully relevant for so many in the ongoing, protracted crises of the global pandemic and global warming, and the capitalism that fuels them. Surely, after the last few years, many can relate when Veysel says, "I don't know what state I'm in, but I keep going, day and night."

The other one was more explicitly motivational. Knowing I was working on this project, someone I love sent along a track by the popular psychedelic fusion artist Baba Zula called "Asiklarin Sozu Kalir" (Lover's words are eternal). The song became the star of the soundtrack to my writing, as it is a passionate love letter to ashik poetry tradition, repeating core themes in its verses. Amid rollicking guitars, rippling synths, samples of horses neighing, and a thick bass line, the two vocalists, one from Turkey, one from North America, echo each other: The ashik's words are eternal." The lyrics even quote directly from the words of Pir Sultan Abdal:

> Go on, Hizir Pasha
> your wheel will break one day
> the padishah you trust
> will be overturned one day.

When I learned more about the backstory of Murat Ertel, the vocalist and electric saz player in Baba Zula, it became even clearer that traditional methods of religious transmission, like student-pupil and father-son relationships, did not disappear in the second half of the twentieth century. Like Ashik Veysel, Ertel credits the ashiks who would visit his house as a child as the impetus for his participation in the music industry and his choice to play saz in particular. In fact, his father, Mengü Ertel, was a graphic designer whose work included the cover art for the album *Koroglu* by Ruhi Su. So, when I hear the horses neigh in the Baba Zula track, I see the drawing of the horse that graced the cover of the *Koroglu* album, which mediates the story of a powerful truth-telling duo: the lute, and the lyric. In drawing this connection, I'm not definitively proscribing whether Baba Zula or even Ruhi Su even fit a label of *ashik* in the historic sense. Instead of trying to draw boundaries, my focus has been on the question of "how" individuals participate in continuities of Alevi traditions.

As I've endeavored to demonstrate in this chapter, it isn't just a song's words, but the lives that are informed by them—the humans that carry them and speak them, sometimes at great cost—that are the real center of the Alevi ashik tradition today. The words of ashiks are eternal not because they've been written down, but because humans verbally transmit them, carrying them on their tongues and in their hearts, in relationship with one another, flying from one generation to the next, from living rooms to protest assemblies to concert halls, echoing in prison cells and even ricocheting across oceans. The ashik tradition among Alevi in Turkey is not the story of one or a few men, but of thousands of people in motion, in conversation, and in relationship with each other.

At present, the manifold influences of the ashik tradition on contemporary popular culture in Turkey are difficult to understate. Thanks to a long tradition of lyrical flexibility and polyvalence, Alevi culture not only survives but also continues to inform the contours of musical cultural production across the world today. Amid a century of rapid sociopolitical change, a whole host of institutions and leaders, especially ashiks, preserved the verses of the past while continuing to create new poems that interpret the meaning of Alevism and the struggles of its members for today. Scholars and community members debate the origins, development, and contemporary status of the Alevi, which continues to defy categorization. But that conversation, the very disagreements in which participants engage, are exactly elements that constitute a tradition. As historian of religion W. C. Smith argues, religious people often disagree about the most fundamental aspects of the tradition they share, but it's often shared arguments that make them a community, not the agreements.[43]

Despite all of the opposition and oppression that Alevism has faced, ashiks have persisted in improvising from their positions of relative marginality to speak on behalf of the oppressed and downtrodden, the poor and the hungry—the people. Alevi ashiks use lute and lyric as a technology of gnosis as well as liberation. Even as some insist that the ashik is really a kind of folkloric shaman, those drawing such circumscribed boundaries have not been able to limit the imaginations of those who maintain a more complex view of the ashik tradition, in which ashiks have been central in speaking from the margins as sites of resistance within and beyond an indexical or categorical relationship to Islam. The words of poets speaking truth to power fly intertextually across generations and continents, returning as litany, as liturgy, as lyrical and melodic refrain, to call for more just tomorrows.

NOTES

Epigraph: "Kaygusuz Abdal: A Medieval Turkish Saint and the Formation of Vernacular Islam in Anatolia," trans. Ahmet Karamustafa, in *Unity in Diversity: Mysticism, Messianism, and the Construction of Religious Authority in Islam*, ed. Orkhan Mir-Kaismov (Leiden: Brill, 2014), 340.

1. bell hooks, "Marginality as a Site of Resistance," in *Out There: Marginalization and Contemporary Culture*, ed. Russell Ferguson, Martha Gever, Trinh T. Minh-ha, and Cornel West (Cambridge, Mass.: MIT Press, 1990), 341.
2. A more thorough accounting can be found in Markus Dressler, "Genealogies and Significations," in *Writing Religion* (New York: Oxford University Press, 2013), 1–28.
3. Besim Can Zirh, interviewed by Murat Es, "Alevi Struggles," in *Authoritarianism and Resistance in Turkey: Conversations on Democratic and Social Challenges*, Esra Özyürek, Gaye Özpınar, and Emrah Altındis (New York: Springer, 2018), 186.
4. See Ayse Baltacioglu, "One Word, Many Implications: The Term 'Kızılbaş' in the Early Modern Ottoman Context," in *Ottoman Sunnism: New Perspectives*, ed. Vefa Erginbaş (Edinburgh: Edinburgh University Press, 2019), 47–70.
5. Ayfer Karakaya-Stump, *The Kızılbash/Alevis in Ottoman Anatolia: Sufism, Politics and Community* (Edinburgh: Edinburgh University Press, 2019).
6. Ahmet Yaşar Ocak, "Alevi," in *TDV İslâm Ansiklopedisi*, (Ankara: TDV İslâm Araştırmaları Merkezi, 1989), https://islamansiklopedisi.org.tr/alevi (accessed September 26, 2022).

7. The Alevi in Turkey are distinct from the Alawites in Syria, who adopted the term "Alawite" against the term "Nusayri" in the 1920s, as the former was seen as derogatory and was deployed amid accusations of heresy. See Kais M. Firro, "The Alawis in Modern Syria: From Nusayriya to Islam via Alawiya," *Der Islam* 82 (2005): 1–31. On the distinctions between Alevi and Alawite communities, see Marianne Aringberg-Laanatza, "Alevis in Turkey–Alawites in Syria: Similarities and Differences," in *Alevi Identity*, 2nd ed., ed. Tord Olsson, Elisabeth Ozdalga, and Catharina Raudvere (Istanbul: Swedish Research Institute in Istanbul, 1998), 151–65.
8. The entry cites *Kizilbash* (lit. redhead) and *rafizi* (schismatic) as terms by which Anatolian Alevis are identified in Ottoman sources, obfuscating quite a bit of history and contentious politics by stating simply that they "chose instead to call themselves Alevi." Irene Melikoff also notes the usage of other derogatory terms, including *zindik* (heretic), *mulhid* (atheist), and Shi'ite (which she describes as directly regarded as a hostile label in the Ottoman context after the sixteenth century). Irene Melikoff, "Bektashi/Kizilbas: Historical Bipartition and Its Consequences," in *Alevi Identity*, 2nd ed. (London: Routledge Curzon, 2003), 5.
9. Ruşen Cakir, "Political Alevism Versus Political Sunnism: Convergences and Divergences," in *Alevi Identity*, 64.
10. Dressler, "Genealogies and Significations," 17.
11. David Shankland, "Anthropology and Ethnicity: The Place of Ethnography in the New Alevi Movement," in *Alevi Identity*, 20.
12. Ayfer Karakaya-Stump, "The Wafā'iyya, the Bektashiyye, and Genealogies of 'Heterodox' Islam in Anatolia: Rethinking the Köprülü Paradigm," *Turcica* 44 (2012–2013): 279–300.
13. A rich argument for how Alevi poetry challenges attempts to define Islam has been made by Zeynep Oktay-Uslu, in "Alevism as Islam: Rethinking Shahab Ahmed's Conceptualization of Islam Through Alevi Poetry," *British Journal of Middle Eastern Studies* 49, no. 2 (2020): 305–26.
14. As historian Ayfer Karakaya-Stump has noted, when the "syncretism" label is unevenly applied in a taxonomic manner, it further foments Othering of the Alevi. Ayfer Karakaya-Stump and Chris Gratien, "Beyond Heterodoxy: Kizilbash/Alevis in Ottoman Anatolia," *Ottoman*

History Podcast, March 8, 2014, http://www.ottomanhistorypodcast.com/2014/03/alevi-kizilbash-history.html.

15. Following field research conducted in an Alevi village in Central Anatolia in the 1990s, David Shankland observed that "many villagers claim also that Haci Bektas is descended from the twelve imams, and through them to Ali himself. Haci Bektas is thus at once a spiritual focus, and also an orienting figure through which the Alevi build up and link and define their place in the wider world of Islam as a whole." Shankland, "Anthropology and Ethnicity," 19.

16. Kristina Kehl-Bodrogi, "The New Garments of Alevism," *ISIM Newsletter* 5, no. 1 (2000): 23.

17. Shankland, "Anthropology and Ethnicity," 153.

18. Nurettin Albayrak, "Âşık," in *TDV İslâm Ansiklopedisi*, 3rd ed. (Ankara: TDV İslâm Araştırmaları Merkezi, 1991).

19. Vernon Schubel, "From the Dutar to the Electric Guitar: Exposing Students to the Music of the Muslim World," Religious Studies News: Spotlight on Teaching, 2001, http://rsnonline.org/indexeard.html (accessed September 26, 2022).

20. Markus Dressler, "Alevīs," in *Encyclopaedia of Islam*, 3rd ed., ed. Kate Fleet, Gudrun Krämer, Denis Matringe, John Nawas, and Everett Rowson, http://dx.doi.org/10.1163/1573-3912_ei3_COM_0167 (accessed October 24, 2022).

21. Ahmet T. Karamustafa, *God's Unruly Friends: Dervish Groups in the Islamic Middle Period, 1200–1500* (London: Oneworld, 2006); Ahmet T. Karamustafa, "Anadolu'nun Islamlasmasi Baglaminda Aleviligin Olusumu," in *Kizilbashlik, Alevilik, Bektasilik: Tarih, Kimlik, Inanc, Rituel*, ed. Yalçın Çakmak and İmran Gürtaş (Istanbul: Iletisim Yayinlari, 2015) 43–54; Ahmet T. Karamustafa, "Antinomian Sufis," in *The Cambridge Companion to Sufism*, ed. Lloyd Ridgeon (Cambridge: Cambridge University Press, 2015), 101–24.

22. Hande Saglam, "Textual Characteristics of Alevi and Sunni Âşıks in Sivas/Turkey," in *Diversity and Contact among Singer-Poet Traditions in Eastern Anatolia*, ed. Martin Greve, Wendelmoet Hamelik, and Ulaş Özdemir (Ergon: Würzburg, 2018), 131–48.

23. Ozan Aksoy, Ceren Erdem and Chris Gratien, "Kurdish Alevi Music and Migration," *Ottoman History Podcast*, March 19, 2015, https://www

.ottomanhistorypodcast.com/2015/03/music-kurdish-alevi-migration
.html.
24. John H. Renard, *Seven Doors to Islam* (Berkeley: University of California Press, 1996), 25.
25. Ulas Ozdemir's important study of itinerant zakirs in Istanbul provides a generative and detailed ethnographic examination of how the mobility of these religious music performers participates in an emphasis on both horizontal leadership and the charisma (ask) of particular teacher (dede) and performer (zakir), in contrast to prior studies that emphasized traditional (village) social organization. Ulas Ozdemir, "Rethinking the Institutionalization of Alevism: Itinerant Zakirs in the Cemevis of Istanbul," in *Landscapes of Music in Istanbul: A Cultural Politics of Place and Exclusion* (Bielefeld: Transcript-Verlag, 2017), 141–66.
26. Many versions of this text exist, and indeed variations of a Koroglu story are prevalent across the Perso-Turkic world. The version of the text I accessed, which corresponds to the text of the Ruhi Su lyrics, can be found at https://www.siir.gen.tr/siir/r/ruhi_su_turkuleri/prolog.htm (accessed September 26, 2022).
27. Mustafa Balbay, *Gönül Gözümde Binbir Renk: Aşık Veysel* (İstanbul: Halk Kitabevi, 2018), 19.
28. Balbay, *Gönül Gözümde Binbir Renk*, 20–21.
29. Sivas Valiliği, "Âşık Veysel," http://www.sivas.gov.tr/asik-veysel (accessed August 31, 2021).
30. Vernon J. Schubel, "From the Dutar to the Electric Guitar: Exposing Students to the Music of the Muslim World," *Religious Studies News* (Spring 2001), http://rsnonline.org/indexea1d.html (accessed November 8, 2022).
31. Paul Koerbin. "Pir Sultan Abdal: Encounters with Persona in Alevi Lyric Song," in *Oral Tradition* 26, no. 1 (2011): 191–220.
32. Balbay, *Gönül Gözümde Binbir Renk* 21.
33. My translation of Mahzuni Serif, "Kizilbas," https://sarki.alternatifim.com/sarkici/asik-mahsuni-serif/kizilbas-ister-sovun-ister-asin (accessed September 26, 2022).
34. Ulas Ozdemir, "Between Debate and Sources: Defining Alevi Music," in *Alevism Between Standardisation and Plurality*, ed. Benjamin

Weineck and Johannes Zimmermann (Berlin: Peter Lang Verlag, 2019), 170.

35. Paul Koerbin, "Players in the 'Web of Poetic Tradition': Interpreting Self-Naming in Turkish Alevi Sacred and Secular Sung Poetry," 43rd ICTM World Conference, Astana, 2015, https://koerbin.files.wordpress.com/2011/11/koerbin_2015_ictm_paper.pdf (accessed September 26, 2022).

36. My translation of "Saying 'Allah Allah Comrade,'" which is in my possession.

37. For more on this narrative, see Vernon Schubel, "When the Prophet Went on the *Mirac* He Saw a Lion on the Road: The *Mirac* in the Alevi-Bektaşi Tradition," in *The Prophet Muhammad's Ascension: New Cross-Cultural Encounters*, ed. Frederick Colby and Christiane Gruber (Bloomington: Indiana University Press, 2010), 330–43.

38. Ozdemir, "Between Debate and Sources," 170.

39. "Kul Olayım Kalem Tutan Ellere," Turku Dostlari, https://www.turkudostlari.net/soz.asp?turku=714 (accessed October 20, 2021).

40. See Hande Saglam, "Textual Characteristics of Alevi and Sunni Âşıks in Sivas/Turkey," in *Diversity and Contact Among Singer-Poet Traditions in Eastern Anatolia*, ed Martin Greve, Wendelmoet Hamelik, and Ulaş Özdemir (Ergon: Würzburg, 2018), 134, 145.

41. Hande Saglam, "Textual Characteristics," 135.

42. Eliot Bates, *Digital Tradition: Arrangement and Labor in Istanbul's Recording Studio Culture* (Oxford: Oxford University Press, 2016).

43. Wilfred Cantwell Smith, *Toward a World Theology: Faith and Comparative History* (Maryknoll, N.Y.: Orbis, 1981), 4–5, 27–28.

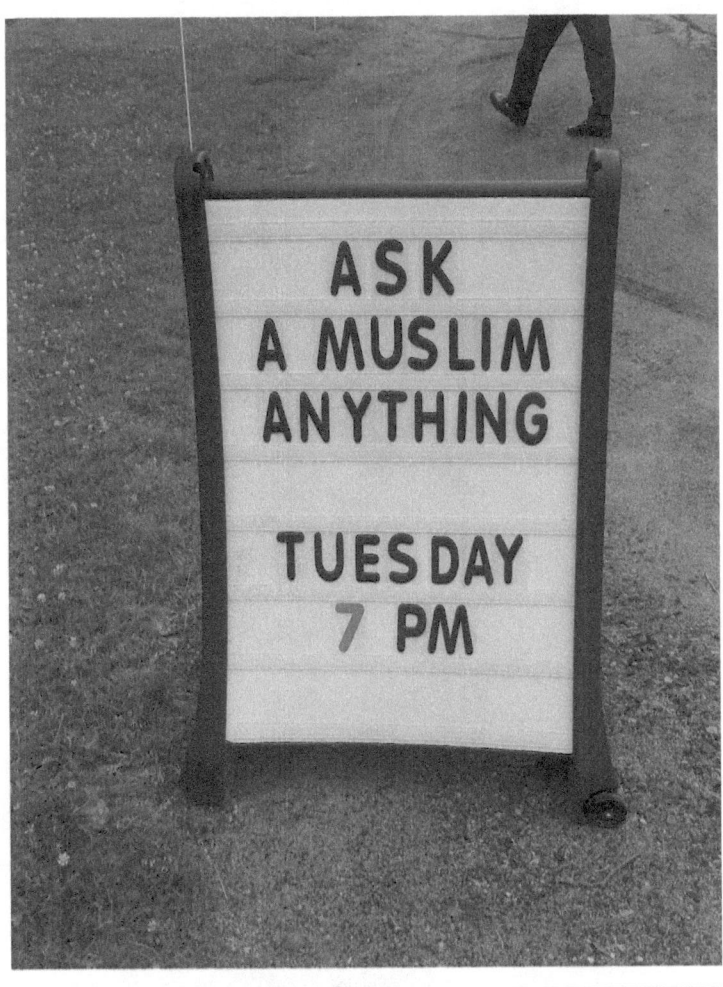

FIGURE 1 In the post-9/11 era, Muslim Americans devoted significant time and resources to public outreach, including "Ask a Muslim" sessions. Events like this one, held in 2018 in New Hampshire, were meant to dispel stereotypes about Islam and reduce anti-Muslim violence. Farah Bakaari.

FIGURE 2 Rep. Ilhan Omar (D-Minn.) often challenges anti-Muslim bias and discrimination even as she faces multiple threats to her own safety and well-being. Kristie Boyd; U.S. House Office of Photography.

FIGURE 3 The Sunan Abu Dawud is one of the six collections of hadith, or reports of what the Prophet Muhammad and his companions did and said, broadly accepted as canonical by most scholars of Islam. But these six canonical collections do not present a unified, monolithic portrait of Muhammad and his companions. Abu Ta'ib.

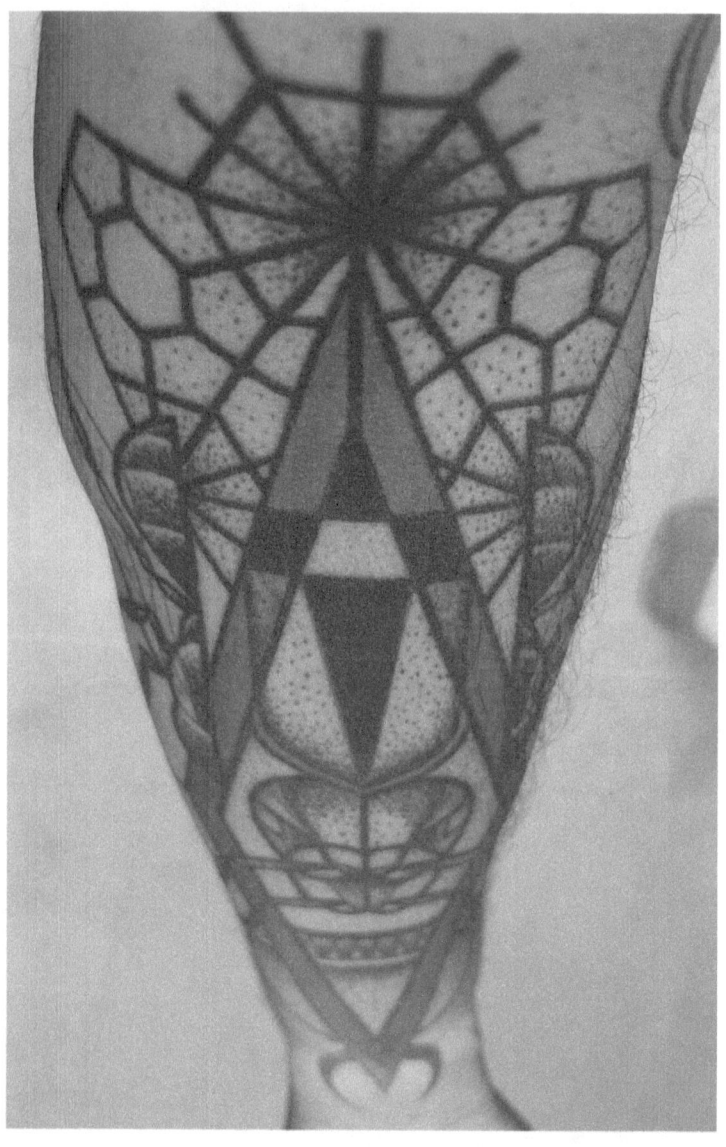

FIGURE 4 Muslim tattoos can feature calligraphy, geometric shapes, or images. This tattoo features two ant heads inside a mosque with the body of a bee on the outside. According to the Sunni Muslim man on whose left arm it appears, it is "meant to signify my complicated relationship with the mosque and the tradition writ large." Edward E. Curtis IV.

FIGURE 5 Ashik Veysel (1894–1973) plays the *baglama*, a seven-stringed instrument used to accompany the poetic songs at the center of Alevi Muslim religious life in Turkey, in 1948. Şarkışla Belediyesi.

FIGURE 6 In Turkey, Alevi Muslim music and poetry appear not only in religious but also in secular settings. In the early 1970s, singer Selda Bağcan, seen here in an Istanbul street mural, became famous for her interpretation of Turkish folk music that included Alevi poems. J. W. S. Lubbock.

FIGURE 7 Members of the Fruit of Islam, the male auxiliary of the Nation of Islam, provide security as boxer Muhammad Ali watches leader Elijah Muhammad address his followers in 1964. Muslims in the group were known for their smart, elegant dress: men in suits and bow ties, women in long-flowing white gowns. Library of Congress.

FIGURE 8 Food was a focus of religious and political liberation in the Nation of Islam, headquartered in Chicago, Illinois. One of the group's most noted culinary contributions to the United States was its popularization of the bean pie, which was often made by Muslim women in their homes and sold to supplement family incomes. WikiCommons.

FIGURE 9 In Lucknow, India, the eighteenth-century Bara Imambara complex includes a mosque for salah, or prayer, and a shrine where worshippers seek blessings. It also hosts a large number of commemorations of Husayn during the Islamic month of Muharram. Matt Stabile.

FIGURE 10 The Hazrat Abbas Dargah is a shrine in Lucknow, India, where Muslims and people from other communities, including women hoping to become pregnant, visit for the purposes of spiritual intercession. Aou Naqvi.

FIGURE 11 Depicted in a brown-and-white checkered turban, fifteenth-century Sufi teacher Khwaja Ahrar, born in what today is Uzbekistan, was a major figure in the Naqshbandi Sufi Muslim network with which Turko-Mongol historian Mirza Muhammad Haydar Dughlat (d. 1551) associated himself. Wiki Commons.

FIGURE 12 Young Alevi Muslim men and women perform *semah* in the city of Sivas, Turkey. Semah is a form of Islamic dance generally accompanied by *saz*, or lute, music. The turning of the dancers can be seen a symbol of the belief that human beings come from God and they return to God (Qur'an 2:156). Vernon James Schubel.

FIGURE 13 Qawwali musicians on the streets of Multan, Pakistan. Popular on the world music scene for decades, qawwali is devotional Islamic music sung in praise of God and the Prophet Muhammad. Often performed in or near the shrines, such music is a central element of South Asian Muslim religiosity and culture. Vernon James Schubel.

5

ON THE MARGINS OF ISLAMIC DOCTRINE, AT THE HEART OF ISLAMIC ETHICS

Elijah Muhammad's Nation of Islam
and Black Liberation

EDWARD E. CURTIS IV

At the end of his life, El Hajj Malik El Shabazz, or Malcolm X (1925–1965), articulated a powerful Islamic ethics of Black liberation. Confronting Muslim audiences in North America, Europe, North Africa, and the Middle East with the realities of anti-Black discrimination and white supremacy, Shabazz argued that Muslims had a moral obligation to engage in the struggle to help Black people—Muslim or not—free themselves from the bonds of second-class citizenship wherever they lived. Malcolm X saw this struggle as part and parcel of the larger effort of what he called the "dark world" to defeat colonialism, both mental and physical.[1] Though Shabazz is often rightly seen as having undergone a second conversion to what he called so-called orthodox Islam in the 1960s, the memory of him as a Black freedom fighter burns less brightly in some quarters, especially among Muslims and non-Muslims who want to credit him as having seen the errors of his ways as a Black nationalist. These memories emphasize a softer, less political, and more "correct" Muslim, effectively marginalizing him as a Black freedom fighter.

This chapter is not primarily about Malcolm X, but it invokes his memory here in order to make clear that looking at Islam primarily through the lens of theology can obscure how ethics, rather than theology, is sometimes at the heart of Islam. Malcolm X's pilgrimage to Mecca in 1964 has been seen as a miraculous and wholesale transformation for the leader. In reality, some of Malcolm X's commitments stayed the same after he became a Sunni Muslim. Focusing exclusively on the interracialism of his pilgrimage can cover up the fact that, even after he denied the doctrinal claims of the Nation of Islam's theology, what did not change was his belief in Islam as a pathway to human freedom.

Malcolm X exemplifies the power of Islam in Black America as a lifeway of liberation. This understanding of Islamic religion has been typical for Black Muslims in the United States—whatever their doctrinal commitments—from the 1920s until his time and today. Islam has been a many-splendored thing in Black America: its aesthetics, beliefs, rituals, organizations, mythologies, sacred texts, and leadership have assumed many diverse and beautiful forms. But the institutionalization of Islam among African Americans in the United States during the 1920s, when Ahmadi, Sunni, and Moorish communities first took root as voluntary associations in Black America, has been united for the most part by an imagining of Islam as a discursive heritage of freedom. In their preaching and outreach, the foreign missionaries and American-born Black people who helped to establish Muslim groups in the midst of the Great Migration of African Americans from the rural South mainly to the urban North built on decades of anticolonial Islamic thought. From the 1880s until World War I, African Americans in Black schools, churches, clubs, and mutual aid societies read coverage of Muslim resistance to colonialism. In his well-circulated articles and speeches, Liberian nationalist and educator Edward Wilmot Blyden argued forcefully that Islam was the religion best suited to achieve Black freedom and liberation from white supremacy. Dusé Mohamed Ali's *African Times and Orient Review* amplified that message, and, after World War I, Ali became the foreign affairs correspondent for Marcus Garvey's *Negro World*. By 1921, when Ahmadi missionary Muhammad Sadiq began to preach to Black audiences that Islam was a religion of racial equality and Black liberation, he was building on a theme already established in Black American intellectual culture. When Noble Drew Ali created his Moorish Science Temple of America in 1925, which was based on the idea that adopting Islam as a religion was a pathway toward full citizenship rights in the United States, he was building on Islam's association with freedom in Black life.[2]

There were already Sunni, Ahmadi, and Moorish communities when W. D. Fard Muhammad created the Temple of Islam, later the Nation of Islam, in Detroit in 1930. Though Farad Muhammad, as he is also called, disappeared just a few short years after the group's establishment, he planted yet another Black Muslim community that saw Islam as coterminous with Black freedom. After World War II, that group emerged under the leader of Elijah Muhammad, born as Elijah Poole in Sandersville, Georgia, in 1897, as the preeminent Muslim community or "denomination" in the United States.[3] In terms of the number of mosques, schools, and members and the amount of press coverage, it dwarfed all other national networks of Muslims, including the Federation of Islamic Associations of the United States and Canada, the second-largest association of Muslim communities. During its rise, most other Muslims, as well as sociologists of religion, journalists, and the U.S. Federal Bureau of Investigation (FBI) went to great efforts to define the group as heretical; it wasn't actually Islamic, they said.[4] It was criticized as a cult, and, to this day, religious studies scholars often understand it to be a "new religion."[5]

This chapter explains instead how putting this marginal Muslim group at the center of our study of Islam reveals that, despite the incredible doctrinal gulf between it and other interpretations of Islam, the struggle for Black dignity, hope, and liberation can rest at the very heart of Islamic ethics. In the 1950s and 1960s, the Nation of Islam nurtured an Islamic identity that had begun to take root in the hearts, minds, and bodies of thousands of African Americans in the 1920s as an international freedom discourse. The organization had tens of thousands of members, but its appeal and influence could be felt by millions across the United States as its message of Islamic liberation fueled Black dissent to racism and colonialism during the Cold War and the war in Vietnam. As intellectuals and everyday practitioners imagined and embodied Islam, this religion became a powerful form of personal and communal transformation that freed Black people—mind and body—from internalized racism while challenging foundational American myths that served as a foundation for white supremacy.

ISLAMIC MYTHOLOGIES OF BLACK SUFFERING, FREEDOM, AND PRIDE

Starting from the 1920s premise that Islam was, above all things, an ideology of Black freedom, and thus of social, political, and cultural power, the Nation of Islam added its own original mythologies to historically traditional interpretations of Islam.

Like other new religious movements, the movement recognized the legitimacy and importance of the tradition from which it took its name—it was, after all, the Nation of *Islam*, not some other religion. The adoption of this name was no small thing. When someone who is born into a different social group—in this case, a religious community—explicitly rejects or sets aside the religious identity of their family and begins to call themselves something else, this is a social crossing of great import; it can have immediate implications for one's communal affiliations, social status, and political loyalties. As Devin DeWeese points out in his study of the Golden Horde, "To adopt a name is to change one's reality, and in this sense there is hardly a *deeper* 'conversion' than a *nominal* one."[6] Understanding Islamization from the point of view of Nation of Islam members means shifting a scholar's geographic perspective toward Islam as well. Historian Richard Eaton describes this reorientation as one that centers the margins of the global community of Muslims: "Instead of adopting the perspective of one standing in Mecca, looking out upon an ever-widening, ever-expanding religious tide that is uniform and monolithic, one adopts the perspective of someone standing in a remote and dusty village, incorporating into his religious system elements considered useful or meaningful that drift in from beyond the ocean, from over the mountains, or simply from the neighboring village."[7]

Looking at the center of Islam from the perspective of African American Islam means looking toward Mecca from the largely urban milieu of Black life during the Great Migration and after World War II. This rich environment for the flourishing of Islam as a religious community among Black Americans was awash with the increasing use of Islamic symbols among Black metaphysical groups and Black Shriners, the development of Muslim immigrant and missionary associations, and the appropriation of Islamic and Muslim images in consumer culture and mass entertainment. These resources provided the materials out of which Black Muslims imagined an Islam that was useful and meaningful to their particular circumstances. One common element of the 1920s Black Muslim communities, whether Ahmadi, Sunni, or Moorish, was the idea, for example, that Islam was part and parcel of Black history. Repeating themes articulated in the 1880s by Edward Wilmot Blyden and perpetuated in Garvey's Universal Negro Improvement Association (UNIA), African American Muslims spoke and wrote about the involvement of Black people with Islam from the very beginnings of its history. Figures such as Bilal ibn Rabah, the companion of Prophet Muhammad and first prayer-caller in Islam, made frequent appearances in Black Muslim discourse. Prophet Muhammad himself and the Qur'an were not framed as foreign elements but rather as part of Black history and culture.[8]

As movement leader Elijah Muhammad built on the prewar foundations laid by Fard, he saw the Qur'an and Prophet Muhammad as authorizing his unique claims about the nature of God, prophecy, time, and space. Elijah Muhammad had a special place in his home for his Ahmadi translation of the Qur'an, and the picture of him holding it as a sacred object circulated widely in the movement. But the Qur'an and the Bible, which he quoted more frequently, were, according to him, largely prophecies that predicted the appearance of Fard as God in person and his role as the Messenger of Allah. The basic Islamic profession of faith, the *shahada*, was used in the movement. But when members recited it, it was clear that the statement "There is no god but God" referred not only to Allah, but also to Fard, and "Muhammad is His Messenger" actually pointed not toward Muhammad ibn Abdallah but to Elijah Muhammad.[9] The idea that a human being might be God or God-like was not new in the the history of Islam; mystical theologies that attributed divine characteristics to human beings such as the Prophet Muhammad's family or Sufi masters are part and parcel of Islamic tradition. But in the twentieth-century United States, such teachings were framed by both non-Muslim scholars and many Muslim leaders as outside the boundaries of Islam. The opponents of the movement successfully convinced most American opinion makers, politicians, and other Black religious leaders familiar with the Nation of Islam that it was not "truly" Islamic.

Most members of the Nation of Islam thought that these critics were just denying the truth. The Qur'an and the Bible, they said, had to be read in light of Fard's and Elijah Muhammad's teachings. Doctrines about the nature of the universe and humankind could be found in several sources, including catechisms that had been memorized by members of the movement such as *Actual Facts* and *Student Enrollment* in addition to the speeches and writings of Elijah Muhammad, including *The Supreme Wisdom* (1957) and, most importantly, *Message to the Blackman* (1965).[10] These teachings introduced mythologies that utilized Islamic idioms in new ways. Like other historians of religion, I am not calling these teachings mythological as a way of claiming that they are untrue; that's the street definition of "myths," which are often time things that are supposed to be "busted." Rather, I understand a mythology to be a story about the beginning and ending of the universe, the creation of human beings, the fate of humankind, and other fantastic phenomena. For religious studies scholars, then, stories about Adam and Eve, the resurrection of Jesus, and the destruction of the world are all myths, which says nothing about whether or not they are true. Elijah Muhammad's Islamic myths created meaning that was not simply useful—for those who applied their ethical lessons in their lives, such myths were about survival and protection from fellow American citizens and the institutions of state and society that physically and psychologically hurt or killed them.

Like most good mythological systems, Elijah Muhammad's myth began with the origins of the universe. Black scientists, described as gods or godlike creatures, created the cosmos trillions of years ago. Black people also came to be the original people of the Earth. To be human was to be Black. There were no other colors among the human race. They lived in the holy city of Mecca. They practiced Islam and spoke Arabic. It was like Eden. Elijah Muhammad's "fall of man" story explained why bad things happened to these good people. Around 4600 BCE, an evil, mad, and big-headed scientist by the name of Yakub (Jacob) launched a series of horrifying genetic experiments that resulted in the making of the white man. Yakub deployed some of the same techniques of U.S. eugenics and Nazism's final solution. When a lighter-skinned baby was born, then that child would be allowed to live, but when a Black baby was born, the baby would be killed. In some cases, nurses killed the child by "picking its brain"; in other cases, the child was sent to a crematorium. Elijah Muhammad's myth of the fall of humankind was thus clearly situated in and influenced by twentieth-century events: it reflected the truth that the medical establishment and the U.S. government had abused or stood silent as Black people were victimized by phenomena such as the Tuskegee syphilis experiment, state-run programs to reduce the number of children born to poor mothers through forced sterilization (which continued into the 1970s), and complicity with vigilante and police torture and murder of Black people. Elijah Muhammad's Islamic myth recognized the suffering of Black people as something deeply part of the human experience.[11]

Over time, Yakub's evil science won the day. He made a new people: the brutish and violent white man. He was a blue-eyed devil who first lived, like the Neanderthals, in the caves of Europe for thousands of years. But around 2000 BCE, at the beginning of recorded history, the white man came out of the caves and viciously attacked Black people. The white man destroyed human civilization. In making these claims, the Nation of Islam's myth adopted the terms by which Black people had been rendered inhuman—the idea that Blacks were uncivilized—and offered a mirror in which Blacks and whites were challenged to see themselves in a reverse ontology, an alternate reality. In truth, went the myth, it was actually the murderous, genocidal societies of white people that were savage and ignorant. Elijah Muhammad thus offered secret knowledge, a truth that had been covered up. The white man overtook the Black man in this real version of what happened and then wrote the history that submerged the truth that Black people were the original owners of the Earth.[12]

Elijah Muhammad's myth of the origins and the fall of man had no appreciable resemblance to traditional Islamic teachings, whether Sunni or Shi'a. In addition, his radical reinterpretation of God as having appeared in the person of Fard and his claiming the mantle of prophecy for himself were deeply troubling to many other Muslims. Among his loudest opponents in the 1950s were African Americans who subscribed to a modern Sunni interpretation of Islam, an interpretation that was especially committed to ideas about God's transcendence and Prophet Muhammad's status as "just a man." Prompted by the FBI, the mainstream press also rejected the Islamic legitimacy of the movement, and then, in 1961, the first edition of C. Eric Lincoln's *Black Muslims in America*—the most important book ever written about the Nation of Islam—said that the movement was neither authentically Islamic nor religious (by the second edition, that interpretation changed).[13] In response, in the 1950s, but especially in the 1960s, a whole cadre of movement intellectuals, men and women, developed a literature of apologetics—that is, a literature that defended the legitimacy of their leader in Islamic terms.

First, movement intellectuals sought the endorsement and support of foreign and immigrant Muslims. Imams and others from Pakistan, the United Kingdom, and the United States were cited as evidence if not of the Islamic legitimacy of Elijah Muhammad's teachings then of the overall importance of a nascent movement of Muslims in the West. Pakistani Abdul Basit Naeem became a regular columnist for *Muhammad Speaks*, and Imam Muhammad Abdul Rauf of Washington, D.C., a very prominent Muslim leader, joined a Nation of Islam protest against police violence in 1972. Second, Elijah Muhammad and leaders Louis Farrakhan, Tynetta Deanar, Eugene Majied, and Malcolm X mined verses from the Qur'an to prove Elijah Muhammad's Islamic legitimacy. Movement intellectuals created original interpretations of Islamic theology and scriptural exegesis that explained how the Qur'an itself pointed to Elijah Muhammad's prophecy and proved the accuracy of his teachings. If other Muslims rejected his authority, that was their problem.[14]

Elijah Muhammad's original Islamic myths were the dominant narratives through which members in the Nation of Islam viewed Black history, but these myths were not the only stories that members told one another about their shared past as Muslims. New religious movements, often pejoratively called "cults," are sometimes blamed for brainwashing followers, for taking away their ability to think for themselves or to think outside of the narrow boundaries of the "cult leader." By that definition, the Nation of Islam was not a cult, because the same movement intellectuals who defended the Islamic legitimacy of Elijah Muhammad pursued their own study of Islamic history. Elijah Muhammad was not a student of traditional Islamic history and did not express great interest in the topic. (What need would he have for it, since he received his knowledge directly from Allah?) But many of his followers studied and published articles about the history of classical and medieval Islam. Under Elijah Muhammad's religio-racial definition of Blackness, all of these figures were considered Black even if they had no African lineage. Such stories were integrated into the other mythologies that Elijah Muhammad had revealed. By reading *Muhammad Speaks*, one could learn about Umar ibn al-Khattab, the second caliph of Islam; Bilal ibn Rabah, the Ethiopian freedman and beloved companion of Prophet Muhammad; Khawlah Bint al-Azwar, a female Muslim warrior; and Sunni Ali, founder of the Songhay Empire in the fifteenth century.[15]

Elijah Muhammad taught that, despite the greatness of Islam and the historical achievements of Islam, Muslim power declined. White people enslaved Black people, who forgot their original religion, Islam, and their language, Arabic. Incorporating Black vernacular and folk wisdom into his myth, Elijah Muhammad proclaimed that Black people were transported to America in a slave ship called the *John Hawkins*. Slave masters used "tricknology" to make Black people hate themselves—that is, they used false knowledge to convince Black people that they were unintelligent, violent, and ugly. The religion of Christianity, which taught slaves to be obedient to their masters, was the foundation of this internalized oppression. Black people imitated their masters. They lived dirty, drinking, fornicating, eating pork.[16]

But, according to the Nation of Islam's mythology, God did not abandon God's people. In 1930, Fard, whose roots can be traced to Pashtun areas of Afghanistan and Pakistan, appeared in Detroit to resurrect the so-called Negro from his mental slavery.[17] His followers understood him to be their Savior and also the Islamic Mahdi, the figure in Islamic tradition that will appear at the end of the world to usher in justice and righteousness. Elijah Muhammad became the Messenger who underwent great trials and tribulations, eventually emerging to lead the lost-found in the wilderness of North America. Elijah Muhammad believed that he was not a true citizen of the United States; U.S. citizenship did not really apply to African Americans. He was, instead, a citizen of the *Nation* of Islam. Thus, he did not serve in World War II, and he spent three years in a Michigan federal prison for refusing to do so.[18]

During the 1940s, Clara Muhammad helped to convey messages from Elijah Muhammad, and when he got out of prison in 1946, the movement took off. In dozens of communities around the country, urban African Americans began to proclaim not only their belief in Fard as Allah but also in Elijah Muhammad, His Messenger. Fard had chosen Muhammad for this purpose. The Messenger, as he was often addressed, did not adopt the preaching style frequently associated with African American culture: the chanted sermon featuring dramatic variation in the volume and pitch of the voice. In fact, he taught that such emotionalism, which led people to believe that they would be rewarded after death rather than in this life, contributed to Black internalized oppression. Elijah Muhammad was more of a college lecturer, imparting actual facts and wisdom to his followers. And there was one follower above all who helped to build Elijah Muhammad's movement. Without Malcolm X, who became the leader's national spokesman and one of his chief organizers, it is doubtful that the movement would have grown into the largest Muslim American organization.

As central as Malcolm X was to the movement's growth, however, it is important to remember that it was Elijah Muhammad who provided the sacred narratives that held power for the group's "card-carrying members." In addition to teaching a countercultural myth of Black origins and the fall of (Black) man, Elijah Muhammad's teachings about the end of the world had clear postwar cultural influences. The official stance of the movement was that Allah had revealed all of this truth to the Messenger, but there were narrative elements that are better dated to the late 1940s and 1950s, long after Fard had gone. For example, UFOs became central to Elijah Muhammad's prophecies. Though the idea of alien invasion had already been popularized through H. G. Wells's *War of the Worlds*, the assumption that UFOs would take the form of flying saucers became popular only after World War II.[19]

The Mother Plane, later the Mothership, was the deus ex machina, the God out of a machine, of the movement. It was a powerful tool of justice-making. Like Ezekiel's wheel, the Mother Plane would rain fire upon the Earth at the end of the world; it would destroy white civilization and make it possible for Black people to reign once more. During the 1950s and 1960s, mainstream press accounts and scholarship claimed that this belief was literal—that all white people would be killed in this apocalypse. In the early 1970s, Elijah Muhammad told the Associated Press that white people would not actually be killed. Rather, the Mothership would kill the whiteness in them. It would be like strong medicine that makes you sick at first, but then cures you of a horrible disease. In this case, it would alter the very structure of the white man, who was a genetic anomaly. This strange science had an appeal that went far beyond the Nation of Islam. For example, George Clinton, the king of funk music, built a showy Mothership that was central to his stage performances; today, it sits in the National Museum of African American History and Culture in Washington, D.C. Beyond this, allusions to the Mothership are still made in hip hop and other African American cultural forms.[20]

The idea that the Mothership would make things right again in the world meant that members of the Nation of Islam were expressly forbidden from participating in wars on behalf of the United States or in any offensive violence. Despite the rhetorical and symbolic power of the Nation of Islam, which sought an independent state for Black Americans, harshly criticized Christianity, and proudly opposed U.S. military interventions in brown and Black countries, it was a nonviolent movement. The fact that the FBI's Counter-Intelligence Program (COINTELPRO), operated during the Johnson and Nixon administrations, and the mainstream press associated the Nation of Islam with political revolution, had everything to do with the moral power of its mythologies, rhetoric, and pride. The Nation of Islam imaginatively and peacefully assaulted the ideological pillars of U.S. society and politics. The group was effective enough to attract repression from the government, not only through COINTELPRO but also in the Bureau of Prisons, the Justice Department, and other offices of state.[21]

BODILY AESTHETICS AND RITUALS OF LIBERATION AND RECLAMATION

It was precisely the idea that Black people should wait on the Mothership that began to frustrate Malcolm X in the late 1950s and early 1960s. He found it too passive, and when he left to become a Sunni Muslim, the change freed him to articulate a more forceful endorsement of revolution in the struggle against colonialism and racism. Though El Hajj Malik El Shabazz's example is essential to the history of Islam and to the United States, it must be stated that Malcolm X's departure did not hurt the Nation of Islam's ability to expand its reach in the United States. If Muhammad Ali had also left, history might have unfolded differently—but perhaps not. In any case, Muhammad Ali remained loyal to Elijah Muhammad, and his willingness to give up his world heavyweight boxing crown and go to jail rather than join the U.S. military in 1967 brought Elijah Muhammad and the Nation of Islam to the attention of even greater numbers of people around the globe.

Many of those who followed Elijah Muhammad as their Messenger of Allah did not think of themselves as passive. Waiting on the Mothership, just like waiting on the return of Jesus, does not necessarily make people complacent. The Mothership meant the end of the white world, not the end of the world. According to Elijah Muhammad, the teaching that heaven was a place one goes after one dies was untrue, a form of tricknology invented by the white man to keep the Black man pining for heaven in the hereafter. Like many other metaphysical groups popular at the time the Nation of Islam was formed, including New Thought, Elijah Muhammad proclaimed that heaven and hell were states of mind on Earth. Living according to Muslim principles would free a person from the chains of the old, white world, and they could enjoy being who they were made to be: free, strong, pure, and naturally beautiful. Instead of organizing armed resistance to white supremacy, members of the Nation of Islam participated in a complex set of ritualized activities that often restructured their day-to-day lives to achieve this heaven on Earth. Like other religions, the Islam of the Elijah Muhammad sought not only to encourage attendance at congregational meetings but also to transform one's mind and body through the performance of daily activities. These embodied rituals were full of meaning; they actualized the lessons learned in Elijah

Muhammad's speeches and writings as well as lessons learned in one's local temple/mosque (the movement used both terms for their congregations).[22]

For example, diet was a central focus of life in the Nation of Islam community. If part of the fall of Black man was the polluting of Black bodies, then reforming one's diet was a key component of following one's true religion, Islam. Christian slave masters, Elijah Muhammad said, had poisoned Black people with the swine, which was a genetic mélange of cat, rat, and dog. In fact, the enslaved were not even permitted to enjoy the best parts of the pig, but had to settle for the intestines and other less desirable parts. According to Elijah Muhammad, this explained Black people's love of chitterlings, which were banned in the Nation of Islam. Because slave masters had also addicted enslaved people to liquor, the movement enforced the traditional Islamic ban on alcohol. Many elements of African American culture associated with slavery were similarly prohibited, including eating certain kinds of beans and greens, but navy beans, which were said to be high in nutritional value, were allowed and ended up becoming the basis for one of the most important Black Muslim culinary contributions to the world: the bean pie. Overall, the point of this attack on slave culture was to separate contemporary Black people from any false nostalgia for slavery. By demanding a total break with the slave past, the Nation of Islam was trying to remake Black men and women in the image of the original human, the owner and maker of the Earth.[23]

In the late 1960s and early 1970s, Elijah Muhammad published a two-volume work entitled *How to Eat to Live*, which were edited versions of his various columns and lectures on diet. Many of these teachings incorporated contemporary dietary and medical advice; some of them were ahead of their time. Elijah Muhammad was also aware that obesity was leading to poor health among many African Americans. His solution to this problem was to reduce caloric intake, so he directed his followers to eat only one meal a day. This was obviously difficult, and many were unable to put it into practice, but the movement newspaper, *Muhammad Speaks*, was full of detailed testimonials about how the one-meal-a-day plan had cured followers of high blood pressure and other ailments. In addition, Elijah Muhammad directed followers to consume only whole grains and to eliminate processed sugar in their diets in order to avoid diabetes. Fasting during Ramadan was embraced by the Nation of Islam, but Elijah Muhamad ordered that it be observed during Advent so that African Americans in the United States had something to replace Christmas. All of these revelations pointed toward an interpretation of Islam that was synonymous with and supportive of Black freedom in the United States. As a means of recovering from anti-Black racism, Elijah Muhammad was depicted as a healer who could free the Black mind and body from the burdens of physical and psychological internalized racism.[24]

It is hard to underestimate the role of food in the ways that Islam was actually lived inside of the Nation of Islam in the postwar period. It became more and more central to the ways that members spent their time, and more important to their economic lives as well. As the Nation of Islam grew in membership in the 1960s, temples and sometimes individuals would open restaurants, grocery stores, and bakeries at precisely the same moment that many white-owned businesses were beginning their flight to the suburbs. Some women supplemented family incomes by selling bean pies. These food businesses paid attention to the dietary regulations issued by Elijah Muhammad. Whole grain bread was served instead of white bread, for example, and sometimes desserts were made with less sugar—but not always. For example, a believer in Baltimore would say later that the cakes and bean pies had plenty of sugar in them and even used artificial flavoring at times. Nation of Islam members did not have to believe in or follow every single prophetic commandment in order to be religious members of the movement; there is no religious community where everyone does everything they are supposed to do. The point is that the overall tenor of the movement directed believers toward food preparation, distribution, and consumption as a central rather than marginal activity.[25]

By the 1970s, food had become a vertically integrated component of movement life. Elijah Muhammad purchased farms to source produce and meat for the restaurants and the groceries, then launched a multimillion-dollar fish import business. Emphasizing that white fish was better for one's health than meat (or catfish, which was banned), the Nation of Islam developed a national distribution system for fish sales. This business became well known in Black America and was memorialized in Kool and the Gang's song "Whiting H & G" (1974). Elijah Muhammad, who was in relatively poor health by the 1970s, did not pay attention to every detail of movement business, but he was supportive of the expansion of his business empire, most of which he personally owned (and for which be borrowed millions of dollars).[26]

Food, like other important elements in the Islam of these Black Muslims, had clear religious, economic, social, and cultural meanings, all pointing toward Black freedom, as the movement defined it. Both men and women made and prepared food, but it is clear that the making of food by women supplemented family incomes and thus gave them more power and independence in their marriages. Food had obvious economic implications, as it created ownership and income that circulated largely in a Black urban economy, offering some degree of control in a labor market where Black people were last hired and first fired. In a way, religion clothed these social and economic activities with special meaning, since all this was being done in response to the directions of the Messenger of Allah. But, besides offering the chance for these members to submit their will to God, it is clear that one's redemption from the slave mind—one's resurrection—depended on changing most parts of one's life.

In addition to participating in the food culture of the Nation of Islam, believers paid great attention to their ethical behavior and ritual discipline in the realms of dress, coiffure, and adornment.[27] Ethics, generally speaking, are the rules that guide more and less appropriate human behavior. In the Nation of Islam, how one dressed was an issue of the greatest moral concern. The religious aesthetics of dress were, like food, a way to "Islamize" one's self, to exhibit the respectable and civilized nature that, according to the movement, was at the heart of Black being. Men in the Fruit of Islam, the male auxiliary, became familiar in urban America for their suits and bow ties. Women wore modest clothes, sometimes long-flowing white gowns, and tended to avoid makeup, which was said to obscure their natural beauty. *Muhammad Speaks* columnist Tynetta Deanar wrote in 1962 that there was "nothing wrong with the white woman's dress because it is her dress and she has the right to wear it as short as she desires." But Black women should also be themselves, Deanar argued, and they were naturally beautiful and modest. Bleaching the skin was seen as especially horrific; it was a "grotesque caricature of our open enemy," according to Ermine X Lowe. Conking, frying, greasing, or processing the hair was also taboo. As the Black Consciousness movement took hold in the early 1970s, some members of the Nation of Islam donned dashikis and sported large Afros, choosing the style of Black "soul" over the more buttoned-up, bourgeois fashions favored by Elijah

Muhammad. Women leaders in the Nation of Islam tried to bring the sisters with short skirts back into the fold, praising longer hemlines. But official dress in the movement did change in response to the times. The slimmer-cut polyester Fruit of Islam uniforms, and the official and sometimes hand-sewn dresses of female members looked slick, not frumpy. In Washington, DC, during the early 1970s, immaculately dressed Fruit of Islam members "looked sharp in their dark blue suits with a thick white stripe running down the pant legs, a high collar on the jacket, and the matching cap that bore a backward star and crescent." And the women were "equally dazzling in their special uniforms: a long white skirt, a knee-length cape, white gloves, and a white box-hat with flaps tied under the chin."[28] This Islamic dress was different than what had been worn in the early 1960s, but it still embodied practices of Black freedom, beauty, and self-love.

While Islamic ethics and rituals concerning diet and dress were focused on individuals' bodies, members of the Nation of Islam were also devoted to the life of their local Nation of Islam congregations. The centrality of the temple or mosque in the lives of Black Muslims is unsurprising, perhaps even commonsense, for most Americans, who often associate religion in general with membership in and attendance at a particular congregation. When viewed from a global perspective, however, it is important to keep in mind that Muslims elsewhere are not generally members of a particular mosque; they go to the mosque, shrine, or *jamatkhana* to pray, but they do not generally "join" an incorporated organization. America is different. In the United States, the religious congregation is, historically, the best funded and most popular form of voluntary association in the society. Congregations are not only places of worship but also business networks, educational institutions, mutual aid societies, social networks, and performance venues, among other things. Thus, all things being equal, one would expect to see Nation of Islam congregations, like American congregations more generally, play a large role in the lives of members.

The local Nation of Islam mosque often became the center of Black Muslim life. It was the location of meetings in which rituals were deployed to produce a feeling for those in attendance that they were entering both sacred space and sacred time, something set apart from everyday life. First, one had to show up on time. If one was late too many times, there could be consequences, including suspension from movement activities. Punctuality was an Islamic value, according to Elijah Muhammad, a sign of civilized, respectable behavior. Second, before entering the temple, one had to go through a bodily search meant to purify the person and the space in which they were entering. The search was not only for weapons but also for cigarettes and other items understood to be taboo. You were then shown to your seat—unlike most other mosques, these meeting halls had seats—often by a uniformed member of the Fruit of Islam. Saluting one another in a variety of ways, the Fruit "moved with swift precision, walking straight lines swiftly, turning corners sharply with a clock of their heels."[29] Once everyone was seated, and members of the Fruit of Islam had staked out positions around the room, it was time to begin the ceremony, which was taken up mainly by the minister's lesson. Unlike a lot of African American Protestant worship, Nation of Islam meetings emphasized what was framed as the logic, rationality, history, and truth of Elijah Muhammad's teachings. His revelations were the gnostic key to mental resurrection. This was knowledge that could truly save a person, and so it was put at the ritual center of the congregational meeting.[30]

In many ways, the congregational meeting was geared toward recruitment, as it was the first thing a man or woman with interest in the Nation of Islam would do after being "fished" by a Nation of Islam member in their neighborhood or on the street. Once someone converted to Islam, the mosque offered activities most days of the week, if not every day. As E. U. Essien-Udom has documented, classes were often held on Monday evenings, and, depending on the city, a Muslim could study Arabic, math, Elijah Muhammad's revelations, or other topics. Members of the mosque might socialize together on Tuesday nights and attend the regular meetings on Wednesdays, Fridays, and Sundays. Women would meet on Thursday nights, and some of the men would provide protection and assistance. In some cases, people slept at the temple. In St. Louis, Abdul Shabazz remembers, "fifteen to twenty brothers would stay above the mosque. It was like a dormitory."[31]

The Nation of Islam built an entire culture in which Black people could reclaim their true Muslim selves through the performance of rituals, the care of their bodies, and the nurturing of their minds. Even if the general tone of movement life was sober, and emotion was to be carefully controlled, there were still religious moments of intense feeling, the kind of spiritual connection that makes one experience ecstasy, or at least a little bit of it. Some of those moments came in more private settings, when a neophyte of the movement suddenly realized through lots of study the truth that Black people could be free if they came to Islam. Films of various private meetings and celebrations that exist from the 1960s and 1970s also show laughter and smiles when children at Nation of Islam schools would perform plays, or when female members of the movement would step together, chanting, "Two, four, six, eight, who do we appreciate? / Elijah / Once more / Muhammad / Break it down / Elijah [step, step] Muhammad [step] M—U—H—A—M—M—A—D." Even Malcolm X, not a man prone to showing a great deal of emotion, reported in his autobiography that tears would well up in his eyes during the moment when Elijah Muhammad first entered an arena to address thousands of cheering followers during Nation of Islam conventions. Accompanied by a phalanx of Fruit of Islam members, "the gentle, meek, brown-skinned Lamb . . . carried his Holy Bible, his Holy Qur'an" as people shouted out "All Praise be to Allah," according to Malcolm X. "I think that my life's peaks of emotion, until recently at least, were when, suddenly, the Fruit of Islam guards would stop stiffly at attention, and the platform's several steps would be mounted alone by Mr. Muhammad."[32]

I have been met with a variety of responses when sharing my scholarship on Elijah Muhammad's Nation of Islam with predominantly U.S. Muslim audiences over the past two decades. There has been genuine sympathy, bordering at times on paternalism, expressed for those people who once believed what Elijah Muhammad taught. Then, those already knowledgeable about Muslim American history are quick to point out that Mohammed, Elijah Muhammad's son, corrected his father's mistakes and led his people toward what they consider to be "true Islam." Some Muslims, aware that Elijah Muhammad's doctrines and mythologies still live, in altered form, in Louis Farrakhan's version of the Nation of Islam are upset that I am not more critical of these teachings as illegitimate. Still others, both old and young, Black and brown, take a more positive view of Elijah Muhammad's movement; they can appreciate what people created in the Nation of Islam. For example, Shakeela Hassan, who provided Elijah Muhammad with his unique fez, has written an affectionate, ebullient memoir of her experience with the Nation of Islam.[33] In addition, the community of Muslims who associate with Fard's teaching are diverse, but among them I have discovered a real love and respect for Elijah and Clara Muhammad. These believers have told me how good the movement was for them personally, that they don't regret their involvement, and that it must have been God's plan that they came to Islam through the Nation of Islam.

I have known about the Nation of Islam since I read Malcolm X's autobiography as a teenager, and I have been professionally studying the movement since the 1990s. The mythologies of Elijah Muhammad no longer seem any stranger to me than other religious myths. Over time, I have understood the feelings of love that many of Elijah Muhammad's followers have for him; I have also come to understand the foundation of my own deep interest in the Nation of Islam and its long-time leader. This movement responded without apology and with such courage to the ways that racism not only limits one's life opportunities but also one's imagination, self-love, and dignity. Leon Forrest called it a "miracle drug," implying, at least to me, that there was something too easy about the Nation of Islam's solution. To be sure, the movement had its problems; it was as coercive and conservative as many other religious movements and communities. But it was more than a cheap drug. It was liberating.

For me, the key to understanding the lives of those who valued their membership in the Nation of Islam, as they also surely questioned it or resisted various elements of it, is its interpretation of an Islam that loved Black people and that was synonymous with their freedom—not just political freedom, but economic, social, and psychological freedom, too. Other Muslims may debate the validity of these teachings, as is their right, but, looking away from doctrinal disputes toward Islam as a religion of liberation, justice, and love, there could hardly be anything more Islamic than the Nation.

NOTES

1. Edward E. Curtis IV, "'My Heart Is in Cairo': Malcolm, X, the Arab Cold War, and the Making of Islamic Liberation Ethics," *Journal of American History* 102, no. 3 (December 2015): 775–98; Manning Marable, *Malcolm X: A Life of Reinvention* (New York: Viking, 2011).
2. Richard Brent Turner, *Islam in the African-American Experience*, 2nd ed. (Bloomington: Indiana University Press, 2003).
3. Claude Andrew Clegg III, *The Life and Times of Elijah Muhammad* (Chapel Hill: University of North Carolina Press, 2014).
4. Classic treatments of the Nation of Islam include E. U. Essien-Udom, *Black Nationalism: A Search for an Identity in America* (Chicago: University of Chicago Press, 1962); and C. Eric Lincoln, *The Black Muslims in America*, 3rd. ed. (Grand Rapids, Mich.: Eerdmans, 1994).
5. Islam in America specialists have often defied marginalizing the groups as such. See, for example, Kambiz GhaneaBassiri, *History of Islam in America* (New York: Cambridge, 2010); Zareena Grewal, *Islam Is a Foreign Country: American Muslims and the Global Crisis of Authority* (New York: New York University Press, 2014); Aminah Beverly McCloud, *African American Islam* (New York: Routledge, 1995); and Juliane Hammer and Omid Safi, eds., *Cambridge Companion to American Islam* (New York: Cambridge University Press, 2013).
6. Devin DeWeese, *Islamization and Native Religion in the Golden Horde* (University Park: Penn State University Press, 1994), 55.
7. Richard M. Eaton, *Essays on Islam and Indian History* (New York: Oxford University Press, 2000), 35.
8. Edward E. Curtis IV, "African-American Islamization Reconsidered: Black History Narratives and Muslim Identity," *Journal of the American Academy of Religion* 73, no. 3 (September 2005): 659–84.
9. Elijah Muhammad, *Message to the Blackman in America* (Chicago: Temple No. 2, 1965).
10. Mattias Gardell, *In the Name of Elijah Muhammad: Minister Louis Farrakhan and the Final Call* (Durham, N.C.: Duke University Press, 1996).
11. Muhammad, *Message to the Blackman*; see also Edward E. Curtis IV, "Science and Technology in Elijah Muhammad's Nation of Islam:

Astrophysical Disaster, Genetic Engineering, UFOs, White Apocalypse, and Black Resurrection," *Nova Religio* 20, no. 1 (August 2016): 5–31.
12. Muhammad, *Message to the Blackman*.
13. Harold Dean Trulear, "Sociology of Afro-American Religion: An Appraisal of C. Eric Lincoln's Contributions," *Journal of Religious Thought* 42, no 2 (1985–1986): 44–55.
14. Curtis, *Black Muslim Religion*, 36–65.
15. Curtis, 77–86.
16. Muhammad, *Message to the Blackman*.
17. For more on the person whose identity has been such a subject of scholarly and popular curiosity, see Fatimah Abdul-Tawwab Fanusie, "Fard Muhammad in Historical Context: An Islamic Thread in the American Religious and Cultural Quilt" (PhD diss., Howard University, 2008); and Patrick D. Bowen, *A History of Conversion in the United States*, vol. 2: *The African American Islamic Renaissance, 1920–1975* (Leiden: Brill, 2017), 240–76.
18. Clegg, *Elijah Muhammad*.
19. Edward E. Curtis IV, *Islam in Black America* (Albany: State University of New York Press, 77–78.
20. Curtis, "Science and Technology."
21. Frank J. Donner, *The Age of Surveillance: The Aims and Methods of America's Political Intelligence System* (New York: Knopf, 1980).
22. Curtis, *Black Muslim Religion*.
23. Curtis, 98–109.
24. Curtis.
25. Curtis.
26. Curtis.
27. Curtis, 109–18.
28. Tate, *Little X*, 49–50.
29. Tate, 49–50.
30. Curtis, *Black Muslim Religion*, 160–62.
31. Curtis, 167–68, Essien-Udom, *Black Nationalism*, 225–26.
32. Alex Haley and Malcolm X, *The Autobiography of Malcolm X* (New York: Ballantine, 1965), 252; Curtis, 148; *This Far by Faith: African-American Spiritual Journeys* (Boston: WGBH, 2003).
33. Shakeela Z. Hassan, *Starry Crown: Making of a Fez* (privately published, 2020).

6

LOVE AND CARE AT THE MARGINS OF FUTURE GENERATIONS

HOLLY DONAHUE SINGH

Who cares about how many babies Indian Muslim women have? It was a question I heard frequently at the beginning of my graduate studies, and one that I learned to address from many different perspectives. The question itself grew out of my interest in everyday life in South Asia, rooted in attention to the margins and in fascination with the ways religious tenets, stories, and traditions, as well as the artistic expression that grows out of religious practice in particular places, shape the embodied, situated experiences of people through the ups and downs of daily life. I was interested in the ways people attempt to enact future communities, starting with making families and making kinship.

These ideas have carried me into social spaces, into classrooms, into clinics, into activist networks, and into literature and movies saturated with cultural content. They have led me to spend years in a north Indian city with strong local Muslim heritage, but changing politics, a place where appreciation of Islam and Muslims can lead to conflict. In this chapter I aim to not only notice the margins through focusing on Muslim women's reproductive experiences but also to understand better what building future generations looks like from the standpoint of people whose reproduction draws stigma, and whose infertility remains unfathomable—and the idea of it perhaps desirable—to many of their fellow citizens. First, I historically situate how the issue of Muslim reproduction in India has become such an important issue to people in South Asia and beyond. Then, I engage in the act of scholarly reflexivity, explaining how I came to be interested in this work, what my training was like, and how that background influences the way I engage in ethnographic study. Finally, I explain how focusing on the margins of reproduction has helped me draw attention to the roots of contemporary conflicts about population, care, and the potential for justice in our shared global futures.

SITUATING ISLAM IN PRACTICE ACROSS GLOBAL CONTEXTS

Laughter. The first encounter with my descriptions of an interest in infertility in India, and especially the infertility experiences of Muslims, has often produced immediate, knee-jerk responses of laughter, then disbelief. How could infertility be a subject worthy of study in a country with over one billion people? Or among a minority population reputed, among non-Muslims and in popular discourse, to have prodigiously large families? "Go to the old city, it's overflowing with children." Looked at through a frame of abundance of children, often cast as an *over*abundance of children unwelcome in a crowded country aiming to modernize the economy and, for some, to create a new, more Hindu, India. The idea that Indians, especially Muslims, but also poor people, rural people, low-caste people, were *too* fertile overshadowed infertility as a problem. Jokes about Gandhi and *khadi* condoms, made from the loose-weave cotton of local homespun cloth, ensue. Take the conversation a bit further, and the laughter might die away, making room for more personal engagement, perhaps recollection of stories of people who didn't have children. What happened to them? This kind of recognition could open up a deeper understanding of the significance of the topic; it might create the potential to access a connection to the humanity of people beyond their religious, caste, or class identity, but history, resentment, or privilege could stand in the way.

In Lucknow, the old city is home to the greatest concentration of historical monuments—the most distinctive traces of its era of rule by the Nawabs, Shiʻa Muslims whose legacies remain in Lucknow's built environment and cultural ethos, even though the Nawabs were deposed by the British colonial enterprise in the mid-nineteenth century and the area badly damaged by fighting in the uprising of 1857 that has variously been labeled a mutiny, rebellion, or war of independence. People from many different backgrounds have made their homes in the densely populated small lanes of the old city, but contemporary residents of Lucknow often imagine those lanes as places where Muslims live—a partially accurate, yet incomplete, vision. People who practice Islam have been part of the social fabric of South Asia for over a thousand years. They have identified as Muslim in various ways, as part of a constellation of identity that also incorporates region, language, gender, sexuality, foodways, and culture to make up rich and colorful tapestries of the diversity of human lived experience that massively exceeds the bounds of a flattening category of "Muslim." In Lucknow, Urdu, Hindi, common blendings of vocabulary and register sometimes known as Hindustani, and, to varying extents, English, are primary languages of daily life for people of all backgrounds. Once held up as the language of elites, Urdu is more recently known as a sweet language (*meethi zaban*) popularly identified with Muslims and with movies, although it is only one among many languages spoken by Muslims in South Asia. In practice, Urdu has been used by people from across the entire social landscape to different degrees and for a variety of purposes, and people from all over India, as well as contemporary Pakistan, still imagine Lucknow as a place where people know and use true, clear Urdu. The politics of Urdu over time are instructive about the politics of religion, identity, and belonging of each era.[1]

Rulers from the medieval Mughals to the eighteenth- and nineteenth-century Nawabs of Awadh, through the early twentieth-century Nizams of Hyderabad, left traces of their own embrace and use of a wide range of religious and cultural practices through their policy decisions, support of artistic production, and contributions to the built environment. Those contributions echo in the present across many domains of social life and matter not only as matters of history but also, for some, as markers of proximity to faded power and pride, and, for others, indicators of connections to past oppression. Relatively few contemporary Muslims have strong claims to those elite connections, and even fewer retain (or ever had) tangible privilege based on those ties.

The idea of Muslim glory and flourishing can serve as a positive touchpoint for Muslims and as examples of their accomplishments, while the idea of Muslim dominance and threat invigorates discriminatory discourse and action against them, which can extend even to people marginalized by class and caste-like status, gender, and sexuality. Historical events, from the Partition of India upon independence from Britain in 1947—which led to the creation of Pakistan and later, Bangladesh, and disputes over the regions of Kashmir and northeastern India—to the Islamophobia fueled by the 9/11 attacks on the United States have added to the social marginalization and precarity of Muslims in India. In between and continuing to the present, Muslims have also migrated temporarily or permanently around the world, with labor migrations to Gulf states particularly reverberating back to influence religious and social life in South Asia.[2]

In the face of the growing challenges of this century, the urgent and persistent need for structures of care that transcend divisions of race, class, caste, gender, religion, ability, sexuality and other human hierarchies are becoming progressively more apparent. As pandemic illness and climate crisis threaten individual lives and collective survival for humans and for many other species and planetary systems, the responses of institutions and individuals seem poised to either aid in fostering human flourishing or ensuring human suffering on massive scales. Global challenges demand global cooperation, yet nationalism, the global and local distribution of wealth, and other human divisions repeatedly foil true collaboration. These crises demonstrate the limits of humans' care for one other and show the consequences of withholding or withdrawing care from others for the future potential of human communities. Though these consequences may be made newly visible by events such as the spread of the virus that causes COVID-19 and its variants, they are certainly not novel in the world, nor in world religions. High value on acts of nurture and care toward others lie at the heart of many traditions, though they may be interpreted differently—for example, as part of an individual journey toward salvation or self-realization, or toward becoming more fully part of a community or fostering a just society.

So, who cares about how many babies Indian Muslim women have? When someone in the United States first asked me this question, it gave me pause. Since I had already spent over a year in India and listened to lots of people talk about population as one of the biggest problems facing India in the future, and I had started to explore scholarly literature and other sources on this issue, I knew that, actually, many people cared. They cared in different ways and for different reasons, but, yes, there was a great deal of interest in the fertility of Indian Muslims. At the international level, programs on population aimed at reducing the number of children people gave birth to around the world had been operating for decades and had accelerated since the late 1960s, when environmental and economic concerns drove population control to the top of many international health agendas, eclipsing other needs.[3] The Government of India had also been promoting "family planning" through national programs since the 1950s, aiming to slow population growth. Although these efforts have produced uneven results across regional, class, and religious groups, they have led to dramatic drops in the average number of children born to women in India.[4] Demographers and other population scientists still track births over the course of individual lives at the population level to understand the dynamics of reproduction.[5] In the late twentieth and early twenty-first century, these gaps in fertility rates have found their way into national political discourse that targets people made vulnerable by their class, caste, or religious status and configures their higher fertility as a social problem and evidence of their deficiency as proper citizens. These dynamics have not only inspired social science research but also a feature-length film by one of India's most prominent artists, Shyam Benegal, called *Hari Bhari (Fertility)*, starring two luminaries of Indian cinema, Shabana Azmi and Nandita Das, and funded through the national health agency.[6] Grounded in social science research conducted in and about north India, the film weaves together fictional stories of several generations of women living in a single rural north Indian Muslim landholding family. It shows the real stakes of marriage, fertility, infertility, and labor migration in women's lives. At the same time, it dramatizes and demonstrates how changing expectations wrought by rapid social change and intergenerational interactions shape individual action.

International and national programs certainly matter for the services they make available to local residents. These programs shape how the public perceives social issues such as reproduction whether or not they affect people's reproductive behaviors. They can influence people on the levels that are most salient to their daily lives: their local communities, their families, and their selves. Individuals have their own desires about the number of children they wish to have, as well as the sex of those children, their skin, hair, or eye color, their physical and mental ability, and other characteristics. Societal discourses tend to influence these desires, even when people disavow them with platitudes such as "As long as they're healthy," or "Whatever God wills." And in India, as in many other places around the world, those desires get bound up with the desires of partners, and here, with the desires of many members of extended families, especially if they live together in joint, multigenerational households. People of reproductive age may hear advice—usually unsolicited—from family members belonging to two or three generations about what shape their own reproduction ought to take, expressed, for example, by desires to assume a new kinship title: grandmother, uncle, auntie, or sibling. Family members may express their desires through the idiom of having someone to light up the home, to carry on the family line, to bring fame to the family name, to help in the household, or to assist with agricultural chores. They may articulate worries about the division of property through inheritance, the depletion of resources through dowry, or the need to feed more mouths. In big, interdependent families, lots of people care about how many and what sort of babies come into the family. As one woman in my field research in Lucknow between 2005 and 2007 put it, whether people perceived the number of children to be too many or too few, they would always have something to say, and they would most likely direct their criticisms at women, refusing to just "let them live" (*jine den*). There are commonalities across many different identity categories, as well as nuances associated with being part of groups whose reproduction attracts stigma at larger collective levels.

ETHNOGRAPHY AND DOCUMENTING MUSLIM LIVES

As a scholar, I have always been drawn to understanding human creativity in many different forms, but especially the art of getting by from day to day, as well as through expressive life in stories, music, and even legislation and public health campaigns, as evidence of self-cultivation and community-making. By inquiring into how people make meaning through crafting their own selves, families, and larger collectivities in their daily lives, as well as in the ways they document what life is and what they imagine life could be, ethnographers add to the richness of understanding human experience. Contextualizing contemporary human life within the historical and religious frames that ground individual experiences and influence their ideals, dreams, and actions helps show what it means for people situated differently by as gender, economic and social hierarchy, and sexuality to live, in this case, as Muslims—whether identified by belief, practice, or social category—in a particular place, time, culture, and society. Not only does such an approach humanize religion but it also puts human culture and society in motion; it creates opportunities to delve deeply into the diversity, complexity, and dynamism of how human lives intersect with religion in time in ways that may not be accessible through historical perspectives and that may generate new questions about historical perspectives, while attending to power relations within specific circumstances.

In anthropology, ethnography is both an orientation toward certain research methods and one kind of product of inquiry. Grounded in participant observation, or "deep hanging out," usually through immersion over an extended period of time with plenty of opportunities for listening, ethnographic methods can intersect with other methods of scholarship, such as archival research, interviews, survey research, or literary analysis. At their heart, ethnographic research methods constitute an expansive approach to learning through as many senses as possible, with openness to following where evidence and experience lead, while documenting experiences and encounters along the way. Although anthropologists have led the way in creating and using ethnographic methods, they are not now the exclusive tool kit of anthropologists, and I first learned about them through the study of religion, especially with reference to Islamic and South Asian histories, religious traditions, and literature, in the work of scholars such as Vernon Schubel, Meena Khandelwal, Wendy Singer, and Shuchi Kapila, either through their published writing or through their courses.[7] As I engaged more deeply, I discovered that these contributions grew from the foundational work of early-to mid-twentieth century anthropologists such as Bronislaw Malinowski, E. E. Evans-Pritchard, Franz Boas, Margaret Mead, and Zora Neale Hurston. They flowered through conversation with leaders in symbolic anthropology, such as Victor and Edith Turner, who transformed the study of ritual and fostered such inquiry in humanistic social sciences.[8]

The writing and other publications scholars produce find their genesis in the intellectual communities that foster (or stymie) their development, inspire their work, guide it in particular directions, and help secure funding to pursue it. These histories matter, and they help us understand how fields of study change over time. At the University of Virginia, for example, the Turners and their colleagues encouraged new generations of scholars to take seriously the people, contexts, and perspectives they encountered, which their students did through careful fieldwork and through the study of other evidence of human lives and creative production. For those interested in religion and South Asia, they found a vibrant interdisciplinary center that brought together experts in history, religion, culture, society, politics, language, and more, with core faculty such as Walter Hauser, Richard Barnett, Abdulaziz Sachedina, R. S. Khare, and H. L. Seneviratne and in weekly seminars that featured world-renowned guests.

The faculty from whom I learned as an undergraduate had participated in those intellectual conversations at the University of Virginia, also developing their own areas of expertise. They embraced core common threads of deep investigation into the nuances of human lives, whether focused on religion, gender, or history. They all used ethnographic methods, such as conducting participant observation, collecting oral histories, or learning popular stories and songs, during long-term in-country research, along with learning about historical events and cultural and religious practices through other methods, such as studying texts or visiting archives. In each area, these approaches resulted in creating more humanistic accounts of the people and traditions they encountered. Schubel's work on religious performance among Shi'as in Pakistan created a path for other scholars to study Islam more deeply through the ways that people practiced it.[9] He did not focus solely on religious texts, institutions, or the everyday lives of Muslims, but instead on the ways religious traditions—in this case, Shi'a Islam—manifest in particular contexts and through the messiness of getting by. That ability to toggle between a rich religious tradition and the details of everyday life has drawn others toward accounts of Muslim life as embodied experiences, complex in all the ways human identities can take shape.

These roots persisted when I made my own way to the University of Virginia for graduate study and grew with the diversification of the intellectual community and of research interests among faculty and students. As an undergraduate, I had learned with and from their students. As a doctoral candidate, I studied with these experts in a later era of their own research careers, when, for example, Khare focused his attention on hierarchy and human survival and Sachedina on Islamic bioethics. I brought my own questions and situated experience, learning kinship studies with Susan McKinnon, critical medical anthropology with Wende Marshall, and Hindi and Urdu language and South Asian Studies with a plethora of the university's experts. At the same time, I was immersed in a community, Charlottesville, which in the early 2000s was still struggling to grapple in meaningful ways with national, institutional, and local legacies of slavery and white supremacy, gender and labor relations, and its own contemporary instantiations of hierarchy and power. Listening intently to the ways people articulated their ways of understanding and experiencing their worlds, participating in daily life, and attending to the margins—whether doctrinal, social, political, or economic—still mattered. These approaches had something to offer toward understanding the world as it is and has been, and toward creating a more just world for future generations.

Carrying these lessons into my own scholarship, I valued immersion, paying attention, listening and watching, as events unfolded around me, as I took part in them, and as I read history, learned languages, and studied cultural patterns, literature, popular media, and public discourse. Study and research required adapting to new environments in the field, from the very mundane and physical to the existential. Moving back and forth between India and the United States, between classroom environments and family and community immersion, people suggested sources in literature and popular culture that helped me understand better the lives of Muslim women as embodied beings working with, around, and in defiance of religious and cultural expectations. Writers of twentieth-century Urdu short stories, plays, and novels fearlessly wove tales about the intimate lives of Muslim women imagined out of the foundation of their own gendered lives, from Ismat Chughtai's *Lihaaf Aur Digar Afsane* (*The Quilt and Other Stories*) to Rashid Jahan's *Aurat* (*Woman*) and Khadija Mastoor's "Dada."[10] Under cover of veiled language enabled by the ambiguities of Urdu, Chughtai dared to write about same-sex sexual encounters, among other aspects of the lives of women. Jahan, a physician, worked in maternal health and wrote fiction and nonfiction through the lens of that profession, while Mastoor told the tale of a woman nicknamed "Dada," who was rejected by her baby's father's family and torn away from her breastfeeding infant son while imprisoned. These fictional sources offered insights into how women might construct meaning in order to survive and thrive within their local physical, emotional, and moral worlds, as well as to critique their social and religious surroundings. Morever, they helped me begin to understand the many different ways religion can be represented and can infuse the rhythms of a day, especially in a place like India, where so many people embrace religion, while others reject it, and religious life takes many different forms.

In Lucknow, which eventually became both my primary fieldwork site and one of my homes, people identifying as Muslim, Hindu, Christian, Sikh, Buddhist, and non-religious live together, often in the same neighborhood or apartment complex. Religious sites such as mosques, Hindu temples and roadside shrines, and Christian churches may be situated within the same local area, the bells, sounds of *azan* calling people to prayer, and songs that accompany Hindu *puja* and Christian worship services resonate in the same lanes. Sites such as *dargah*s, *mazar*s, and *imambara*s are identifiably Muslim and attract visitors and supplicants from many different religious backgrounds. It is common in Lucknow for people to offer holiday greetings to people of all religious backgrounds and to share special holiday foods, to the extent possible, given dietary preferences. While strains and conflicts have not been absent in Lucknow, the city has been renowned for the capacity of its diverse residents to live and work together amid the buzz of getting by from day to day. I determined to pay attention how these contours played out in actual lives, while focusing on a particular topic of research: on the reproductive experiences of women living in Lucknow, a place that I've been connected with for more than twenty years now.

As may seem evident from the intellectual trajectory outlined here, my grounding in anthropology and paths into fieldwork grew through interactions with scholars who themselves had varied relationships to their fields of study through geography, heritage, community membership, and interest. In my case, the geographic and topical orientations that led to my course of study and research grew slowly out of curiosity, rather than out of a preexisting connection, something I have been repeatedly asked to explain over the years within academic settings, social circles, and fieldwork interactions. How did I learn to speak and read Hindi and Urdu? Why would I want to leave my family and travel to India? Starting from my curiosity and desire to learn, I would talk with people I encountered, some of whom became friends, and some of whom became family in one way or another; I would share stories about the scholarship-funded travels that led me from my white, working-class hometown in western Pennsylvania (more like a village, in north Indian terms) to rural Bihar, then to Lucknow, with short visits to many other parts of India.

Rooted in my academic courses on religious studies, as well as in broader contexts of the liberal arts, my curiosity both broadened and deepened over time, across disciplines and directed toward the dynamics of family life, health, and community. I lived for months in a Buddhist monastery, a women's university hostel (dorm), and a local guesthouse frequented by local and international scholars, between short stays with families who invited me to spend time with them. Eventually, my *sasural*, my partner's family's household, became my primary place of residence in India, the place that I have gone out from, returned to, and stayed emotionally connected with even when I have been geographically distant while employed as a peripatetic professor.

Fieldwork involves a great deal of listening. Learning to listen carefully and to fully attend to rich immersive contexts of people and places are key skills for ethnographers—especially for feminist researchers—as are practical matters such as attaining some degree of fluency in the local language and finding ways to connect with people and their local worlds that can generate insight into a chosen topic. I have visited hospitals, private physicians' offices, free health camps, the offices of nongovernmental organizations, local historical sites, museums, archival collections, and religious sites, as well as concert halls, shopping malls, coffee shops, schools, and universities. I have lived on my own, in a local university hostel, and, after my marriage, with extended family—all told, more than four years so far. I have spent time in homes with friends and interlocutors, as well as attending lectures, seminars, and workshops. Listening to local religious leaders, social activists, and scholars talk about their perspectives on religious and social life, often in public events directed at people who sought their views as a model for their own behavior, has helped me understand the many layers of messages that influence human behavior, religious conduct, and reproductive journeys. Interviews with and observations of physicians and other medical professionals show me how they mobilize religion in their practices in some ways, while discounting it in others, as well as how visible religious identity might shape their patients' experiences of seeking health care.

Frequent visits to spaces of public discussion have led me to other people, very often Muslim women who lead local nongovernmental organizations, teach in local colleges, or work in various less formal ways to support and lead their communities. That, too, has fostered deeper connections and friendships and led to invitations to spend time talking about other aspects of life, family, and homes—conversations that have become a source of joy, no matter where I happen to be. It has helped me listen better and ask better questions about reproduction and the experiences of individuals, families, and communities that are at the same time quite political and extraordinarily private. For me, attending to the margins in this place meant—and means—primarily paying attention to the perspectives of women, of people with less financial and social capital, and of Muslim women in particular across all other identity categories. These deeply immersive experiences in a place with a strong local Muslim heritage and shifting politics that have made appreciation of Islam and Muslims a more radical act leads me back to literature, films, and songs saturated with rich cultural content about family, fertility, and the future. Equipped with a critical eye, I find more nuanced ways to attend to how these creative works present cultural norms and engage the emotional aspects of how families get made in contemporary India. In my work, embracing the margins of Muslim lives has meant learning about and from Muslim women's reproductive journeys—not to pry or expose, but to understand better what life looks like from the grounded, situated, intimate lens of their experience and to further the possibility of expanding love and care for one another.

There are many ways to do ethnography. Learning in holistic, sensorially rich ways whenever possible and to the degree possible, contributes to vibrant ethnography, itself a practice that entails several different sorts of translation, depending upon the audience. It also involves thinking with theoretical models to see how they help in interpretation or fail to do so. In the case of my work, showing how women's experiences of infertility matter in a context in which India and the world have been primary focused on high fertility helps to contextualize their experiences. It provides a different lens to understand how relationships among population, economic development, nationalism, and environmental sustainability and human lived experiences of reproduction manifest, resulting in expansive or restricted visions of human futures, or, in this case, of India's possible futures. Examined through comparative or theoretical frameworks, there are opportunities to understand, for example, what it might mean for people to be part of the "invisible infertile" in different places.[11]

There are chances to try out theoretical frameworks: How might the reproductive justice framework articulated by women of color activists in the United States, led primarily by Black women, provide helpful ways to understand reproductive oppressions experienced by people in India? What potential advantages and limits might that framework have for understanding the unique aspects of reproductive unfreedoms and organizing for positive change?[12] At the largest scale, how do we humans, through our institutional and ideological systems, encourage some among us to flourish, while we leave others to suffer and die? These are some of the questions scholars might examine through theoretical lenses of abandonment or necropolitics.[13] Such explorations can yield insights that may be translated into small acts of care and collective acts of policy change in a variety of realms, as well as illuminating the real-world implications of the intricate webs we humans weave, entrap ourselves and others in, and work to expand, reform, or escape.

CENTERING MUSLIM WOMEN'S PERSPECTIVES ON REPRODUCTION

Historically, in my home discipline of anthropology, the study of kinship as one major foundation of human societies formed the center of cultural inquiry. These days, people often take for granted the ways that people imagine themselves as related to one another, and not because genetics has provided irrefutable answers—it hasn't, and kinship is much more than that and different than that. Rather, all too often, even scholars gloss over kinship as something that has already been figured out, as systems operating in the background rather than an aspect of human life in need of further study. In our buzzingly diverse world of constant and rapid transformation, that is anything but true, as researchers in anthropology and adjacent areas such as demography, sociology, population studies, and even literature continue to document. Kinship is something that people make and do, even when they create kin by choosing to engage with archives and technologies such as 23andMe that claim to help people discover their relations. The grounds on and the means by which we make and break family ties and other social bonds shift over time. Changes in how we as humans make our gender expression and family forms, how we create and preclude community through structures such as citizenship, and how we influence reproductive trajectories and outcomes through a variety of reproductive strategies, show the need to continue learning about how we humans make ourselves and the worlds we inhabit.

At various levels of analysis, scholars seek to understand how reproductive options and ideologies in specific local and overall global contexts impact reproductive decisions, compulsions, and oppressions that shape families, communities, and, ultimately, human populations. They use a variety of quantitative and qualitative methods—statistics, surveys, and stories—and analyze reproduction according to categories such as religion, race, ethnicity, race, sex, gender, sexuality, nationality, and global location. These strategies together are meant to help us understand human reproductive ideologies, experiences, and trends, and, perhaps, to give us new ways to imagine human futures.

Among the social sciences, anthropology tends most toward the humanistic, and, among the humanities, it tends most toward the scientific. Practitioners of this border-edging and boundary-crossing discipline have excelled in noticing all kinds of social margins, whether or not their inquiries spring from or result in love. In any case, it has been well suited to learning by putting the experiences of Muslim women at the center, in a place where they often experience social marginalization both as women and as Muslims, and sometimes in other ways as well. Spending time in spaces where Muslim women lead has helped me study how health care provision could come together with cultural norms and religious advice to influence not only access to health care—in the case I have in mind, through a low-cost camp hosted by a nongovernmental organization every weekend—but also the distribution of alms, gendered access to education, employment, and solidarity or separation across economic and social classes.[14] In another example, a prominent social activist whom I call Shabana *baji* led a women's organization and organized monthly meetings in a park in the old city of Lucknow, in addition to meeting people at her own home.[15] These meetings provided, first and foremost, a space for women to gather away from their families and enjoy the company of people outside their households, without other demands making claims on their attention, opening up a time for laughter, learning, joy, and sadness. Attendees and guests shared knowledge and educational resources and discussed important issues of the day, while observing special occasions with poetry, song, prayer, food, and games like *baitbaazi*, which allowed participants to show off their skill and speed with Urdu poetry. Women came looking for marriage partners for their relatives as well as for information to help them get by in situations where their gender, religion, or financial status might pose difficulties.

Shabana baji graciously gave me a platform to introduce my work while I searched for people to interview about infertility and infertility treatment, as well as to share what I found. In that forum with so many other women—a hundred or more—present, she responded to the framing I presented in ways that helped me think more deeply about kinship and reproduction from her perspective, which reflected common local logics of relatedness that accord high value to biological connection, most often talked about through the language of shared blood (*khun*), and especially paternity. In that sense, her views aligned with popular understandings of Islamic formulations of kinship, which anthropologists and religious studies scholars have studied in practice in other local contexts.[16] What stood out was how she framed the links between children and their families, and in particular the status of children whom parents embrace as *aulad*, a category whose local definitions are subject to local contestations and disagreement, but, generally imagined as those (usually male) who would "light the lamp" and carry on the family. People hope for aulad, wait for them, and make their own efforts to obtain them.

The vagaries of reproduction mean that aulad may be hard to get, as in cases of infertility, or when multiple pregnancies do not result in the birth of a son. They also lead people to seek aulad through less conventional means, or to redefine the category to include daughters, or to incorporate children into their families even though they may not meet socially or religiously accepted methods of reproduction. For example, child adoption or the use of assisted reproductive technologies, especially conception with donor gametes or gestation through surrogacy, create controversy about kinship, especially if these methods cannot be kept secret from others. Some people may be persuaded to accept their childless state rather than to try for a child that might fail these cultural or religious tests of relatedness. All of this is to say that the vast majority of people I talked to found aulad to be an essential part of living a successful life and an important part of envisioning their own future, as well as that of their families and their communities. These reproductive desires persisted even though (and perhaps because) the state and people outside of their families might not think their reproduction mattered and actually might be happy if they could not have children. Shabana baji cautioned the attendees at her meeting, even those with aulad, about the precarity of reproduction. She said that people understood the nature of the relationship between parents and children incorrectly, that they think that children are their own (*apna*), as if their children are their property. This logic, which makes some sense from a capitalist worldview, fits the analyses of scholars in demography and interdisciplinary population studies who have written for decades about the "value" of children and applied economic principles to reproduction, especially with reference to things like the number and sex of children people say they want.[17]

Speaking to the women gathered before her, Shabana baji rejected the idea of children as property and distanced herself from a capitalist view of reproduction. "An aulad is a trust (*amaanat*) of God," she said. "It's not ours. Whenever He feels like it, He will take it away."[18] In a place where many people have experienced the loss of pregnancies, infants, and children due to any number of environmental hazards, pathogens, and forms of social and economic marginalization that are part of the historical legacies of South Asian histories of colonization and discrimination, there are no guarantees of successful reproduction. Recognition of its fleeting nature and a measure of humility are fitting. In the midst of dominant public discourse about the dangers that high fertility pose to national flourishing and popular perceptions—often stigmatizing and disparaging views—that Muslims have large families, such recognition often falls to the wayside. I noted this often while documenting public discourse, interacting with Muslim and non-Muslim academics and social activists, and observing health care provision in medical offices and low-cost health camps.[19]

Statistical data produced from large-scale surveys about reproduction can provide insight into general beliefs, desires, and preferences held by people in a particular place about birth control, pregnancy, birth, and the ultimate shape of their families. Some examples include the Demographic and Health Surveys, the National Family Health Survey, and the India Human Development Survey.[20] These are massive and expensive ventures, often funded by national governments and international organizations, which can be vulnerable, in many national contexts, to suspicions of the government or nongovernmental agencies, often rooted in histories of colonization, perceived or actual discrimination or violence against minority populations, and abuse of reproductive technologies in the service of population control targets. Still, when broken down into nuanced categories of analysis and brought together with individual narratives, religious and cultural perspectives, and other qualitative research, a more complete picture begins to emerge that can more fully account for the rich tapestries of human experiences in creating families.

The relationships between religion and reproduction are—as is almost always the case in anthropology, when looking at the ways theory and practice relate—complex and contingent. Perspectives from textual sources matter; their interpretation over time matters. These sources may inform practice, but they do not dictate it in any religious tradition. In practice, people are dealing with situations quite different in terms of economic and social conditions from the foundational texts and interpretive traditions of their religions. They are often bound up with novel possibilities involving reproductive technologies: for instance, modern medical options for contraception, abortion, fetal surgery and surgical birth; assisted reproductive technologies such as in vitro fertilization; and neonatal intensive care. Legal strictures and local and global differences in access grounded in financial factors, as well as structural and institutional discrimination, contribute to disparities in terms of who can realistically take advantage of these technologies. Religious leaders continually offer recommendations, but technologies change rather quickly, and people may or may not follow their guidance anyway. In my fieldwork, women undergoing infertility treatment often said that their issue was a medical one, and that they sought advice from physicians, not from religious leaders. Alternatively, they might state a very general religious idea, such as that birth control or abortion were wrong, because people should have as many children "as God wants," without getting into details. Among the Muslim women who were social activists, previous encounters with religious leaders and texts, as well as their lifetimes of grounded experience as women living in north India, shaped the recommendations they gave. This wealth of experience led some of them to argue for leaving religious leaders out of the reproductive decisions and actions of women and their partners.

Meeting women across fields such as social work, medical service, and education not only helped me appreciate the diversity of their lives and of the experiences of women across different social locations but also provided clues about the variety of their religious perspectives and their level of engagement with and differences with religious leaders, who were most often men. The ways they grounded their religious advice in the care activities central to most women's lives, whether speaking from their own personal experience or drawing on their history of interactions with others, their appreciation for the practical, pragmatic realities of nurturing families and communities drew other women to them.[21] At the same time, some of them made the most of the opportunity to increase the reach of their messages through the local press, which attended meetings and seminars.[22]

Thinking with religious categories as one important aspect of identity, while being careful not to let it subsume all other aspects of lived experience, led me toward greater inclusivity and important lessons in my field research. One day in a government clinic—the first day I spent there—I met two women who were seeking treatment for infertility problems, one among many services the clinic provided. Both women found themselves in this medical space, asked by the staff to talk with a researcher, and they both identified as Muslim women. Apart from these two aspects of their lives, it quickly emerged how different their day-to-day, embodied experiences were. One of them was married to a rickshaw driver and sought treatment whenever she could scrape together the money, leading to procedures frequently repeated, only to be abandoned again and again when money ran short. The other, whose appearance suggested that she was at least comfortably middle-class, had been married for several years and running a business with her partner before thinking of having children. Both women had been unable to give birth to a child and ended up seeking help, at least temporarily, in the same place.

Beyond religious conceptions of appropriate reproduction, the emotional aspects of making family loomed large for women I met who were hoping to become mothers. Their sentiments included love for children, the idea of children they could claim as their own who would provide an outlet for their feelings of motherly love and attachment, even as those affectionate yearnings might be mixed with fear of the social implications of reproductive failure and loss. Still, religious views and cultural ideals could provide limits that some women said that they would not cross—such as using donor sperm in order to conceive—and led others to explore such options under cover of secrecy. Shared elements of life as women, or as people with a common level of access to financial resources, health care infrastructure, or common experiences of the labor required to get by, within or beyond the domestic sphere, as well as mostly shared cultural grammar around reproduction, create broader categories of commonality that exceed religious divisions. Exposure to governmental and nongovernmental programs about population may contribute to some shared views, practices, and sense of common cause as Indians, but also lead to resistance and rejection of those programs' aims and methods, often linked with distrust of the state or of international agencies.

Growing into awareness from my rural starting point, a very white and mostly working-class-to-working-poor Christian environment, I had learned viscerally that policy can marginalize people who already live on the edges of society. Questions like "Whose lives matter?" and "Whose futures matter?" were always implicitly part of my analysis of any particular social situation, even when I didn't articulate them in just this way. At any given time, they were more likely to be grounded in observations of what was happening, how people comported themselves, and who could readily speak or act or move, unimpeded by finances or gendered expectations. Developing skills of participant observation started out as a way to get by in my familiar world, but these skills prepared me for learning the nuances of unfamiliar worlds. And learning more about the lives of Muslim women led me back to those questions about how the structures of human life favor expansive or restricted possibilities for the flourishing of future human communities, inflected by the hierarchies we humans create while living with one another, and that we can perpetuate, exacerbate, resist, navigate around, or work to dismantle, even as many of us attempt to ignore them.

As an anthropologist, it is fitting that, in my case, studying Islam has meant attending to the contexts in which people practice Islam, identify as Muslims, and create not only literary and other artistic works but also the world, in conjunction with, in opposition to, or in evasion of the humans and environments that surround them. Even more fundamentally, this work of attending to the margins through the experiences of Muslim women across the social spectrum of India, and particularly of Lucknow, has given me many opportunities to learn how ideas about love and justice and hope and action, as well as oppression and discrimination, manifest in reproductive life, from literature to lived reality and back again.

The life that I have been creating along the way is deeply connected to multiple places, such that all kinds of translation—of language, cultural practices, food, political systems, and interclass and interreligious interactions—are integral to my own daily experience. Studying humanity through embodied experience and cultural production in comparative perspective, and deeply in one location, has generated more questions about how we live as humans, as well as about what new worlds we could imagine and work toward. Living through a time when toxic nationalisms, global health crises, and climate disruptions have upended daily life has brought me deeply and critically into examining the global net of human connections, from rural Pennsylvania to Lucknow, and radiating out to discover how threads hold together, knot, break, and get severed. Responding to seemingly simple questions like "Who cares how many babies Muslim women have?" has drawn me toward mundane local details of daily life to make visible the injustices that surround us, while thinking with a global vision and, lately, with the frameworks of reproductive justice so useful to mapping the margins and beginning to make the world different. It has required me to turn toward where the hurt has been, attending to the disorders of my own home region, which are, in part, emblematic of ongoing struggles in the contemporary United States, as well as to the intimate lives of women half a world away.

These intellectual and physical journeys have taught me that what appears to be a margin may not actually be so. It may, rather, be an indication of power relations. After all, conflicts over reproduction—whether in the form of birth control, abortion, assisted reproductive technologies, surrogacy, adoption, childcare, or collective social support—are both intensely local and of critical importance to global human futures. How we see ourselves and as connected and obligated by those bonds to care for one another, or not, underlies our policy as well as our potential to flourish or fail in the difficult project of both surviving as a species and cultivating our potential to become fully *insaan*, as Shabana baji often reminded the women who gathered together with her: humans who not only seek to become the best versions of themselves but also to cultivate the capacity to recognize and uplift one another in their full humanity.

NOTES

1. See Kavita Saraswathi Datla, *The Language of Secular Islam: Urdu Nationalism and Colonial India* (Honolulu: University of Hawai'i Press, 2013); Jennifer Dubrow, *Cosmopolitan Dreams: The Making of Modern Urdu Literary Culture in Colonial South Asia* (Honolulu: University of Hawai'i Press, 2018); Shamsur Rahman Faruqi, "Strategy for the Survival of Urdu in India Through School Education," *Annual of Urdu Studies* 21 (2006): 120–38; Asha Sarangi, ed., *Language and Politics in India* (New Delhi: Oxford University Press, 2009); and Ulrike Stark, "Politics, Public Issues, and the Promotion of Urdu Literature: *Avadh Akhbar*, the First Urdu Daily in Northern India," *Annual of Urdu Studies* 22 (2007): 66–94.
2. Andrea Wright, *Between Dreams and Ghosts: Indian Migration and Middle Eastern Oil* (Stanford: Stanford University Press, 2021).

3. Paul Ehrlich, *The Population Bomb* (New York: Ballantine, 1968); Betsy Hartmann *Reproductive Rights and Wrongs: The Global Politics of Population Control and Reproductive Choice* (New York: Harper and Row, 1987).
4. Roger Jeffery and Patricia Jeffery, *Population, Gender, and Politics: Demographic Change in Rural North India* (Cambridge: Cambridge University Press, 1997); Roger Jeffery and Patricia Jeffery, "'We five, our twenty-five': Myths of Population Out of Control in Contemporary India," in *New Horizons in Medical Anthropology: Essays in Honor of Charles Leslie*, ed. Mark Nichter and Margaret Lock (New York: Routledge, 2002), 172–99; Sriya Iyer, *Demography and Religion in India* (New Delhi: Oxford University Press, 2002).
5. This method is known as the total fertility rate (TFR). See Samuel H. Preston, Patrick Heuveline, and Michel Guillot, *Demography: Measuring and Modeling Population Processes* (Malden, Mass.: Blackwell, 2001).
6. Shyam Benegal, dir., *Hari Bhari (Fertility)*, National Film Development Corporation and Ministry of Health and Family Welfare, New Delhi, 2000.
7. Shuchi Kapila, *Educating Seeta: The Anglo-Indian Family Romance and the Poetics of Indirect Rule* (Columbus: Ohio State University Press, 2010); Meena Khandelwal, *Women in Ochre Robes: Gendering Hindu Renunciation* (Albany: State University of New York Press, 2004); Vernon Schubel, *Religious Performance in Contemporary Islam: Shi'i Devotional Rituals in South Asia* (Columbia: University of South Carolina Press, 1993); Wendy Singer, *Creating Histories: Oral Narratives and the Politics of History-Making* (New Delhi: Oxford University Press, 1997).
8. Victor Turner, *The Forest of Symbols: Aspects of Ndembu Ritual* (Ithaca, N.Y.: Cornell University Press, 1967); Edith Turner, *Heart of Lightness: The Life Story of an Anthropologist* (New York: Berghahn, 2005).
9. Schubel, *Religious Performance in Contemporary Islam*.
10. Ismat Chughtai, *The Quilt and Other Stories*, trans. Tahira Naqvi and Syeda S. Hameed (New Delhi: Kali for Women, 1990); Rashid Jahan, *Aurat aur Digar Afsane [Woman and Other Stories]* (Lahore: Fairoz, 1937); Khadija Mastoor, "Godfather" [Dada], trans. Shahrukh Husain, *Hoops of Fire: Fifty Years of Fiction by Pakistani Women*, ed. Aamer Hussein

(London: Saki, 1999), 24–38; originally published (in Urdu) in *Thake Haare* (Lahore: Glad, 1962), 315–40.

11. Jasmine Fledderjohann and Liberty Walther Barnes. "Reimagining Infertility: A Critical Examination of Fertility Norms, Geopolitics, and Survey Bias," *Health Policy and Planning* 33, no. 1 (2018): 34–40.

12. To learn more, see, for example, ACRJ (Asian Communities Reproductive Justice), "A New Vision for Advancing Our Movement for Reproductive Health, Reproductive Rights, and Reproductive Justice," 2005, http://strongfamiliesmovement.org/assets/docs/ACRJ-A-New-Vision.pdf (accessed September 27, 2022); Loretta Ross, "Understanding Reproductive Justice: Transforming the Pro-Choice Movement," *Off Our Backs* 3, no. 4 (2006): 14–19; Loretta J. Ross and Rickie Solinger, *Reproductive Justice: An Introduction* (Oakland: University of California Press, 2017); and Karen A. Scott, "The Rise of Black Feminist Intellectual Thought and Political Activism in Perinatal Quality Improvement: A Righteous Rage About Racism, Resistance, Resilience, and Rigor," *Feminist Anthropology* 2 (2021): 155–60.

13. João Guilherme Biehl, *Vita: Life in a Zone of Social Abandonment* (Berkeley: University of California Press, 2013); Achille Mbembe, *Necropolitics*, trans. Steve Corcoran (Durham, N.C.: Duke University Press, 2019); Emma Varley, "Monsoons and Medicine: The Biopolitics of Crisis and State Indifference in Gilgit-Baltistan." *South Asian History and Culture* 10, no. 1 (2019): 78–96.

14. Holly Donahue Singh, "Numbering Others: Religious Demography, Identity, and Fertility Management Experiences in Contemporary India," *Social Science & Medicine* 254 (June 2020), https://www.sciencedirect.com/science/article/pii/S0277953619305283?via%3Dihub (accessed November 4, 2022); Holly Donahue Singh, *Infertility in a Crowded Country: Hiding Reproduction in India* (Bloomington: Indiana University Press, 2022).

15. In Urdu, *baji* means elder sister. Holly Donahue Singh, "Fertility Control: Reproductive Desires, Kin Work, and Women's Status in Contemporary India," *Medical Anthropology Quarterly* 31, no. 1 (2017): 23–39.

16. Morgan Clarke, *Islam and New Kinship Reproductive Technology and the Shariah in Lebanon* (New York: Berghahn, 2011); Carol Delaney, *The*

Seed and the Soil: Gender and Cosmology in Turkish Village Society (Berkeley: University of California Press, 1991); Marcia C. Inhorn, *The New Arab Man: Emergent Masculinities, Technologies, and Islam in the Middle East* (Princeton, N.J.: Princeton University Press, 2012); Marcia C. Inhorn and Soraya Tremayne, eds., *Islam and Assisted Reproductive Technologies: Sunni and Shia Perspectives* (New York: Berghahn, 2012); Robert Matthew Tappan, *Beyond Clerics and Clinics: Islamic Bioethics and Assisted Reproductive Technology in Iran* (PhD diss., University of Virginia, 2011).

17. Ramesh C. Mishra, Boris Mayer, Gisella Trommsdorff, Isabelle Albert, and Beate Schwarz, "The Value of Children in Urban and Rural India: Cultural Background and Empirical Results," in *The Value of Children in Cross-Cultural Perspective: Case Studies from Eight Societies*, ed. Gisela Trommsdorff and Bernhard Nauck (Lengerich: Pabst Science 2005), 143–70; Monica Das Gupta, "Life Course Perspectives on Women's Autonomy and Health Outcomes," *American Anthropologist* 97, no. 3 (1995): 481–91; Amartya Sen and Jean Drèze, *The Amartya Sen and Jean Drèze Omnibus* (New Delhi: Oxford University Press, 1999); Carol Vlassoff, "The Value of Sons in an Indian Village: How Widows See It," *Population Studies* 44 (1990): 5–20.

18. Singh, *Infertility in a Crowded Country*.

19. Nilanjana Chatterjee and Nancy E. Riley, "Planning an Indian Modernity: The Gendered Politics of Fertility Control," *Signs* 26, no. 3 (2001): 811–45; Kalpana Ram, "Rationalizing Fecund Bodies: Family Planning Policy and the Modern Indian Nation State," in *Borders of Being: Citizenship, Fertility, and Sexuality in Asia and the Pacific*, ed. Margaret Molly and Kalpana Ra (Ann Arbor: University of Michigan Press, 2001), 82–117; Singh, "Numbering Others"; Singh, *Infertility in a Crowded Country*.

20. DHS Program, Demographic and Health Surveys, http://www.measuredhs.com; National Family Health Survey, India, http://rchiips.org/nfhs/; India Human Development Survey, https://ihds.umd.edu/ (accessed September 27, 2022).

21. Asghar Ali Engineer, *Problems of Muslim Women in India* (Bombay: Orient Longman, 1995); Zoya Hasan and Ritu Menon, *Unequal Citizens: A Study of Muslim Women In India* (New Delhi: Oxford

University Press, 2004); Zoya Hasan and Ritu Menon, eds., *The Diversity of Muslim Women's Lives in India* (New Brunswick, N.J.: Rutgers University Press, 2005).

22. Holly Donahue Singh, "'The World's Back Womb?' Commercial Surrogacy and Infertility Inequalities in India," *American Anthropologist* 116 (2014): 824–28; Holly Donahue Singh, "Surrogacy and Gendered Contexts of Infertility Management in India," in *International Handbook on Gender and Demographic Processes*, ed. Nancy E. Riley and Jan Brunson (Dordrecht: Springer, 2018), 105–16.

7

WRITING MONGOL HISTORY ON THE MARGINS

Sufi and Kinship Connectivity in the *Tarikh-i Rashidi*

HENRY D. BRILL

> *With my lack of ability, what right had I to put my destitute pen to the page of composition? However, it was out of necessity, since a few narratives of the Moghul khans who were Muslims have been heard from reliable sources, and there are also those whose careers I have witnessed myself. Now that I look around myself, I see that among my peers there is no one left who knows these narratives or who could recite them. If I were not so bold, the Moghuls and the Moghul khans would become so neglected that they would lose their own heritage, not to mention the history of their ancestors.*
>
> —Mirza Haydar Dughlat

Historian and Turko-Mongol aristocrat Mirza Muhammad Haydar Dughlat (d. 1551) wrote his 1546 Persian-language history, the *Tarikh-i Rashidi* (History of Rashid), which became a major source for the study of Central and South Asia between the fourteenth and sixteenth centuries, for many reasons. Above all, Mirza Haydar was worried that the memory of the Moghul khans—by whom he meant members of a particular lineage descended from the world conqueror Chinggis Khan (d. 1227)—would be forgotten and lost to time. This was a history written out of an anxiety about erasure, not only of others but also of the historian himself.

Given the circumstances, such fears were reasonable. The early modern period about and during which Mirza Haydar wrote was a time of great transformation, as political culture turned away from norms established during the medieval period. Beginning in the late fourteenth century, Central Eurasia saw the emergence of new forms of political legitimacy as the unified Mongol Empire splintered into separate territories governed by competing Chinggisid royals.[1] In a milieu of political fragmentation, aristocratic families began to play a larger role in the ebb and flow of sovereign rule. Take, for example, Amir Temür (d. 1405), the eponymous founder of the Timurid dynasty, a major polity that at its height ruled much of Central Asia and Iran, as well as parts of South Asia. Temür, a Turko-Mongol aristocrat, introduced a variety of legal, religious, and military innovations that positioned his own family—rather than the Mongol royalty—at the center of political culture.[2] Although the Timurid dynasty fell from ascendency toward the end of the fifteenth century, Temür and his descendants left a lasting political legacy: the slow but steady shift from traditional Mongol modes of political legitimation that became a defining feature of the early modern period in the region.

New forms of imperial authority emerged around the turn of the fifteenth century, long after the victories of the Chinggisid and Timurid dynasties. The Ottoman, Safavid, and Mughal empires each fashioned new modes of political, cultural, and religious authority to create what became new royal houses responsible for ruling Anatolia, Iran, and South Asia into the modern period.[3] With the emergence of these empires came dramatic changes to the political topography of the region and to religious institutions and intellectual production in the Islamicate world. Around the sixteenth century, Sufi orders—a key Islamic institution—underwent a process of crystallization, evolving from loose networks into far more demarcated organizations in which the teaching and practices of a shaykh or pir, a single charismatic and authoritative leader, formed the basis of a communal consciousness.[4] A similar sort of innovation occurred around literary and artistic production as competing empires sponsored historians, painters, and poets in producing creative works reflecting and propagating imperial authority.[5] These formative changes to political culture, religious organization, and intellectual production lie precisely at the center of the *Tarikh-i Rashidi*.

That Mirza Haydar authored a historical narrative during and about the early modern period is not entirely unique in and of itself, especially given the wealth of these texts in the archives. What is special about the *Tarikh-i Rashidi* is how Mirza Haydar wrote the text. The subject matter is wide ranging, addressing a variety of different dynasties across an expansive geography, in no small part because Mirza Haydar traversed the political terrain of Central and South Asia—quite literally from Kashgar to Kashmir, from Tashkent to Tibet—in the service of various royal families. As a Turko-Mongol aristocrat, Mirza Haydar was at the center of many of the events he records in the *Tarikh-i Rashidi*, perhaps explaining why it is such a personal text: part historical narrative and part memoir, with stories of childhood uncertainty, political betrayal, and spiritual experience. Because he was historian and aristocrat, analyst and participant, Mirza Haydar provided a rich and highly personal view into a rather turbulent period of political and cultural history. His work was also an urgent, perhaps desperate, attempt to save the historian himself from social, political, and even spiritual marginalization.

This chapter presents a sustained treatment of Mirza Haydar as both aristocrat and historian to explore the dynamics of early modernity in Central Asia. It makes an important contribution to the study of Muslim margins in at least three ways. First, Mirza Haydar's story is that of an elite who felt increasingly marginalized during his lifetime. The mere fact that he was able to write history, however, indicates that, while he may have no longer been at the center of political power, he possessed a kind of privilege that most in his society did not. His life thus exemplifies how one can occupy social margins and centers at the same time. In order to explain his status, the chapter charts where Mirza Haydar and the Dughlat aristocracy fell within the broader landscape of Turko-Mongol family life during a period marked by changes in the practice and theory of kinship.

After unpacking how broader transformations in the aristocratic-royal relationship shaped life for Mirza Haydar, we will then explore how the Dughlat historian found affective and political support through Sufi teachers during a time of personal crisis. Both Sufi and kinship networks defined the Turko-Mongol world of the sixteenth century, influencing Mirza Haydar's approach as a historian. In tracing how he asserted the importance of Sufi Muslims to the political foundations of his Turko-Mongol society, we can see how the writing of Islamic history claimed an important social status for the historian as well as for his kin. This—what might be called the "hidden transcript" of the text—highlights why scholars should read the *Tarikh-i Rashidi*: not only to learn about the events that Mirza Haydar recorded but also to understand what he hoped to gain by narrating history in a certain way. Rather than direct our gaze at what is right in front of us, we will step back and look from the margins, asking what motivates his approach to the writing of history.

Finally, the chapter examines Mirza Haydar's account of Moghul conversion to Islam. He sees the writing down of this history as urgent, given what he identifies as a preference in his society for oral storytelling over written accounts. Mirza Haydar's book thus serves as an attempt to rescue history—and his own place in it—from fading memory, and from the margins of Islamic history. It does so by writing his own lineage into the greater story of the conversion of the Moghuls to Islam.

SUFI AND KINSHIP NETWORKS: EARLY MODERN AFFECTIVITY IN PRACTICE

In order to understand the fear of marginalization of Mirza Haydar himself and the political regime about which he wrote, we must first explore his social status—that is, where he stood in the aristocratic and royal circles of the Turko-Mongol world.

Kinship relationships crisscrossed royal houses and aristocratic families, connecting members of the Turko-Mongol elite in complex—and, at times, even surprising—ways, with Mirza Haydar serving as a case in point.[6] Through his father, Muhammad-Husayn (d. 1508), Mirza Haydar was a member of the Dughlat family, one of the key aristocratic families in Central Asia during the period. Mirza Haydar also shared a matrilineal connection to the Chaghatayid-Moghul royal family, members of which were descended from the second son of Chinggis Khan, Chagatay Khan (d. 1241). Because Turko-Mongol systems of kinship were built on a patriarchal and patrilineal logic, Mirza Haydar identified as a Dughlat.[7]

Dughlat identity is situated firmly at the center of the *Tarikh-i Rashidi*. Early in the history, Mirza Haydar outlines how the Dughlat line came to be one of the leading aristocratic families in the Moghul khanate. As Mirza Haydar recounts, Chinggis Khan gave Amir Ortu Bora, the apical—or foundational—ancestor of the Dughlat lineage, "seven privileges," ranging from ceremonial honors, such as a privileged place in the royal court, to military liberties, such as the unique freedom to bring arms into the royal assembly.[8] But if Chinggis Khan played a central role in giving the Dughlat family a claim to elite status in the Mongol Empire of the early thirteenth century, the relationship between the royal house and the Dughlat family looked rather different by the time of Mirza Haydar some three hundred years later.

While Mirza Haydar traces the historical origins of the Dughlat lineage to Ortu Bora, the historian does not identify himself using the title of "amir."[9] Instead, Mirza Haydar lays claim to a related but more specific title. At the outset of the *Tarikh-i Rashidi*, he identifies himself as "Muhammad-Haydar," who is "known familiarly as Mirza Haydar."[10] The Persian title of *mīrzā* is an abbreviation of *amīrzāda*, meaning "son of an amir"—a significant title in that it stakes a claim to aristocratic status.[11] That Mirza Haydar makes a concerted effort to identify as such reflects how the historian understood his position within the broader Turko-Mongol political landscape.

According to Mirza Haydar, the historical connection between the Dughlat line and the Moghul royal house was characterized by emotional closeness. In a particularly memorable scene, he writes of the intimate relationship between his father and Sultan-Mahmud, who was then ruling as khan: "They always did things together. Many times, the khan said to my father apologetically, 'I have to go to my wife for conjugal duties. You will be left alone in the chamber like a night watchman, and this is contrary to friendship.'"[12] Here, Mirza Haydar provides an anecdote illustrating the bonds of friendship shared between his Dughlat father and the Moghul khan. The intimacy of this particular relationship reflects a larger trend identified by Ali Anooshahr in his study of Turko-Mongol political culture—namely, the "long and often arduous process of discipline and mentorship," which was "monopolized by and passed down among important families," royal and aristocratic alike.[13] The underlying political goal of the aristocrat-royal relationship was a central component of the affective intimacy shared between Dughlat amir and Moghul khan.

Following in the footsteps of his father and other Dughlat relatives, Mirza Haydar shared a close bond with members of the Moghul royal house. In the *Tarikh-i Rashidi*, the historian often employs kinship terms to describe his connection to the Moghul royals. For example, he recounts how Abdul-Rashid Sultan (d. 1560), son of the then-ruling khan Sultan-Sa'id (d. 1533), swore to recognize the Dughlat aristocrat as his "elder brother," a source of guidance second only to the khan himself.[14] Mirza Haydar also cultivated a family tie to the royal family through his marriage to Moghul princess Muhibb-Sultan Khanim.

The long-standing proximity between the Dughlat lineage and the Chaghatayid-Moghul royal house ceased rather abruptly in 1533. It was then that Abdul-Rashid, serving as khan after the death of his father weeks before, killed Sayyid-Muhammad Mirza, head of the Dughlat lineage, and ordered for the arrest and death of Mirza Haydar.[15] The move against Sayyid-Muhammad and Mirza Haydar was part and parcel of what the Dughlat historian saw as a radical reorientation in Chaghatayid-Moghul family and political relationships. Specifically, Mirza

Haydar notes that Abdul-Rashid "exiled all his aunts, sisters, and step-mothers. . . . He also made peace and became friends with the Shaybanid Uzbeks, who were old enemies."[16] These significant changes to family life and the political order lead Mirza Haydar to conclude that "the customs of our ancestors have been overthrown."[17] It is difficult to overstate how deeply the newfound animosity between the Dughlat lineage and the Moghul royal house reshaped lived experience for Mirza Haydar.

The sudden change in Dughlat fortune forced Mirza Haydar into exile from both Abdul-Rashid and the Moghul royal court. When he received word of the death of his uncle, the Dughlat historian was in Tibet on a campaign for the royal house. He saw his army quickly disbanded on order of Abdul-Rashid, who made it clear that Mirza Haydar was not to return to Kashgar, the center of the Moghul khanate.[18] In the wake of his falling-out with Abdul-Rashid, Mirza Haydar was left with no option but to remain in political and physical exile from the Moghul court.

But, even as he was forced into exile from the court, Mirza Haydar remained focused on Abdul-Rashid. A case in point is the very title of the *Tarikh-i Rashidi*, a reference in part to Abdul-Rashid, as Mirza Haydar explains.[19] The Moghul historian also frames his composition as a sort of peace offering to Abdul-Rashid. In the dedication of his history, Mirza Haydar references his quarrel with Abdul-Rashid and considers the broader purpose of the text: "Although from his [Sultan-Sa'id's] sons I have suffered that than which there can be no worse, I reciprocate with this poor effort [the *Tarikh-i Rashidi*] and, whether it be accepted or not, I dedicate it to the khan's son [Abdul-Rashid] in order that it may be a memento from me to him."[20] Identifying Abdul-Rashid as a primary audience of the *Tarikh-i Rashidi*,

Mirza Haydar positions the work as a reminder of his once-close relationship with the Moghul khan. In so doing, he highlights a central tension underlying his compositional moment: Abdul-Rashid as source of both suffering and affection.

Mirza Haydar provides a framework for making intelligible the seemingly incomprehensible events of 1533, by placing blame on an amir serving the khan: Muhammadi Barlas. He considers at some length how the "improper acts" often attributed to Abdul-Rashid, from exiling family members to breaking political alliances, were "actually done through Muhammadi Barlas's pernicious influence."[21] Muhammadi was part of the Barlas aristocratic lineage, a competitor with the Dughlat line.[22] By identifying Muhammadi Barlas as the reason why Abdul-Rashid chose to abrogate the long-standing connection between the Dughlat line and Moghul royal house, Mirza Haydar not only attacks a rival aristocratic line but also, in effect, expiates the khan: "Abdul-Rashid Khan, in and of himself, supported justice and equity," concludes Mirza Haydar.[23] Significantly, this explanation presents a logic through which Mirza Haydar could reenter the retinue of Abdul-Rashid—a major motivation of the *Tarikh-i Rashidi* on the whole.

That Mirza Haydar desired to be back in Abdul-Rashid's good graces is not entirely surprising, especially considering how the *Tarikh-i Rashidi* highlights not only the political but also the more emotional contributions of the Dughlat lineage to the khanate. Mirza Haydar indeed devotes no small portion of his text to discussing the affective dimensions of his role as close advisor to Abdul-Rashid. He describes the "affection, unity, and love" between the pair as "reach[ing] a degree higher than which cannot be imagined," with Mirza Haydar and Abdul-Rashid swearing oaths to support each other shortly before Sultan-Saʿid died.[24] Mirza Haydar also highlights how members of his

Dughlat line played a major role in the life course of Abdul-Rashid. As a case in point stands Habiba-Sultan Khanish, a sister to Mirza Haydar; in the words of the historian, Habiba-Sultan raised Abdul-Rashid "like a mother."[25] By chronicling the emotional intimacy once shared between his Dughlat family and Abdul-Rashid in a text dedicated to the khan, Mirza Haydar makes an implicit case for restoring the relationship, presenting *past history* imbued with *future possibility*.

But the possibility of reunification did not change the fact that Mirza Haydar had to grapple with losing access to the Chaghatayid-Moghul network of affectivity exemplified by his once-close relationship with Abdul-Rashid.[26] Here, "network of affectivity" refers to personal relationships that connect people across geographic, political, and familial boundaries by providing members with different types of support and guidance, including emotional, political, spiritual, and economic.[27] The *Tarikh-i Rashidi* serves as a helpful source for the study of such networks. For one, the text is an example of what scholar Nurten Kılıç-Schubel terms the "emotional turn" in Turko-Mongol source material dating to the sixteenth century, which features more frequent non-normative displays of emotion and increased discussion of feelings about feelings.[28] Then there is the case of Mirza Haydar himself, who was isolated—affectively, politically, and geographically—from Abdul-Rashid and the Moghul khanate after the murder of his paternal uncle. Who supported Mirza Haydar following the unsettling events of 1533?

Mirza Haydar coped with the varied challenges of exile by relying, at least in part, on members of the Sufi *awliyā'* (sing. *walī*) or "Friends of God." Sufi networks—the complex matrices of Sufi teachers and followers associated with a particular spiritual lineage—made key contributions to religious life and political culture in Central and South Asia during the early modern period.²⁹ One such network was the Naqshbandi-Ahrariyya, which included Sufi leaders who held sacred authority as well as political influence and extensive economic resources.³⁰ Some Turko-Mongol royals and aristocrats, including Mirza Haydar, were closely connected to Naqshbandi teachers.³¹ In the *Tarikh-i Rashidi*, Mirza Haydar provides a multivalent treatment of Sufi figures. His discussions of Sufi teachers range in theme, from mapping spiritual lineages and describing miracles to recounting day-to-day interactions such as involvement in military campaigns. One contemporary scholar even classifies the text as "hagio-historiography," on account of its rich treatment of saintly lives and miracles.³² The validity of such a reading notwithstanding, the point here is to highlight the extent to which Mirza Haydar speaks to multiple audiences and fulfills various goals in his discussions of Sufi adepts.³³ He also uses a variety of compositional modes to drive the treatment of Sufi *awliyā'* in his text, including both prose and poetry. It is through the inherent multivocality of poetry, a key genre in Sufi thought and practice, that Mirza Haydar provides a fleeting glimpse into his affective circumstances and social imagination during a period of marked change, both personal and historical.

Poetry about Naqshbandi shaykh Khwaja Mahmud (d. 1536), a spiritual mentor to Mirza Haydar, in the *Tarikh-i Rashidi* provides a close look at their personal relationship. One representative instance in which Mirza Haydar provides a poetic treatment of his Sufi teacher comes as part of a discussion of his physical separation from both Sultan-Sa'id Khan and Khwaja Mahmud:

> My beloved departed from my sight, and only horns were left in my heart. As a memento of him there remained a hundred scars of regret in my heart.

Although one can have no expectation of the return of past life,
for many lifetimes my eyes remained expectantly on the road.[34]

Here, the speaker describes how exile from the "beloved" brought great emotional pain and references a number of different tropes in Sufi literature. For instance, in Sufi poetry, the relationship between lover and beloved has historically been understood in terms of earthly and divine love, as well as the connection between disciple and spiritual guide.[35] Much as separation is a feature of many romantic relationships, exile—often understood in terms of distance from the divine—marks the Sufi path to which Mirza Haydar might allude when the speaker references keeping their eyes on a difficult goal while on "the road."[36] Suffice it to say that Mirza Haydar drew from a well-established set of Sufi tropes, such as the lover-beloved relationship and the theme of exile, that would be familiar to members of his intended audience. But his exile was something more than spiritual distance, as the physical separation from his spiritual masters parallels his exile from the royal court. It speaks, at least implicitly, about the pain of his political as well as his spiritual alienation.

By chronicling his own experiences throughout the text, Mirza Haydar also allows for the examination of his poetry through a comparatively more personal framework.[37] He includes these verses at a narrative moment during which he is isolated from both Khwaja Mahmud and Sultan-Sa'id. Thus, when Mirza Haydar describes being "bereft of the privilege of his company," to whose company he refers is unclear.[38] A similar sense of subjective ambiguity marks his treatment of Sultan-Sa'id, who in the *Tarikh-i Rashidi* is often described through Sufi tropes. Narrating Sultan-Sa'id's impending death, for example, Mirza Haydar writes of "the scar of separation on my brow and the flames of hopelessness licking at my heart"—imagery representative of the themes of exile and affection in Sufi thought and practice.[39] The poetic verses quoted earlier then might refer simultaneously to the isolation Mirza Haydar felt from *both* Khwaja Mahmud *and* the Moghul khan.[40]

The rhetorical similarities between the ways in which Mirza Haydar frames his affiliations with the khan and the shaykh seem to reflect the comparably affective functions royal and Sufi figures served for the Dughlat historian. Considered in terms of the sense of exile and isolation underlying the *Tarikh-i Rashidi*, the verses function in part to highlight the close bond between Mirza Haydar and Sultan-Sa'id Khan. Accordingly, the verses are part of a larger compositional goal: to highlight the historical connection between the Dughlat lineage and the Chaghatayid-Moghul royal family. On account of his political exile, however, Mirza Haydar could not look to his Chaghatayid-Moghul kin connections for affective support while writing his history. These poetic verses, then, might highlight his yearning for a close relationship with Abdul-Rashid and the royal family, much like the connection between Mirza Haydar and Sultan-Sa'id Khan of years past.

When their subject is read as Khwaja Mahmud, however, these verses assume a different function, seeming to articulate the ways in which Mirza Haydar appealed to *available* Sufi networks of affection. While writing in exile, Mirza Haydar was still able to appeal to Khwaja Mahmud and similar Sufi figures, who—although often affiliated in some way with royals—lay claim to authority of their own. The *walāya*, or saintly authority, available to Sufi leaders gave them an additional level of agency vis-à-vis members of the Turko-Mongol aristocracy.[41] Aristocrats such as Mirza Haydar were in large part dependent on royal families for political support, as legitimate rule required at least the symbolic backing of a Chinggisid khan. Sufi power and authority, however, was not predicated on royal support.[42] By highlighting his close relationship with Khwaja Mahmud, Mirza Haydar wrote himself back into a Central Asian network of Sufi affectivity—a network made accessible by the distinct modality of Sufi authority. He was trying, in effect, to move himself from the margins of his society to the center through a claim on Islamic religious power. But those claims on religious power need not be seen as merely instrumental or insincerely religious; perhaps they were effective for him precisely because they were both spiritual and political.

That Mirza Haydar situates himself within a Central Asian network of Sufi affectivity is not only meaningful on the individual level but also connected to the broader political dynamics of the post-Timurid period. As Nurten Kılıç-Schubel has argued, the sixteenth century saw a shift in political culture from loyalty-based legitimacy to rule predicated on "familial bonds of affection"—a shift related to the broader transition from non-Chinggisid to Chinggisid rule in Central Asia.[43] The movement of imperial power toward the Chinggisid royalty reflected and shaped more constrictive understandings of kinship across the leading dynasties, as Kılıç-Schubel suggests. While bonds of affection between royal brothers came to define Turko-Mongol political culture, aristocrats were often found at some distance from once-close rulers.[44] That Mirza Haydar appeals to Naqshbandi teachers might suggest how Sufi networks could provide support and guidance to other members of the Turko-Mongol elite who faced similar affective challenges as understandings of kinship changed.

The preceding discussion has attempted to balance the specific circumstances of Mirza Haydar with broader political and cultural changes that were characteristic of the early modern period of Central Asian history. By focusing first on political and kinship connections between the Dughlat lineage and Moghul house, the chapter contextualized the relationship between aristocrat and royal as one of emotional intimacy. The historical closeness between aristocracy and royalty changed as the sixteenth century progressed, with Mirza Haydar serving as a representative example of the broader shift toward the consolidation of royal power. That Dughlat identity and political exile underlie both the motivation and content of the *Tarikh-i Rashidi* allows for a more complex picture of these changes to political culture. The chapter then focused on how Mirza Haydar grappled with the affective consequences of dislocation from the khanate through support from Sufi networks. The analysis suggests that the lived relationship between Sufi teacher and follower could shape the contours of personal and political experience, adding richness to the standard representation of Sufism as a source of political legitimation to be used—rather than experienced—by the elite. Mirza Haydar challenged his feelings of both political and spiritual marginalization through his relationship to Sufi teachers.

FRAMING ISLAMIC HISTORY: A VIEW FROM THE MARGINS

If Sufi and kinship relations shaped lived experience for Mirza Haydar, they can also be said to have impacted the ways in which the Dughlat historian frames the history of Islam. This section—a case study of Islamic conversion as depicted in the *Tarikh-i Rashidi*—provides insight into what it can mean to write a history of Islam for fear that the Muslim past is becoming marginal to the Muslim present.

For a leader of a major polity to convert to Islam often came with significant changes to political culture and religious life in the Mongol world, especially given some of the underlying tensions between Islamic and Chinggisid traditions around a host of issues, ranging from governance to ritual observance.[45] This could help explain, at least in part, why Mirza Haydar situates the Islamic conversion of the Moghul khanate as a framing element in the *Tarikh-i Rashidi*. Specifically, the Dughlat historian begins the work with the reign of Tughlugh-Temür Khan (d. 1363) because "of the Moghul khans it was he who converted to Islam, and after him the Moghuls' necks were freed of the yoke of heathenism, and by the grace of Islam, like all other peoples, they entered among the Muslim peoples."[46] Mirza Haydar highlights the conversion of Tughlugh-Temür as a critical juncture, responsible for bringing the Moghul khanate into the fold of Islam.

Conversion narratives, including that of Tughlugh-Temür, can be read as participating in a broader discussion about the margins of Islam.[47] As Devin DeWeese highlights in his scholarship on Islamization in the Golden Horde, a Mongol khanate in Central Asia, "conversion narratives are themselves central elements in the process of Islamization, as the community articulates its Islamicness and either stresses its break with the past or finds common ground with pre-Islamic traditions or values."[48] In short, a conversion narrative—as an element of the Islamization process—can be viewed as a rich storytelling space that at once reflects and shapes the ways in which a community creates meaning in conversation with Islam.[49] In suggesting a connection between conversion and the margins of Islam, my point is not that Islamization should be understood as a progression toward some constructed "orthodox" Islam, but, rather, that conversion narratives can be located at the *start of a process* of negotiating communal identity in terms of Islam.[50] By narrating the conversion of Tughlugh-Temür, Mirza Haydar can be said to make a critical contribution to the discursive boundaries of Islam.

The fact that Mirza Haydar positions the conversion of Tughlugh-Temür as a central framing element, responsible for shaping the arc of the *Tarikh-i Rashidi* as a history of "the Moghul khans *who were Muslims*," calls for a more contextualized reading of the conversion narrative, a reading attuned to the anxieties underlying the text as a whole.[51] In short, the ways in which Mirza Haydar narrates the conversion emphasize the critical historical agency of, first, Sufi teachers affiliated with the Naqshbandi order, and, second, members of the Dughlat lineage. By so recording the conversion narrative of Tughlugh-Temür, the Dughlat historian was able to push back against the perceived historical erasure of both the Moghul khanate and his own lineage.

In the narrative, Sufi teachers affiliated with the Naqshbandi order play a key role as agents responsible for converting Tughlugh-Temür to Islam. The story starts with the figure of Shaykh Jamaluddin, a "man of inner power" who was descended from a prominent Sufi lineage in Central Asia.[52] Tughlugh-Temür summoned Shaykh Jamaluddin after the shaykh unknowingly disobeyed a royal order for a hunt. As Mirza Haydar relates, when the shaykh was brought before Tughlugh-Temür, the khan was "feeding pig meat to several dogs. 'Are you better or this dog?' he asked angrily. 'If I have faith,' the shaykh answered, 'I am better; but if not, the dog is better than I am.'"[53] In a follow-up encounter, Shaykh Jamaluddin explained Muslim faith to Tughlugh-Temür, causing the khan to weep and say, "If I become khan and achieve autonomy, you must come to me, and I will certainly become a Muslim."[54] The only problem: Shaykh Jamaluddin died before Tughlugh-Temür could secure power.

This is where Mawlana Arshaduddin, the "very pious" son of Shaykh Jamaluddin who was also a Sufi, comes into the story. Based on a dream before his death, Shaykh Jamaluddin issued a charge to his son: "When that young man [Tughlugh-Temür] becomes khan, go to him. He may keep his promise and convert to Islam, and this felicity, by which a population will be enlightened, will be due to your endeavor."[55] And this is exactly what Mawlana Arshaduddin did. As Mirza Haydar writes, "The mawlana ordered the khan to bathe and then offered him the faith. The khan became Muslim, and then they made plans to propagate the faith and spread Islam."[56] While a number of literary elements in the conversion narrative can be viewed in light of political and religious culture in Mongol Central Asia, the point here is to highlight the key role of Sufi teachers from the Naqshbandi order in the story Mirza Haydar tells.[57]

That Mirza Haydar situates Sufi teachers as agents of conversion is not entirely surprising in and of itself, especially since it was common in the post-Mongol era to ascribe such agency to Sufi teachers.[58] What is more interesting, however, is the source from which Mirza Haydar draws in order to tell this story: his own Sufi teacher, Mawlana Khwaja Ahmad, a descendant of Mawlana Arshaduddin. Before narrating the conversion of Tughlugh-Temür, Mirza Haydar provides a biographical gloss of his Sufi teacher: "He was among those who were attached to the Sublime Order of the Khwajas. I myself paid him homage twenty times," he writes.[59] The Dughlat historian then goes on to describe how Khwaja Ahmad "told such wonderful stories of these people [Sufi teachers] that no matter how little devoted to him people were, they were still inescapably affected by him."[60] The conversion narrative of Tughlugh-Temür was one such story related by Khwaja Ahmad.

The significance of Khwaja Ahmad serving as the informant for such a historically and narratively important story in the *Tarikh-i Rashidi* operates on multiple levels. For one, the place of Khwaja Ahmad in the narrative points toward the ways in which Sufi teachers contributed to the very process of writing history. This is of particular significance because stories about Mongol conversions to Islam far more often appear in works of hagiography than in history (*tarikh*), the genre in which Mirza Haydar firmly locates his text.⁶¹ Pushing the boundaries of genre, he gives prominence to a Sufi perspective on Moghul and Islamic history.

The conversion narrative is also one example where the Dughlat historian draws from oral tradition, a methodological tendency that is connected to the larger anxiety over marginalization underlying his project. In the opening of the *Tarikh-i Rashidi*, Mirza Haydar explains his decision to write the history as motivated by the lack of textual sources: the Moghuls "remember their ancestors merely by oral accounts," which the Dughlat historian thought would "disappear entirely from the pages of time" as the khanate fell from political ascendancy.⁶² This fear of historical marginalization leads Mirza Haydar to describe the process of writing the *Tarikh-i Rashidi* as a "grave task" at the outset of the text.⁶³

Mirza Haydar situates the conversion narrative of Tughlugh-Temür as a critical intervention against the marginalization of Moghul historical memory. In particular, he highlights how the narrative added depth to the existing Moghul oral tradition around Tughlugh-Temür: "I heard these stories [the conversion narrative] from Mawlana Khwaja Ahmad, a trustworthy man. Among the Moghuls it is told only that Tughlugh-Temür Khan became Muslim. No one knows anything of Mawlana

Arshaduddin or the particulars of the story."[64] For Mirza Haydar, writing history necessitated combining multiple streams of historical memory—not only Moghul oral tradition but also stories passed down by Sufi teachers—in order to combat the marginalization of the khanate. In short, the conversion narrative of Tughlugh-Temür can be read as a Sufi-derived remedy to the marginalization of both Moghul history and the Islamic history of Central Asia.

Moreover, the conversion narrative accentuates the ways in which the historian incorporates Dughlat voices into the history of Islam. Take, for instance, the immediate aftermath of the conversion as depicted in the *Tarikh-i Rashidi*. The day after Tughlugh-Temür converted, he offered Amir Tülāk, who at the time was head of the Dughlat lineage, the chance to do the same. After being invited by the khan to convert to Islam, "'Amir Tülāk began to weep, saying, 'I converted three years ago at the hand of the pious men of Kashgar, but because of my fear of you I was unable to let it be known. What happiness could be better than this?' The khan rose and embraced him."[65] The role Mirza Haydar gives to Amir Tülāk in the narrative can be said to operate on multiple registers, at once preferential and deferential vis-à-vis the khan. For one, Amir Tülāk is described as having converted to Islam years *before* Tughlugh-Temür, giving the Dughlat leader a sort of upper hand when it comes to personal piety. At the same time, however, Amir Tülāk attributes the secrecy of his conversion to his fear of Tughlugh-Temür, a display of deference to the khan that would be expected on the part of a Turko-Mongol aristocrat. Therefore, the ways in which Mirza Haydar depicts Amir Tülāk give the Dughlat leader a favorable, but appropriate, position relative to Tughlugh-Temür.

In narrating the conversion of Amir Tülāk, Mirza Haydar also situates his Dughlat ancestor against members of rival aristocratic lineages. For instance, according to him, it was only after Tughlugh-Temür approached Amir Tüläk that, "one by one, the amirs were offered a chance to convert."[66] That the Dughlat aristocrat was the first amir approached by Tughlugh-Temür suggests his close relationship with the khan, perhaps even a relationship more intimate than that between the khan and other amirs. His conversion is also described as having predated that of other aristocrats, lending an additional air of piety to Amir Tüläk with respect to rival lineages. This appears to be even more the case when Mirza Haydar relates a story about an amir from the Chiras lineage whose conversion could be described as conditional (in the sense that he would only convert if Mawlana Arshaduddin successfully wrestled a warrior known for his almost otherworldly strength).[67] In short, Mirza Haydar can be said to give Amir Tüläk a preferential position vis-à-vis his political rivals.

That Mirza Haydar lends prominence to Dughlat and Sufi voices in his telling of the conversion is significant because he takes a similar approach in narrating his own experience of personal and political crisis. As discussed earlier, Mirza Haydar was writing at a time when the royal/aristocratic relationship, as well as understandings of kinship, were changing. As a consequence of these broader changes, he was writing the *Tarikh-i Rashidi* while in political and physical exile from the Moghul khanate. The Dughlat historian found a solution to the varied challenges of exile in the form of Sufi teachers affiliated with the Naqshbandi order. Thus, stressing Dughlat and Sufi agency in the conversion of the khanate can be read as a strong parallel with the contemporary experience of Mirza Haydar as the historian who lived and wrote on the margins of Mongol society.

The point here is not to say that Mirza Haydar "made up" the history, inserting his Dughlat and Sufi connections in a display of self-interest. Instead it is to emphasize the significance of his editorial choices in the *Tarikh-i Rashidi* and to explore what those choices meant in their historical context. We could imagine, for instance, a history of the khanate in which the author narrates the conversion of Tughlugh-Temür without bringing Amir Tüläk into the picture; we could also imagine a history of the khanate not framed in terms of Islam, a text in which Sufi oral tradition plays a less prominent role, if even included at all. All of this is to highlight the possibilities of approaching the process of history-writing from the margins—that is, reading between the lines to construct a vision of the social realities behind the text.[68] By focusing on aspects of the *Tarikh-i Rashidi* such as Sufi poetry, the conversion narrative, and tales of authorial hardship, this chapter suggests that telling the story of Central Asia and of Islam is a historically contingent process, tied up in early modern changes to kinship patterns, political culture, and religious life.

By way of conclusion, it is appropriate to end with a word from Mirza Haydar himself. In a concluding section to the *Tarikh-i Rashidi*, he writes: "No one other than a Moghul will derive any benefit from these words and what they convey. It is for that reason that I realized it would be burdensome to impose the composition on a literary person. I did not, however, let my own lack of talent and ability detain me, and insofar as it was possible I ran my untalented pen across the pages of inability."[69] Here, Mirza Haydar assumes an authorial pose of humility, a generic convention of contemporaneous literature, and downplays his contributions as a historian. Given the tendency for early modern historians to self-represent as untalented, it is difficult to gauge the extent to which he understood his role as historian in such a way. Regardless of how he conceptualized his own journey as a historian, it is clear that the *Tarikh-i Rashidi* is valuable far beyond the narrow confines of Moghul history. The work continues to speak in the contemporary moment, providing a valuable window into the challenges and possibilities of including the Moghul khanate and of Islamic Central Asia in how we explain the history of Islam and its margins more generally.

NOTES

Epigraph: Mirza Haydar Dughlat, *Tarikh-i-Rashidi: A History of the Khans of Moghulistan, English Translation*, trans. Wheeler M. Thackston (Cambridge, Mass.: Department of Near Eastern Languages and Civilizations, Harvard University, 1996), 85; cited hereafter as *TR-T*.

1. David Morgan, "The Decline and Fall of the Mongol Empire," *Journal of the Royal Asiatic Society* 19, no. 4 (2009): 427–37.
2. The standard treatment of Amir Temür is Beatrice Forbes Manz, *The Rise and Rule of Tamerlane* (Cambridge: Cambridge University Press, 1989). For later Timurid rulers, see Beatrice Forbes Manz, *Power, Politics, and Religion in Timurid Iran* (Cambridge: Cambridge University Press, 2007); and Maria E. Subtelny, *Timurids in Transition: Turko-Persian Politics and Acculturation in Medieval Iran* (Leiden: Brill, 2007).
3. The ways in which Chinggisid and Timurid legacies played out in the early modern Islamicate empires are far too complex to unpack in full. Ali Anooshahr has considered how these emergent states navigated the question of Turko-Mongol origins in his *Turkestan and the Rise of Eurasian Empires: A Study of Politics and Invented Traditions* (Oxford: Oxford University Press, 2018). On the Timurid heritage, see Stephen Frederic Dale, "The Legacy of the Timurids," *Journal of the Royal Asiatic Society* 8, no. 1 (1998): 43–58; and Maria E. Subtelny, "The Timurid Legacy: A Reaffirmation and a Reassessment," *Cahiers d'Asie Centrale*, nos. 3–4 (1997): 9–19.
4. Rachida Chih, "The Apogee and Consolidation of Sufi Teachings and Organizational Forms," in *The Wiley Blackwell History of Islam*, ed. Armando Salvatore (Hoboken, N.J.: Wiley, 2018), 413–31.
5. The literature on Islamicate history-writing during the early modern period is vast. See Anooshahr, *Turkestan and the Rise of Eurasian*

Empires; Cornell F. Fleischer, *Bureaucrat and Intellectual in the Ottoman Empire: The Historian Mustafa Âli, 1541–1600* (Princeton, N.J.: Princeton University Press, 1986); Kaya Şahin, *Empire and Power in the Reign of Süleyman: Narrating the Sixteenth-Century Ottoman World* (Cambridge: Cambridge University Press, 2013); and Sholeh A. Quinn, *Historical Writing During the Reign of Shah 'Abbas: Ideology, Imitation, and Legitimacy in Safavid Chronicles* (Salt Lake City: University of Utah Press, 2000).

6. Kinship relations continue to play an important role in lived experience across the Islamicate world. For a view from contemporary India, see Holly Donahue Singh's chapter in this volume.

7. Scholars have long noted the patriarchal and patrilineal nature of Turko-Mongol kinship. See Maria E. Subtelny, "Bābur's Rival Relations: A Study of Kinship and Conflict in 15th–16th Century Central Asia," *Der Islam* 66 (1989): 106–7.

8. *TR-T*, 29–30.

9. Scholars continue to debate how to best conceptualize social organization in Central Asia. Anthropologist David Sneath has led the charge against using the categories of "tribe" and "clan" to understand Central Asian societies. Instead, Sneath advocates for the concept of "aristocratic lineage" in attempt to acknowledge the internal conflict within nomadic groups. For his argument in whole, see David Sneath, *The Headless State: Aristocratic Orders, Kinship Society, and Misrepresentations of Nomadic Inner Asia* (New York: Columbia University Press, 2007). For a summary, critique, and response, see David Sneath, "A Response to Critics," *Ab Imperio* 4 (2009): 164–75.

Here, I view the Dughlat as a polity, and the family with which Mirza Haydar affiliates himself as an aristocratic lineage within the larger polity, which comprised multiple lineages (not all of which were aristocratic). When referencing the "Dughlat lineage," I actually mean the line in which Mirza Haydar places himself (*TR-T*, 31).

10. *TR-T*, 3.
11. For the definition of *mīrzā*, see Subtelny, *Timurids in Transition*, 43n1.
12. *TR-T*, 64.
13. Anooshahr, *Turkestan and the Rise of Eurasian Empires*, 117.
14. *TR-T*, 244.
15. *TR-T*, 81.

16. *TR-T*, 83.
17. *TR-T*, 31.
18. *TR-T*, 277–80.
19. *TR-T*, 4.
20. *TR-T*, 5.
21. *TR-T*, 83–84.
22. Members of the Barlas lineage played key roles in establishing Timurid political supremacy vis-à-vis the Chaghatayid-Moghul khanate. For one such amir, see Ali Rıza Yağlı, "Timurlu Devleti Emîrleri I—Barlas Boyu: Caku Barlas" [Amirs of the Timurid State I: Caku Barlas], *Hacettepe Üniversitesi Türkiyat Araştırmaları Dergisi* 32 (Spring 2020): 221–32.
23. *TR-T*, 84.
24. *TR-T*, 81, 244.
25. *TR-T*, 79.
26. The literature on early modern affectivity is rich. For a relevant volume, see Kishwar Rizvi, ed., *Affect, Emotion, and Subjectivity in Early Modern Muslim Empires: New Studies in Ottoman, Safavid, and Mughal Art and Culture* (Leiden: Brill, 2017).
27. Barbara Rosenwein has developed a somewhat similar concept of "emotional communities," defined as "precisely the same as social communities—families, neighborhoods, parliaments, guilds, monasteries, parish church memberships—but the researcher looking at them seeks above all to uncover systems of feeling: what these communities (and the individuals within them) define and assess as valuable or harmful to them; the evaluations that they make about others' emotions; the nature of the affective bonds between people that they recognize; and the modes of emotional expression that they expect, encourage, tolerate, and deplore." Barbara H. Rosenwein, "Worrying About Emotions in History," *American Historical Review* 107, no. 3 (2002): 842. Whereas Rosenwein "seeks above all to uncover systems of feeling," I have a somewhat different goal in mind (i.e., to examine how affective relationships shaped and reflected larger sociopolitical changes).
28. Nurten Kılıç-Schubel, "Familial Affection, Brotherly Love, and the Royal Tears of Grief: Emotions, Sibling Relations, and the Making of New Chinggisid Families in the 16th Century" (paper presented at the annual Central Eurasian Studies Society conference, University of

Pittsburgh, October 26, 2018). Thank you to Professor Kılıç-Schubel for sharing this paper with me.

29. Sufi thought and practice continues to be a critical part of Islamic spirituality around the world. For a view from contemporary Turkey, see Tess Waggoner's chapter in this volume.

30. Jürgen Paul, "The Rise of the Khwajagan-Naqshbandiyya Sufi Order in Timurid Herat," in *Afghanistan's Islam: From Conversion to the Taliban*, ed. Nile Green (Oakland: University of California Press, 2016), 71–86; Jo-Ann Gross, "The Economic Status of a Timurid Sufi Shaykh: A Matter of Conflict or Perception?," *Iranian Studies* 21, nos. 1–2 (1988): 84–104.

31. For a royal connected with the Naqshbandi-Ahrariyya, see A. Azfar Moin, "Peering Through the Cracks in the *Baburnama*: The Textured Lives of Mughal Sovereigns," *Indian Economic and Social History Review* 49, no. 4 (2012): 493–526.

32. Thomas Hayoz, "Hagiographic Tendencies in the *Tarikh-i Rashidi*: Mirza Haydar Dughlat's Hagio-Historiographic Way of Writing History," in *Proceedings of the Ninth Conference of the European Society for Central Asian Studies*, ed. Tomasz Gacek and Jadwiga Pstrusińska (Newcastle upon Tyne: Cambridge Scholars, 2009), 149–56.

33. That Mirza Haydar identifies writing a history of the Chaghatayid-Moghul khanate as his central goal complicates reading the work as hagio-historiography, when Sufi hagiography is understood as making an argument for the sanctity of the *'awliyā'*. For Sufi hagiography so conceived, see Shahzad Bashir, "Naqshband's Lives: Sufi Hagiography Between Manuscript and Genre," in *Sufism in Central Asia: New Perspectives on Sufi Traditions, 15th–21st Centuries*, ed. Devin DeWeese and Jo-Ann Gross (Leiden: Brill, 2018), 75–97.

34. *TR-T*, 247.

35. See, for example, the articulation of this understanding of Sufi poetry as necessarily ambiguous provided by Dick Davis in his introduction to *Faces of Love: Hafez and the Poets of Shiraz* (New York: Penguin, 2012), especially xviii–lxvi.

36. See William C. Chittick, *Divine Love: Islamic Literature and the Path to God* (New Haven, Conn.: Yale University Press, 2013), especially chapter 5.

37. For a similar approach applied to a contemporary and maternal relation of Mirza Haydar, see Stephen F. Dale, "The Poetry and Autobiography of the Bâbur-nâma," *Journal of Asian Studies* 55, no. 3 (1996): 635–64.
38. *TR-T*, 247.
39. *TR-T*, 269–70.
40. It is important, however, not to assign a singular meaning to Sufi poetry. For the centrality of ambiguity in the intellectual world in which Mirza Haydar was writing, see Shahab Ahmed, *What Is Islam? The Importance of Being Islamic* (Princeton, N.J.: Princeton University Press, 2016), especially chapter 5.
41. For the relationship between *walāya* (saintly authority) and *wilāya* (divine proximity), see Vincent J. Cornell, *Realm of the Saint: Power and Authority in Moroccan Sufism* (Austin: University of Texas Press, 1998).
42. The relationship between saint and ruler, however, often did shape the contours of religious and political experience. See Muzaffar Alam, "The Mughals, the Sufi Shaikhs, and the Formation of the Akbari Dispensation," *Modern Asian Studies* 43, no. 1 (2009): 135–74.
43. Kılıç-Schubel, "Familial Affection, Brotherly Love."
44. For more on the broader changes to the Turko-Mongol aristocracy during this period, see Ali Anooshahr, "Mughals, Mongols, and Mongrels: The Challenge of Aristocracy and the Rise of the Mughal State in the *Tarikh-i Rashidi*," *Journal of Early Modern History* 18, no. 6 (2014): 559–77.
45. For a helpful overview, see Peter Jackson, "Reflections on the Islamization of Mongol Khans in Comparative Perspective," *Journal of the Economic and Social History of the Orient* 62 (2019): 356–87.
46. *TR-T*, 4.
47. For a rich discussion on the challenges and possibilities of using "marginalization" as a theoretical frame, see Max Johnson Dugan's chapter in this volume.
48. Devin DeWeese, *Islamization and Native Religion in the Golden Horde: Baba Tükles and Conversion to Islam in Historical and Epic Tradition* (University Park: Penn State University Press, 1994), 10.
49. For another consideration of Islamization from the margins, also drawing from the work of Devin DeWeese, see Edward E. Curtis's chapter in this volume.

50. My thinking here is influenced by the work of Shahab Ahmed, who conceptualizes Islam as meaning-making in terms of hermeneutical engagement with Revelation to the Prophet Muhammad. See Ahmed, *What Is Islam?*, especially chapter 6.
51. *TR-T*, 85; emphasis mine.
52. *TR-T*, 9.
53. *TR-T*, 9.
54. *TR-T*, 10.
55. *TR-T*, 10. For a closer look at the dream narrative, see Sholeh A. Quinn, "The Timurid Historiographical Legacy: A Comparative Study of Persianate Historical Writing," in *Society and Culture in the Early Modern Middle East: Studies on Iran in the Safavid Period*, ed. Andrew J. Newman (Leiden: Brill, 2003), 29–31.
56. *TR-T*, 10.
57. For a helpful contextualization of the conversion narrative in terms of broader trends in hagiography, see Saif Beg, "Religious Conversions and the *Tarikh-i-Rashidi*" (unpublished manuscript, n.d.), https://www.academia.edu/34542227/Religious_Conversions_and_the_Tarikh_i_Rashidi (accessed September 27, 2022).
58. DeWeese, *Islamization and Native Religion*, 137.
59. *TR-T*, 8. The "Sublime Order of the Khwajas" refers to the Khwajagan, a network of Sufi teachers in Central Asia who were active in the medieval and early modern periods. Many within this network were later incorporated into Naqshbandi lineages. For a relevant overview, see Paul, "Rise of the Khwajagan-Naqshbandiyya Sufi Order," 71–86.
60. *TR-T*, 8.
61. Beg, "Religious Conversions and the *Tarikh-i-Rashidi*"; Hayoz, "Hagiographic Tendencies in the *Tarikh-i Rashidi*."
62. *TR-T*, 3.
63. *TR-T*, 3.
64. *TR-T*, 11.
65. *TR-T*, 10.
66. *TR-T*, 10–11.
67. *TR-T*, 11. Saif Beg notes that this type of physical test is common in hagiographic literature, citing similar examples in sources from the Golden Horde studied by Devin DeWeese. See Beg, "Religious

Conversions and the *Tarikh-i-Rashidi*"; and DeWeese, *Islamization and Native Religion*.
68. This approach was first applied to Islamicate literary sources by Marilyn Robinson Waldman in her *Toward a Theory of Historical Narrative: A Case Study in Perso-Islamicate Historiography* (Columbus: Ohio State University Press, 1980).
69. *TR-T*, 85.

8

JOURNEY TO THE TEACHING OF ISLAM

KATHRYN D. BLANCHARD

The award-winning 2020 documentary *My Octopus Teacher* traces the soul-searching journey of South African filmmaker Craig Foster. Suffering from burnout and depression and driven by a longing to be "inside of the natural world," he returned to the ocean of his childhood.[1] While diving in a kelp forest—where "you might as well be on another planet"—he met an octopus, whom he ended up following every day for a year. Over time, watching her in her habitat, learning her patterns, letting her get used to him, building a two-way relationship with her, he grew to better understand her alien behaviors and ingenious survival mechanisms. "Something happens when that animal makes contact," he says. Soon *she* begins to follow *him*, her curiosity piqued. The film ends up a bittersweet example of what scientists call the "observer effect": studying something always changes it, especially if that some*thing* is a some*one*.

When I first stepped into the classroom as a religious studies professor, I had to make decisions about whether I wanted to study someones as if they were somethings, like a zoologist who, according to certain strands of scientific orthodoxy, "does not allow the octopus upon his dissecting table to inquire whether or not it belongs to the family *Cephalopoda*."[2] I agonized over whether religion students should engage the persons whom they study as partners in their research, or if should they instead watch from afar, as if they were merely animal "data" to be mined for information and insights.[3] This dilemma, the so-called insider/outsider problem, was an unavoidable stumbling block to me, as it is to anyone who seeks to learn about religions and religious people from behind proverbial safety glass, without messy entanglements that might mar the purity of our findings.

Students are rightly taught that there are countless ways to study the human phenomenon commonly known as "religion." You can study your own sacred scriptures in a community of faith—the Bible in a church among Christians, the Qur'an in a mosque among Muslims, the Bhagavad Gita in a temple among Hindus. You can study the theology of a single tradition—often via the writings of particularly smart, powerful, and prolific dead men (and perhaps the exceptional woman), whether ancient or contemporary. You can study the history of your own or others' traditions—the traditions of China, India, the Americas, the Mediterranean, or the Middle East—accessed through texts as well as architecture, artifacts, and other pieces of material culture. Or you can study a particular living community as an ethnographer, immersing yourself among them, observing every detail of their behaviors, perhaps even, to some extent, participating. In studying religion, depending upon the approach you take to inquiry and the tools you have at your disposal, there are countless insights to be had or truths to be encountered. Likewise, there are just as many half-truths to be told, whether stemming from accidental misunderstanding or willful ignorance.

In my training as a Christian theologian-ethicist, I studied as an insider, no matter how marginalized I might sometimes feel in my own tradition. When I became a teacher, the insider-outsider problem haunted my preparation. Was I in any position to see religion, religions, or religious people as they "really are," without negative or positive prejudice, without an agenda or axe to grind? Could I teach about Islam and Muslims the same way I taught about Christianity and Christians, especially in classrooms full of mostly non-Muslims? These questions were not merely academic, especially at the height of the war on terror; what people know about Islam can quite literally be a life-and-death matter for Muslims. In Michigan, where I lived and taught, about 2.75 percent of the population is Muslim, but students' knowledge about Islam can also end up affecting Muslims around the world.[4] Today, most students enter college with at least some awareness of Islam and Muslims, but this can be a mixed blessing: "Although U.S. media outlets frequently cover Islam, and stories about Muslims repeatedly dominate the news in the context of religion and politics, the coverage is highly negative."[5] A few students may have learned more than mere stereotypes in a history or social studies class along the way, but it is the rare young adult who comes into a religious studies classroom with any robust understanding even of *their own* tradition (if they have one), much less of Islam or other religions.

My struggles with the insider/outsider problem—and, specifically, with the question of how to teach about Islam—were shaped in dialogue not only with my present but also my past. Whether I was conscious of it or not, my personal history shaped my eventual approach to teaching Islam. Once upon a time, I was myself a college student entering a religious studies course with no prior knowledge of Islam. An Evangelical Christian, I wanted to understand the beliefs of my religious opponents, the better to prove them wrong and persuade them to become Christians. For a teenager, I knew quite a bit about the New

Testament, and mistakenly thought I knew all I needed to know about Christianity and Judaism. But I was fully aware of my ignorance about other traditions. Learning about religions in general, and Islam in particular, changed my worldview radically and with it, the course of my life. It helped turn me away from a career in proselytizing as a Christian missionary and set me on a new course to become a religious studies professor. My own zig-zagging journey as both insider and outsider, in Christianity and in various academic contexts, led to my pedagogical approach, which emphasized diversity and complexity—not just *among* or *between* religions, but, even more importantly, *within* each tradition, including Islam.

INSIDER BEGINNINGS

My religious education before college happened entirely outside of a school setting. I was a product of the public school system, where instruction *about* religion (as opposed to *of* or *for* practitioners of particular religions) has been legal since at least 1963, but where most teachers and administrators would prefer to avoid topics that might provoke angry parents.[6] With the occasional exception of an allusion in literature or major figure in the European wars of Catholics versus Protestants, I have no recollection of learning anything about religion as a subject of academic study. Religion was what I learned at home from my mom, at church from my Sunday school teachers and bible study leaders, and in youth groups, both at my Christian and Missionary Alliance church and in a local Campus Life chapter. Almost to a person, these instructors stressed the *individual* nature of salvation and sanctification, the need for me personally to be humble, loving, pure, and forgiving; to pray, read my Bible, and share my faith with as many people as possible. At the beginning of my first year of college, I was recruited by a Campus Crusade for Christ "discipler," who continued the type of Evangelical Christian study to which I was accustomed. My approach to life wasn't really "religion," I judged; "faith" in Christ was its own thing, more like spirituality, not subject to categories and classifications, utterly distinct from the "ritualistic" and "idolatrous" practices of Catholics and other "nominal" Christians (to say nothing of those who weren't any kind of Christian) who just went through the motions.

It is not unusual for a college sophomore to be naïvely confident, nor to embark upon religious studies or world religions classes as a way of clarifying their own spiritual worldviews by classifying others.[7] Young adults are often actively invested in searching for meaning on their own terms. Like some of them, I took my first religious studies course with a personal agenda, not to have my worldview challenged but in order that I could refute others' wrong beliefs about the universe. I saw myself as an insider to the truth, with everyone except the narrowest slice of fellow Christians as outsiders—destined for eternal damnation if not saved. I couldn't yet truly imagine a world full of people who were as much the protagonists of their own life stories as I was in mine. The fact that my religious persuasion was relatively unusual, even weird, in my upper-middle-class social circles was no reason for discouragement; on the contrary, it seemed to prove that I was right, on the side of the underdogs. "Blessed are you when they revile and persecute you, and say all kinds of evil against you falsely for My sake. Rejoice and be exceedingly glad, for great is your reward in heaven, for so they persecuted the prophets who were before you" (Matt. 5:11–12).

Somehow I made it through my introductory religion course with my faith intact. Sure, I had encountered a host of new traditions that I'd never read about before, perhaps for two to three weeks at a time. I had gone on a Joseph-Campbell-inspired hero's journey through the Five Pillars of Islam as well as Black Elk, the Pentateuch, no self, and terms like "ultimate concern" (via Paul Tillich) and "sacred and profane" (via Mircea Eliade), and arrived right back at Evangelicalism. It was easy enough to dismiss these snapshots of others' rituals and artifacts as cultural groping in the dark, mistakes of those not lucky enough to be born into Christendom. At that point, knowing about others still didn't seem as important as understanding my own tradition better. That is, until I encountered Islam for the second time.

I do not remember ever thinking about Islam before college. As a child I knew about someone in Iran called the Ayatollah Khomeini, who didn't like someone else there called the Shah, and I knew that there were American hostages, and it was all somehow president Jimmy Carter's fault. But the words "Islam" or "Muslim" meant nothing to me. At that stage in my life, I thought everyone in the world was either Jewish, Christian, or Catholic (Christian and Catholic being two different things in my mind, since "we" went to church and Sunday School, and "they" went to mass and CCD, whatever that was). As I grew a bit older, during the Reagan years, I knew there were people in Russia called Communists who were atheists, who didn't believe in God at all. Though I had actually met Muslims (as well as Hindus and Buddhists) in my New Jersey youth, most folks didn't usually talk about religion in polite company, so the world's billion-plus Muslims were still off my radar. What finally made my ignorance uncomfortable was Operation Desert Storm in 1991. (In pre-Google days, a friend took me to the map room of the library to show me where on earth the Persian Gulf was; I also hadn't known Chicago was on a lake until 1988, so my geographical ignorance was domestic as well as international.) I no longer remember why, but I decided it might be important for me, now a junior, to learn more about Saddam Hussein's religion. That was when I enrolled in a semester-long course with Dr. Vernon Schubel, Classical Islam, which would change just about everything I thought I knew about life.

The biggest shock was that Islamic teaching shared so much with Christian teaching. Islam was a matter of voluntary faith rather than bloodlines. Muslims believed in the Jewish God and the Jewish prophets, just like I did; their sacred history was tied to my sacred history. They humbled themselves before God, gave alms to the poor, fasted, and prayed. And they invested Jesus with high significance. Indeed, we Christians seemed to have even *more* in common with Muslims than with Jews—a relationship that had been part of my religious self-understanding since earliest memory—so how could I have never known about this third member of the Abrahamic club? Islam disturbed me in a way Judaism did not, because Muslims felt the need to *correct* Christians' misunderstanding of Jesus's nature as the only begotten son of God. This wasn't a mere difference of opinion; Christians had willfully made idolaters of ourselves by turning Jesus from a human into a god, one with the creator of the universe. Perhaps for the first time, *I* felt what it was like to be the octopus under the microscope; I was the one to be pitied, whose wrong beliefs might send me to hell.[8] I was the outsider to the truth. Ultimately this had the effect not of converting me from one religion to another, but of forcing me to question them both.

Inexplicably, I still spent the following summer with missionaries in Papua New Guinea. (It sounded better than the other option—trying to convert Europeans on the streets of Prague with Campus Crusade.) While these missionaries were self-proclaimed biblical literalists, they disagreed on mission strategy with the Campus Crusade biblical literalists of my acquaintance, a contradiction that added to the slow drip of doubt in my mind. "If they both say they take the Bible literally and still disagree, there must be more to interpretation than I thought. And if reading the Bible is a matter of interpretation . . .": well, that changed everything. In my Mysticism seminar that fall I read St. Teresa's *Interior Castle*, in which she surprised me by sounding Christian, despite being Catholic. (Like many Evangelicals, I did not consider Catholics "real" Christians because they "worshipped" Mary and relied too heavily on "empty ritual.") Some of her thoughts also sounded remarkably similar to those in *The Conference of the Birds* and various Buddhist texts we read, forcing me to ask what it meant that individuals from so many different traditions could have insights and come to conclusions about the universe that seemed so alike.[9] In my Fundamentalism seminar I learned that the brand of Christianity I took for granted was a relatively recent American invention—Christians had not always insisted upon reading the Bible literally—and that it fit a pattern that could potentially be observed among other religious traditions.[10] There were Muslim or Hindu folks who sought to adhere as closely to the "literal" meanings of their sacred texts as I thought I did, for reasons that might or might not resemble my own. If, as an outsider, I could see how historically bound others' sacred texts were, what business did I have trying to protect my own from critical analysis?

Like untold numbers of other students of religion, I found "exposure to Muslims' direct experiences to be some of the most illuminating elements of the class itself," with great "positive affective power and impact," as well as significant disturbance.[11] The slow drip of doubt reached a tipping point in my senior year, and things began to fall apart. With loss of certainty about my faith went certainty about my future. I lost several important relationships with friends who felt betrayed by my lack of faith, who could not or would not entertain the questions that now preoccupied me. I suddenly found myself on the margins of my own group—perhaps even a full-fledged outsider. I am grateful my family and some friends remained true, and that I had my religion classes to provide conversation partners till graduation. Although this change seemed to arrive suddenly in 1992, it didn't happen overnight; it happened because developmental groundwork had been laid, and I was finally ready for change. At the same time, I was not at all ready to lose most of what I had known, and I hadn't yet discerned into what I was changing.

OUTSIDER WANDERINGS

When I left college in a deep depression, I knew for sure that I did not want to be a Christian missionary (or a "missionary's wife," as the option was presented to me), but no new idea for my future had yet taken its place. True to what would become a Generation X stereotype, I moved in with my parents and worked retail (Seattle's coffee trend had not quite made it to the Midwest so "barista" was not yet an option). My liberal arts education had prepared me well to become a bookseller at the late Borders bookstore. It was perhaps meant to be: *The Golden Bough*, which I had read for my Approaches to the Study of Religion seminar with Dr. Schubel, was the answer to a question on the job application test. In those days I sometimes dragged myself to church when I wasn't working on Sundays, just to make my mother happy, but my heart wasn't in it. I didn't know what I believed, and I wasn't sure I even wanted answers anymore.

My coworkers were an intellectually stimulating mix of people with all kinds of viewpoints on the world, and because, for once, I wasn't worried about how to rescue them from their journeys to hell, I could enjoy and learn from them. We recommended books and movies to each other, talked about politics, and never discussed discipleship. But I am a restless person who gets bored when I am not learning new things, so it wasn't long before I began missing school. I come from an educated but not academic family, so I had no idea what my options were. My dad suggested I could get PhD in religion, so I began to prepare. I learned German, took the GRE, studied U.S. News rankings, and applied to three schools: one university, one divinity school, and one seminary, where I happened to know someone from college. In the end I enrolled at Princeton Theological Seminary because it seemed the friendliest. To my surprise, it turned out to be full of Christians who wanted to be church pastors! Everyone's first getting-to-know-you question was, "What's your denomination?" All my coursework was about Christianity; there were disappointingly few options for studying other religions. I feared that I had made a terrible mistake.

And yet. The next three years ended up becoming an exciting and nourishing experience. Instead of being the lone conservative Christian in a secular religious studies classroom, I often found myself the lone "none" in a room full of true believers.[12] (I finally began calling myself "denominationally challenged.") But these Christians, mostly members of "mainline" churches, weren't like the Evangelicals I had known. They took for granted that reading scripture required at least some degree of interpretation (preferably incorporating Greek or Hebrew), and that understanding the history and traditions of Christianity and Judaism was crucial to interpreting the current iterations I saw around me. The coursework challenged me intellectually in ways I couldn't have anticipated. The greatest impact, apart from learning a new mode of biblical study, was learning about various liberation theologies: Latin American, Black, and feminist. A Christianity that put the poor and marginalized at its center was spiritually invigorating and inspiring (once I got over the hurdles of my white fragility and savior complex). By the end of seminary, I was back to seeing myself as some kind of Christian. I took a job in a church-funded food pantry, married a future Presbyterian clergyman, and went to an Episcopal church. The academic study of religion—in this case, of Christianity from the perspective of marginalized insiders—changed the course of my life again, sending me back into the fold, albeit a new one.

After a few years of working in the nonprofit sector, I began to feel restless again, frustrated with the slowness and apparent futility of small band-aid ways of helping my neighbors in need. The problem was the system, I realized, which required systemic solutions and not only stopgap measures. So, with more naivete than I should have had by the age of thirty, I set off to get a PhD as a way to figure out something bigger to do—namely, first to write a world-changing book with all the answers, and then to mold young minds in ways that would shape future generations of system-makers. I applied to several different kinds of programs and vowed to go to the best-name school I got into, just to increase the likelihood of getting a job when I finished. I got accepted into the theology and ethics program at Duke University, where I planned to study globalization and liberation theology.

Upon arrival, I again had the feeling of having made a terrible mistake. While there were subgroups of secular students in the religion department doing secular research on historical, linguistic, and ethnographic projects, the ethicists were embedded in the Divinity School and deeply tied to the insider study of Christian theology. As not-really-a-Presbyterian among mostly Catholics, Methodists, and Mennonites, I felt like a bad fit. The theologians I knew didn't seem to read liberation theologies, much less read religious texts from any traditions that weren't Judaism or Christianity. They certainly didn't talk about globalization, economic policy, or social systems; they talked about liturgy, ecclesiology, and pacifism. Even when 9/11 happened in the first month of the semester, no one seemed to think it important to take a course on Islamic theology, history, or practice. I spent my first year with devastating impostor syndrome, playing catchup and feeling utterly miserable.

Mercifully, things changed in the next couple of years. I began studying economic thought with a historian in the economics department, where I read mostly English-language writers who were practically minded and focused on life on the ground, rather than on ancient philosophies and metaphysical concepts. Additionally, I participated in a program called "Pathways to the Professoriate," which was designed to get graduate students to prepare to be teachers. I was paired up with a nearby college professor close to my own age, a feminist who had written an award-winning book on globalization. She was trained as a theologian, too, but at a seminary steeped in the liberation tradition that dwelt upon economic and political systems as well as race, class, and gender. She mentored me while treating me as an equal, and she helped me see a path from my theology PhD to an undergraduate college professoriate in religious studies—a path I had feared was closed to me forever because of my previous choices. With the help of these folks on the margins of my program, I was able to forge a research project on Christian economic ethics that satisfied the insiders of my department, at least enough for me to graduate. Through a combination of luck, timing, and privilege, I landed one of the last existing tenure-track jobs for a Christian theologian in an undergraduate setting. In 2006 I found myself back in a Midwestern college religious studies classroom.

PROFESSING AND PIVOTING

Thus began a new chapter in my insider-outsider journey in religious studies: professor at a small liberal arts college, one whose religious affiliation did not shape the overall curriculum (i.e., no religion required, beyond the chaplain's prayers at major college ceremonies). For the first time, it was my job to tell other people what to read, to decide what was most important for them to know. At first I thought it was also my job to keep my own religious background a secret from the students; I aspired to be a religious studies professor for outsiders, not a theology professor for insiders. Unlike my seminary and graduate school professors, most of my college professors had maintained outsider personas (at least to my beginner's eye), leaving their religious identities a mystery—or, if not entirely mysterious, at least left on the sidelines. One might be Jewish and teach Buddhism or Quaker and teach Islam, just as legitimately as a Catholic who teaches Catholicism. It shouldn't make a difference to the presentation of course content. Such a perception was not of my own making; historically, the secular study of religion "has either implicitly or explicitly favored 'outsider' perspectives. Even when religious studies scholars happen to be adherents and practitioners of the very religion they are analyzing, the expectation is that the scholar assumes the posture of an outside observer and 'brackets' his/her own religious commitments."[3] Conveniently, this approach would spare me the awkwardness of having to explain my own, marginally Christian religious identity to my students. I did the best I could in my first year to prevent classroom discussions from deteriorating into personal reflections on individual faith and story, so we could do "serious" religious studies.

In time, however, I decided this path was folly. I certainly saw the value of having the instructor keep spiritual disclosures to a minimum, so that students wouldn't feel afraid of offending my sensibilities or feel compelled to agree with me. But I realized the important opportunity I was missing by pretending to be objective and asking students to keep *their* personal lives out of the classroom. Students who took religion, an elective, did so precisely because they had a personal stake in "religious" questions, however defined.[14] The most engaged students were those who—not unlike myself in college—actually cared about "truth," and why different people practice and believe such different things. Asking them to leave their feelings and beliefs at the door was a sure way to hinder their full investment in the course. Requesting their feigned neutrality also meant that I would have difficulty knowing where they were coming from and therefore connecting with them. Whether or not I felt comfortable taking the big questions head on, as opposed to teaching cultural literacy and critical thinking about religion, those big questions were the reason I had students at all. I would need a better approach.

I had many objectives for myself and my students (none of which involved liberal indoctrination per se). The most basic of these, religious literacy, arose because I was teaching in rural Michigan to millennial students who, by definition, remembered 9/11.[15] My earliest generation of students had been in middle or high school when the towers fell, old enough to be traumatized as well as to have picked up many facile and deadly stereotypes about Muslims and terrorism that had proliferated in the years since. Just as I had sought to better understand back in 1991, many of my students—if they weren't Christians seeking affirmation of their childhood faith—were interested in what Muslims were all about. Most of my students would only ever take one religion class, usually to fulfill an arts and humanities requirement for general education. This meant that I might be the only religion professor they ever had, so I saw every class as my one precious opportunity to inform them. Each course, no matter the topic, included texts written by Muslims, whether on Islamic economics, women and gender, Jesus in Islam, Islam in China, or African American Islam. I always gave at least a brief lecture on Islam to provide context, stressing its close relationship with Judaism and Christianity. And eventually I offered a semester-long course on Judaism and Islam that allowed us to venture off the well-trodden path of basics or core content and into the margins, through, for example, feminist discourse or memoir.[16] When my two-person department became a one-person department in 2018, I felt an even greater responsibility to make this one small but meaningful point in the minds of future voters, workers, parents, and citizens: Muslims are people, too.

To help guide my students there, I created structured opportunities for them not only to learn content (prophets, Five Pillars, Qur'an, Mecca, Ramadan, hijab, Sunni and Shi'i, Jerusalem, judgment day, key dates, and population statistics) but also to think deeply about themselves and their own worldviews and habits. On the first day of class, when they introduced themselves, I began asking them to give us the quick version of their "religious baggage" as it related to why they were in the course. Their first essay was to answer some version of the question "What is religion and how do you know?," which was designed to help them sift through some of those assumptions and definitions. And they participated in small group "salons," where they told their religious autobiographies in greater detail to their groupmates, who listened carefully and asked follow-up questions. They then wrote reflection papers on this experience, which usually included either "I was surprised at how different all of our experiences were" or "I was surprised at how similar all of our experiences were," and always some version of "It was hard to talk about myself but it was really cool to hear other people's stories."

The purpose of these exercises was to create space where students could (OK, *had to*) move back and forth between center and margin, insider and outsider territories, while thinking deliberately about the terms they used to describe what they saw, heard, and felt. Learning "facts" as an outsider, just before or after talking about their insider "opinions" and experiences, helped drive home the ways each of us is shaped by our life stories and the contexts in which we find ourselves. If at first students saw Muslims and other religious folks as data to be investigated and comprehended—octopuses on the dissecting table—they were then put into the position of themselves playing the role of religious data for others to try to contextualize and comprehend. These exercises provided important reminders that, just as they saw themselves as individuals who may differ from others within their group, every tradition is internally diverse. If four white Christian adolescents from Michigan don't think and act exactly alike, they certainly can't expect two billion Muslims to do so.[17]

The very good news is that my students, by and large, were ready and willing to learn about Islam and other religious traditions, already accepting the existence of diversity and the principle of pluralism—a hopeful sign, when so much of what we see in mass media is precisely the opposite. Millennials and Gen Z are statistically less religious than previous generations, so they come with little training, open minds, and few defense mechanisms around eternal truth, ritual, or even ethics.[18] They have been steeped in tolerance, moral relativism, and anti-bullying messaging since childhood (at least up until 2016), and they desperately want to avoid offense or conflict with their peers. Many of them are hungry for knowledge, even if they don't want to read too much or are hesitant to talk about personal and political matters. Such students are delightfully easy to teach.

While there are many real dangers to having a non-Muslim, non-Islamicist teaching about Islam to non-Muslims in a non-Islamic context, it was an important part of my job for fifteen years, as well as of my own lifelong learning.[19] The "Islam hates us" trope has been all too prevalent in the past two decades, a sign of the continued need for religious studies in public and higher education.[20] "If 'an educated citizenry' is vital to the health of our democracy," as many of us think it is, "then providing accurate information on Muslim Americans is a civic duty."[21] But to help students be more receptive to absorbing accurate information, at least some effort must be made at self-awareness. Even if there is value in continued distinction between insider "theology," academic "religious studies," and practical "interfaith studies," in the end we are all octopuses, sometimes in the center, other times on the margins.[22] Knowing that gives students an important measure of humility when approaching others as living data.

IN AND OUT OF THE KELP FOREST

Religious studies scholar Russell McCutcheon argues forcefully that scholars of religion "do not exist to . . . help with or even appreciate someone's 'search for the spiritual.'"[23] Rather, religious studies is an exercise in structured curiosity about, and nuanced description of, particular human behaviors, institutions, and traditions. He writes, "As a scholar of religion, my interest is in the ways in which different groups of people attempt to negotiate what might best be called an unregulated social and political economy where competing value systems bump up against each other—sometimes in minor and sometimes in major ways."[24] Islam is a 1,400-year-old social movement, made up of countless subgroups bumping up against each other. The history of Islam provides an opportunity for students of religion to practice their descriptive and comparative skills, ideally without regard for their personal agendas—even to foster the common good. It is not the scholar's job to determine "whose version of Islam counts as authentic Islam."[25]

Readers can by now probably guess where I stand on this. As a student who has always been invested in the big questions that are the bread and butter of phenomena generally known as "religions," I understand the internal motivation such investment provides for many of us. But I am also keenly aware of the ways personal investment can skew the ways we look at other people and phenomena, especially if we don't even try to bracket our biases. "Each perspective is fraught with its own set of challenges,"[26] and, as Jawad Anwar Qureshi writes, "it is no guarantee of balanced insight, to be a Muslim, nor of impartiality, to be a non-Muslim."[27] Coming to see ourselves and our biases more clearly is one of the greatest gifts of the type of critical thinking that liberal arts colleges try to sell. There is tremendous creative possibility in the tension between insider and outsider, center and margin, normative and descriptive study. As Maria Dakake explains the inevitable blurring of ontological borders that occurs in studying religion: "The boundaries between theological/normative and analytical/critical approaches is not always as hard and fast one might expect, and this is especially so in precisely those areas of religious studies research and pedagogy that seem the most 'practical' in their application."[28] Like the South African diver who sometimes observed the octopus from afar and other times allowed her to embrace him, religion scholars—at least those of us not primarily interested in what scientists think of us—can float freely in and out of these modes of seeing and being.

In short, the insider/outsider problem may not be much of a problem after all. My former professor Vernon Schubel, in "Thoughts on Dissecting Octopus: Aaron Hughes, Marshall Hodgson, and Navigating the Normative/Descriptive Divide in the Study of Islam," reflects on what it means to study religion, constituted as it is by living specimens. Not himself an octopus, he rejects an either-or approach to religious studies so well that I quote it at length:

> We all have to negotiate the issue of the relationship of our religious identity (or lack of it) to our scholarship. Religious pre-commitments are certainly not the only pre-commitments that impact our work. I personally see no reason why people cannot teach about traditions to which they belong. Nor is there a problem with non-believers teaching about traditions in which they do not participate. I also have no problem with scholars who are engaging in rigorous 'normative' approaches to the study of religion presenting papers at the same academic meetings as those of us doing more descriptive and historical work. . . . I am even comfortable with people moving back and forth between these two modes of discourse. I, myself, sometimes speak and write as a Muslim, sometimes as a historian of religion, sometimes as both. For those of us who identify as Muslims it strikes me as perfectly natural that there will be times, especially when speaking to Muslim audiences, when we will draw on our knowledge

of the tradition to make statements that are more normative in character. I fail to see why doing so is somehow a violation of one's academic integrity.... It seems to me that as long as we remain conscious of our intentions and our audience, we can sometimes speak normatively and sometimes descriptively without losing our integrity as scholars.[29]

As a Christian ethicist, my written scholarship is generally normative (disagreement among Christians is the ground upon which Christian ethics is built). But as a professor exploring multiple traditions with my students, I have spent much more of my time in outsider mode, focusing on description and analytical critique and comparison, even usually wearing an outsider persona when teaching what is supposedly my own tradition. Sometimes I am an octopus in my natural habitat, sometimes an octopus debating with other octopuses, other times engaging in cross-species communication, as octopuses are known to do. And, sometimes, when I play the role of diver, the octopus "upends" what I think I know about myself.[30]

It was in my very first religious studies course back in 1989 that I heard the term "liminal space," referring to the moment in a rite of passage between what one was and what one is becoming—for example, those in the midst of a wedding, who are no longer single but not yet married, neither here nor quite there. The act of studying religion can perhaps be seen as a liminal space, where one is neither practicing any given religion, nor standing perfectly separate from the people and phenomena one observes. Instead of like a zoologist standing with a dissecting knife over a passive specimen pinned on a table, we are something more like a diver chasing an octopus on her native turf, "stepping into this completely different world." Even if "you realize there's a line that can't be crossed" (you will never *be* an octopus, after all), from a broader perspective "you're part of this place, not a visitor."[31] Once I accepted the creative tension in my role it wasn't a problem at all. Not everyone is comfortable in a liminal state. Some will go to herculean lengths to marginalize the octopus, to try to eliminate the risks that go along with allowing the scholar's data to talk back.[32] But, no matter how hard they might try, insider and outsider students of religion just can't seem to quit each other.[33] We always find ourselves swimming in the kelp pool together again around an ever-shifting center.

NOTES

1. *My Octopus Teacher*, directed by Pippa Ehrlich and James Reed (Netflix, 2020), https://www.netflix.com/title/81045007.
2. Vernon Schubel (paraphrasing J. Z. Smith, paraphrasing William James), "Thoughts on Dissecting Octopus: Aaron Hughes, Marshall Hodgson, and Navigating the Normative/Descriptive Divide in the Study of Islam," *Bulletin for the Study of Religion* 42, no. 4 (2014): 18.
3. See, for example, Matt Sheedy, "Religion Snapshots: On the Uses of 'Data,' Part 1," *Bulletin for the Study of Religion* (October 28, 2013), https://bulletin.equinoxpub.com/2013/10/religion-snapshots/.
4. Rebecca Karam and Muslims for American Progress, *An Impact Report of Muslim Contributions to Michigan* (Dearborn, Mich.: Institute for Social Policy and Understanding, 2017), https://www.muslimsforamericanprogress.org/an-impact-report-of-muslim-contributions-to-michigan (accessed September 28, 2022), 1.
5. Salih Sayilgan, "Unlearning What Is Learned: Teaching Islam in America in Light of Paulo Freire's Pedagogy," *Journal of Feminist Studies in Religion* 36, no. 1 (2020): 175. See also Neha Sahgal and Besheer Mohamed, "In the U.S. and Western Europe, People Say They Accept Muslims, but Opinions Are Divided on Islam," Pew Research Forum, October 8, 2019, https://www.pewresearch.org/fact-tank/2019/10/08/in-the-u-s-and-western-europe-people-say-they-accept-muslims-but-opinions-are-divided-on-islam/.

6. The majority of Supreme Court justices declared in *Abingdon v. Schempp* that "it might well be said that one's education is not complete without a study of comparative religion or the history of religion and its relationship to the advancement of civilization. It certainly may be said that the Bible is worthy of study for its literary and historic qualities. Nothing we have said here indicates that such study of the Bible or of religion, when presented objectively as part of a secular program of education, may not be effected consistently with the First Amendment." U.S. Supreme Court, *Abingdon School Dist. v. Schempp*, no. 142, June 17, 1963, https://caselaw.findlaw.com/us-supreme-court/374/203.html.
7. See Barbara Walvoord's important study of undergraduate religion students, *Teaching and Learning in College Introductory Courses* (Oxford: Blackwell, 2008).
8. It's important to acknowledge that not all Christians are as obsessed with hell as I was in my late adolescence; moreover, it is not a given in Islamic teaching that Christians, who like Jews are *Ahl al-Kitāb* (people of the book), must be eternally damned.
9. In the early 1990s, the "comparative religions" model still prevailed in religious studies, often with emphasis on the common characteristics that different traditions shared. In the twenty-first century this approach has fallen out of scholarly fashion in favor of emphasizing the uniqueness of each tradition, or even each subgroup of any given tradition; see, for example, Stephen Prothero, *God Is Not One: The Eight Rival Religions That Run the World—and Why Their Differences Matter* (New York: HarperOne, 2010). My narrative demonstrates the fact that the academic study of religion is itself a historical phenomenon and therefore in a constant state of change.
10. Again, using "fundamentalism" as a cross-cultural category is now generally frowned upon, since critics have raised our awareness that it is a term that arose in a particular time and place for a particular purpose to describe particular people; see Jonathan Z. Smith, "A Matter of Class: Taxonomies of Religion," *Harvard Theological Review* 89, no. 4 (1996): 402–3.
11. Courtney Dorroll and Phil Dorroll, "Teaching Islam in Contemporary America: Digital Ethnography and the Affective Challenges of Islamic Studies Pedagogy," *Teaching Theology and Religion* 20 (2017): 310.

12. The term "nones," used by researchers to describe people claiming no religious affiliation, wasn't in wide use till the 2010s. See Ryan P. Burge, *The Nones: Where They Came From, Who They Are, and Where They Are Going* (Minneapolis: Fortress, 2017).
13. Dorroll and Dorroll, "Teaching Islam in Contemporary America," 334.
14. This is not an article about definitions of "religion," but those wanting to know more might look at Bradley Herling, *A Beginner's Guide to the Study of Religion* (New York: Bloomsbury, 2015).
15. Dorroll and Dorroll, "Teaching Islam in Contemporary America," 305.
16. I have found feminist texts particularly helpful for students, who often come to class with mental models of oppressed Muslim women. Others concur: "Teaching Islam through feminist internal critique of the religion has the potential to introduce a more processual, contextual, and critical approach to Islam in religious education." Marianne Hafnor Bøe, "Controversies, Complexities, and Contexts: Teaching Islam Through Internal Feminist Critique of the Religion," *Religions* 11, no. 662 (2020): 14.
17. To avoid essentializing, reifying, or otherwise fostering caricatures of Islam, it is important to teach it as a living tradition with internal diversity, rather than a fixed entity that sprung up fully formed and has continued unaltered since the seventh century. See Farid Panjwani and Lynn Revell, "Religious Education and Hermeneutics: The Case of Teaching About Islam," *British Journal of Religious Education* 40, no. 3 (2018):, 268; 275.
18. Pew Resarch Forum, "Religious Landscape Study," 2015, https://www.pewforum.org/religious-landscape-study/ (accessed September 28, 2022).
19. See, for example, Glenn E. Sanders, "Thirty Years Teaching About Islam: Notes on the Classroom," *Fides et Historia* 51, no. 2 (Summer–Fall 2019): 122–26.
20. Jenna Johnson and Abigail Hauslohner, "'I think Islam hates us': A Timeline of Trump's Comments About Islam and Muslims," *Washington Post*, May 20, 2017, https://www.washingtonpost.com/news/post-politics/wp/2017/05/20/i-think-islam-hates-us-a-timeline-of-trumps-comments-about-islam-and-muslims/.
21. Karam and Muslims for American Progress, *Impact Report*, 3.

22. See Eboo Patel, "Toward a Field of Interfaith Studies," *AAC&U: Liberal Education* 99, no. 4 (Fall 2013), https://aacu.org/liberaleducation/2013/fall/patel (accessed September 28, 2022).
23. Russell T. McCutcheon, "And That's Why No One Takes the Humanities Seriously" (lecture at Lehigh University, October 2014), 11. The lecture was later included as a chapter in McCutcheon, *A Modest Proposal on Method* (Leiden: Brill, 2018).
24. Russell T. McCutcheon, "Introductory Remarks on the Academic Study of Islam" (paper presented at the University of Alabama Understanding Islam workshop, January 2003), 2.
25. Russell T. McCutcheon, "'It's a Lie. There's No Truth in It! It's a Sin!': On the Limits of the Humanistic Study of Religion and the Costs of Saving Others from Themselves," *Journal of the American Academy of Religion* 74, no. 3 (September 2006): 730.
26. Jawad Anwar Qureshi, "Being Bilingual: Thoughts on the Insider/Outsider Problem in Teaching Islam," *Muslim World* 108 (2018): 214.
27. Qureshi, "Being Bilingual," 216.
28. Maria M. Dakake, "Teaching Islam in the Public University: Facilitating and Embracing Critical Conversations," *Muslim World* 108 (2018) 330.
29. Schubel, "Thoughts on Dissecting Octopus," 20.
30. One naturalist says, "I am certain of one thing . . . if I have a soul . . . an octopus has a soul too." They play with toys, recognize individual faces, express like and dislike of different people—a.k.a. friendship. Ezra Klein, "How Octopuses Upend What We Know About Ourselves: Interview with Sy Montgomery," *The Ezra Klein Show*, July 13, 2021, https://www.nytimes.com/2021/07/13/opinion/ezra-klein-podcast-sy-montgomery.html.
31. *My Octopus Teacher*.
32. "Anytime 'data' can answer this question [Are you my data?], the stakes increase." Monica Miller, "Yes, You ARE My Data!," *Culture on the Edge*, July 30, 2014, https://edge.ua.edu/monica-miller/yes-you-are-my-data/.
33. I'm thinking here of the short-lived divorce between the Society of Biblical Literature and the American Academy of Religion, which came as a relief to some and grief to many more. According to the director

at the time, "religious studies, apart from faith-based studies, has emerged in a vibrant way" that caused some in AAR to want "to enhance the independent identity of the AAR." Jennifer Howard, "Split Between Two Academic Organizations Has Religion Scholars Fretting," *Chronicle of Higher Education*, November 20, 2007, https://www.chronicle.com/article/split-between-two-academic-organizations-has-religion-scholars-fretting-237.

Conclusion

LET THE MARGINS BE THE CENTER

VERNON JAMES SCHUBEL

There is an old anarchist slogan that has long served as a touchstone in both my teaching and scholarship: "Let the margins be the center." I share it with my students early on in most of my courses and encourage them to keep it in mind as a reminder to allow the voices of those who have been marginalized or treated as peripheral to speak and be heard—to realize that the best and most obvious answer to Gayatri Spivak's famous question "Can the subaltern speak?" is "Yes, but only if we are willing to listen."[1]

I have been a college professor for more than thirty years. I have spent most of that time at Kenyon College, a small liberal arts college in rural Ohio known for its English program, the prestigious *Kenyon Review*, and as the alma mater of Paul Newman, Jonathan Winters, and, more recently, the YA novelist John Green. Historically, Kenyon's student body has been predominantly white and privileged, although it has made efforts to change that situation for three decades now. I have thus spent most of my academic career attempting to teach rooms full of overwhelmingly white, non-Muslim students about the lives of largely non-white Muslim people. It has made for an interesting career.

To be perfectly honest, I did not initially set out to become an academic. In the early 1970s, after a mediocre first year at Oklahoma State University, where I had planned to follow my father's recommendations and major in engineering, a discipline for which I frankly had neither aptitude nor inclination, I dropped out in pursuit of a career as a professional musician. After several years on the road, struggling to make a living as a singer-songwriter and performer in rock and roll bands, I made the obligatory trip to California in search of a recording contract. Suffice it to say, I was unsuccessful in that quest and returned disappointed. Looking back decades later, I see it as perhaps the luckiest moment of my life.

I entered a new phase in my life upon returning to Oklahoma State University, this time to study Asian humanities and religion—something for which I was much more temperamentally suited. As a result of that decision, I have had a tremendously rich and fascinating life, one that I would not change for any of the dreams of my youth. Over the years, I have had the opportunity to study with remarkable teachers and travel the world, exploring Islam in all of its amazing diversity. I might also note that, had I not returned to the academy, I would never have met my wife and colleague, the historian of Central Asia Nurten Kilic, whom I first encountered while we were both doing research in post-Soviet Uzbekistan. Furthermore, I would never have had a decades-long teaching career, which has allowed me to exercise the performative aspects of my personality that I had initially sought to satisfy through a career in music.[2]

When asked how I define my academic discipline, I usually reply that I consider myself a historian of religion who focuses on Islam and the experiences of people who identify themselves as Muslims. I do not describe my field of inquiry as "Islamic studies." I neither consider myself, nor do I wish people to see me as, an "expert" on Islam. I avoid the label of "Islamicist" and all of the Orientalist baggage that goes along with it. Furthermore, I have never seen myself as a "textual" scholar, although I certainly use a variety of texts in my scholarship. Unusual for scholars who work on Islam, my work has been largely ethnographic and deeply influenced by the discipline of anthropology. I have been particularly interested in the lives of ordinary Muslims, and I have always been drawn to the study of Islam as it has been practiced outside of the Arab world.

My research interests have focused primarily on aspects of Islam and Muslim communities that others might consider marginal. My first published article examined the annual commemorations of the martyrdom of the Prophet Muhammad's grandson Imam Husayn in the lunar month of Muharram in North America.[3] My dissertation, which served as the basis for my first book, focused on Muharram performances in South Asia and was based on intensive fieldwork in Pakistan in 1983.[4] Several years later, I returned to Pakistan to observe pilgrimage (*ziyarat*) at Sufi tombs in Multan. Following the collapse of the Soviet Union, I began learning Uzbek and eventually traveled to Tashkent to examine the reemergence of the Sufi tradition in Central Asia. Upon returning to America, I began studying Turkish and have for the last few decades been studying the Anatolian Alevi-Bektaşi community. As one can see, the content and trajectory of my scholarly life looks very different from that of most of my colleagues in the field of Islamic studies much of which is still dominated by a Sunni-Arabo-*fiqh-kalam* centric paradigm of Islam so ably critiqued by Marshall Hodgson in his groundbreaking opus *The Venture of Islam*.[5]

I should point out that there is nothing objectively marginal or peripheral about the topics I have listed. After all, the largest concentration of Muslims on the planet live in South Asia in the countries we now call India, Pakistan, and Bangladesh. Devotion to the family of the Prophet Muhammad (*ahl al-bayt*) is in no way peripheral to Muslim piety; while it is central to Shi'i Islam, it plays crucial roles in the lives of Sunni Muslims as well. The Sufi tradition is arguably the beating spiritual heart of Islam, and the influence of Central Asian and Anatolian Sufis on that tradition is immeasurable. In reality, the topics I have chosen to study and write about are neither peripheral nor marginal; they have only been made to seem so by the ways that the academic study of Islam has defined itself.

Looking back, I can see many reasons for my attraction to what others have (to my mind, incorrectly) considered to be marginal or liminal. For one thing, I have always identified more with the so-called counterculture than with the mainstream of American society, always felt more personally comfortable on the edges and margins than at the center. My decision to leave college at the age of seventeen to play music was indicative of that aspect of my character. Years later, in graduate school, when I read Victor Turner's description of wandering minstrels as bearers of *communitas* and anti-structure, I was better able to understand both the romantic attraction that life on the road as an itinerant musician held for me, and the connections between that mode of existence and my next career as a scholar and an ethnographer.

Anthropologists and ethnographers, like minstrels and troubadours, are inherently liminal, living on the edge of worlds in which they do not and can never fully belong, freely accepting a role that is both inside and outside of the social realities they are observing and about which they are writing. It was thus not surprising, perhaps, how many of my fellow students in Victor Turner's graduate seminars at the University of Virginia had had previous careers as performers—dancers, musicians, actors. Such professions are themselves inherently liminal, blending and blurring the normally distinct binary worlds of work and play. It is therefore not surprising, either, that I would be drawn to the study of those aspects of Islam and the civilization connected to it that others find marginal.[6]

MY SCHOLARLY PRE-COMMITMENTS

As a scholar of Islam, I am clearly the product of what the historian Marshall G. S. Hodgson would call my "scholarly pre-commitments."[7] First of all, my undergraduate and graduate mentors, professors Azim Nanji and Abdulaziz Sachedina, respectively, came from non-Arab Shi'i backgrounds. Unlike most scholars of Islam of my generation, I never studied closely with anyone who assumed that Sunni Arabs were somehow "the real Muslims" or that sharia-minded Sunni Islam constitutes some kind of orthodoxy to which other kinds of Islam should be compared.

Unlike many of my contemporaries, I was initially drawn to study Islam through an interest in South Asian religions rather than the Arab world or "the Middle East." My first intensive exposure to the academic study of Islam in particular, and religion more generally, came in the 1970s in an undergraduate survey course on South Asian religions taught by Hyla Converse. Professor Converse had grown up in Lahore in pre-Partition India and was intimately familiar with religion and culture in South Asian culture. Her discussion of Islam began not with the familiar five pillars, as I had expected, but, rather, with a slide show and discussion of the Islamicate nature of the Taj Mahal and, most strikingly, the *'urs* celebration of the death anniversary of the great South Asian Sufi Mu'inuddin Chishti. These images provided me with a view of Islam I had previously never imagined. Not long after, I decided I would one day study Urdu and travel to South Asia to experience these things for myself.

I was lucky not only to have had remarkable teachers as an undergraduate but also to come of age intellectually at a particularly fascinating time. I began my graduate studies at the University of Virginia in 1978, the same year Edward Said's *Orientalism* was published; thus I come from the first post-Said generation of scholars of Islam. In fact, my dissertation adviser, Abdulaziz Sachedina, and I read *Orientalism* at the same time, shortly after its publication. Said's work, along with my conversations about it with Professor Sachedina, had a profound impact on the shaping of my ideas about how to study Islam, and religion in general. Furthermore—and perhaps even more importantly—I am from the first generation of scholars whose thinking about Islam was shaped by the historian Marshall Hodgson, whose work in many ways both predicted and foreshadowed Said's critiques of Orientalism.

In my opinion, one of the most important dividing lines among scholars of the Islamicate world is that between those who have read and been influenced by Hodgson's *Venture of Islam* and those who have not. More than any other scholar of the twentieth century, Hodgson demonstrated the error of assuming that there is an easily definable, essential Islam to which other schools of thought must be compared. For Hodgson, there is no inherent teleology baked into the first generation of Islam to ensure that it would turn out in any one particular way, in the manner that previous generations of scholars seemed to assume that Sunni sharia-minded Islam was inevitably destined to become the mainstream of the religion.

Hodgson, whose identity as a Quaker—a minority within Christianity whose impact on history and religion is far greater than their relatively small numbers might suggest—deeply influenced both his scholarship and politic opinions, used his scholarship to decenter the world. This tendency in his work goes back all the way to his days as an undergraduate, when he wrote an article criticizing the Mercator Projection maps of the world, ubiquitous in American classrooms, that both artificially enlarged North America and placed it at the center.[8] Most importantly, Hodgson took the Shi'a and Sufi traditions seriously, treating them as integral to the larger history of Islam and describing them on their own terms rather than by comparing them to an idealized Sunni Islam. His brilliant scholarly neologisms like "Islamicate," "agrarianate," and "Oikumene" are remarkably useful additions to the vocabulary of world history. Concepts he developed, like sharia-mindedness, *'alid* loyalism, and *tariqat* Shi'ism, have been incredibly important to my understanding of the diversity of the Islamic world. As I tell my students when they begin reading it, while *The Venture of Islam* is a history of the Islamicate world, it is simultaneously a history of the world with the center moved from Europe and located instead in Baghdad or Isfahan.

Beginning my graduate studies by reading Said and Hodgson was a deeply formative experience, so much so that I wrote my master's thesis at the University of Virginia on the similarities between them. Perhaps most significantly, the fact that both saw clear connections between their scholarship and social justice issues affirmed for me the necessity of recognizing the moral and political aspects of our work as scholar and teachers. This was to become a model for how I was to think about my own career.

I am, of course, forever indebted to my dissertation adviser, Abdulaziz Sachedina, from whom I learned so much more than I could possibly list here. He led me to see and understand the beauty and power of the affective tradition of Islam, especially the Shi'i and Sufi traditions, where devotion and love for the Prophet, the *ahl al-bayt*, the Shi'i Imams, and Sufi *awliyah* provide chains of devotional allegiance that lead inexorably back to the experience of ineffable Divine Reality (*Haqiqat*). Through him, I learned to see Islam as a universe of symbols and presences that continuously reveals the sacred in the context of human history through the presence and actions of embodied human beings.

To single out one extremely important concept among the many I learned from him, he showed me the importance of the *usul al-din* (roots of religion) as a key for understanding Islam, especially the three *usul* shared by both Sunni and Shi'i Muslims: *tawhid* (belief in the unity of God), *nubuwwat* (belief in Prophets), and *qiyamat* (belief in the day of judgment). These multivalent concepts define the boundaries of Islam as a religion while simultaneously allowing for its tremendous diversity. While all Muslims accept the unity of God as the essence of Islam, they have interpreted tawhid along a wide spectrum, ranging from the austere monotheism of Ibn Taymiyya to the mystical conception of unity of being (*wahdat al-wujud*) associated with Ibn 'Arabi. Similarly, while all Muslims accept the prophethood of Muhammad, for some he is primarily the deliverer of the Qur'an and a model for ritual and ethical practice, while for others he is much more. For them, he is the preexistent light (*nur*) for whom God created the universe and an ongoing spiritual presence in the world. For some, *qiyamat*—which for all Muslims is an affirmation of human moral responsibility—implies a Heaven (*jannat*) that is literally a garden and a Hell (*jahannam*) of literal fire, while for others these concepts contain a far more allegorical and mystical meaning, implying an eternity in each individual moment. The multivalence of the *usul al-din* has been the organizing principle of nearly every course I have taught on Islam over the course my career.

Another crucial influence on my thinking as a scholar has been the work of the anthropologist Victor Turner, with whom I had the opportunity to take multiple seminars at the University of Virginia. Turner's work has had a deep and abiding impact on my scholarship. His concept of "root paradigm" as a cultural analogue to DNA pre-dates Richard Dawkins's similar but more familiar concept of "meme," but is, in my opinion, much more sophisticated and far more useful for understanding religious phenomena, especially in the way it foregrounds the concept of self-sacrifice.[9] It has been particularly crucial to my understanding of Islam, in particular the affective piety of the Sufi and Shi'i traditions.

Importantly, Turner's work emphasizes the critical role of the liminal and marginal in the study of religion. The liminal, the space betwixt and between binary social realities, the realm of communitas, anti-structure, possibility, and humility, has been crucial to my understanding of religion. More than any other thinker of the last century, Turner championed the necessity of turning our attention away from the center and toward the margins, which for him was source of human inspiration and imagination.[10] Turner is sometimes misread as a Durkheimian, for whom the primary purpose of the anti-structural liminal phase of the ritual process is to facilitate the reaffirmation of the hierarchical categories of social structure. In actuality, he saw the anti-structural character of the liminal as an engine of creativity, rooted in the subjunctive mode of "what if," which, despite the overwhelming power of social structures, allows for social transformation and change.

My scholarship is very much rooted in Turner's understanding of the liminal. My work on Muharram in South Asia focused on the liminal aspect of Karbala as a root paradigm in Islam. Similarly, my research on the Sufi tradition draws on his notion of structure and anti-structure. If the animal soul, or *nafs*, is the progenitor of structure—the realm of pride, hierarchy, acquisitiveness, status—the *ruh*, or spiritual soul, is that aspect of humanity that yearns for communitas, humility, egalitarianism, poverty, and simplicity, all of which are Sufi virtues. Although terms like liminality, communitas, and anti-structure may be "etic" categories, they resonate closely with emic categories within the Islamic tradition and thus are valuable analytical tools.[11]

SOCIAL AND POLITICAL ACTIVISM

I would be remiss to not mention the role of political and social activism in my scholarly development. When I was a graduate student at the University of Virginia, I became involved in the anti-apartheid movement, the Nestlé boycott, the anti-interventionist movement related to Central America, and other social justice causes. I am particularly proud of having been one of the cofounders of the Socialist-Feminist Alliance at the University of Virginia in the 1980s. My engagement in social activism has continuously reenforced the importance of affirming the voices and the agency of those who have been marginalized and dismissed on the basis of class, ethnicity, race, religion, or gender.

Had it not been for my association with feminists both as an activist and a scholar, I would never have thought to include a chapter on women's household rituals and the reading of miracle stories (*mujizat kahanis*) in my dissertation and, later, book on Shi'ism in Pakistan. My interactions with my feminist comrades had a profound impact on the ways in which I approached the study of religion in another way as well. Feminist theory showed me that the marginalization of women and the devaluation of their experiences was connected to a larger rejection of the body, which, in my opinion, is in many ways at the core of the academy. The historical and cultural association of women with the body, as somehow more tied to the corporeal than men because of the ways in which their lives are impacted by the physical realities of menstruation, pregnancy, and lactation, is, I believe, one reason that women and their experience as human beings have been Othered and diminished.

One of the things I find most pleasing about this volume is its centering of women as embodied human beings. The fact that Max Johnson Dugan begins his essay on tattooing with a quote from the late bell hooks is indicative of the changes that have occurred in the field since I started graduate school in 1978. Holly Donahue Singh's remarkable article audaciously centers women and their reproductive lives, and Farah Bakaari's "Islam and its Others" foregrounds Muslim women in ways that were far too rare when I began my career.

Clearly my desire to learn about Islam by speaking to ordinary people and including their voices in my work, rather than rely solely on texts, emerged in part out of both my social and political activism and scholarly pre-commitments. If I am honest, my current interest in and attraction to the Turkish Alevi community was facilitated by that community's general support of progressive politics, rooted in their vision of Imam Ali and Imam Husayn as revolutionary figures, not to mention the astonishing power of their musical tradition of *nefes* and *deyiş*, discussed so effectively in Tess Waggoner's essay in this volume, which in many ways has become the music of the student Left in Turkey. In fact, it was my experience watching young socialist Alevi college students singing the songs of Pir Sultan Abdal in the Kizilay neighborhood of Ankara during the international Day of Women in 1996 that initially lead me to begin my study of Alevi Islam, with which I am still involved all these years later.

THERE IS NO "CENTER," THERE IS NO "OTHER"

As I stated at the beginning of this chapter, in the study of Islam and the study of religion and culture more generally I believe we should "let the margins be the center." To be more precise, we should always begin our inquiry by recognizing that "centers" are, in fact, illusory. If we study human history with Europe at its center, as most of us who have been educated in North America have done, we see things from one perspective, but if, like Hodgson we instead put Baghdad or the Arabian Peninsula at the center, history looks very different. While neither is "the Truth" per se, neither is entirely false. However, I would argue that the Eurocentric perspective is inherently more dangerous, because it reaffirms commonly held biases and thus is more easily falsely perceived as "the Truth."

Whenever we assume a center, we inevitably wind up seeing the world in terms of essentialist binaries—male/female, East/West, us/them, Sunni/Shi'a. But, as poststructuralist critics of this mode of thinking have pointed out, whenever we see things as binaries, the poles of that binary are never value free; we inevitably privilege one of the two poles, assigning it positive attributes and treating it as real and essential, while defining the Other in opposition to it. One of the two poles of the binary is inevitable defined as "the Other." Thus, "the West" is commonly defined as masculine, rational, dominant, and adult while "the

Orient" is categorized as its opposite—nonrational (read "intuitive" or mystical"), submissive, and childlike. When we look at the world through a binary lens that deems white male Europeans to be normal, and everyone else to be the the Other, we cannot help but see the nature of historical reality in a dangerously distorted way. In fact, whenever we see the world through any kind of binary lens we inevitably distort reality.

We should, therefore, instead try to perceive the world as if there is no center, and thus no Other. This is the primary insight that I took away both from Edward Said, who in *Orientalism* demonstrated the danger in the East/West binary, and from Marshall Hodgson, who similarly critiqued the tendency to privilege Sunni Arab Islam as the center of the Islamic tradition.[12] All of the authors in this collection have striven in their own unique ways to move away from this kind of binary understanding of Islam.

Of course, one cannot deny the importance of Arabic within Islam. As the language of the Qur'an and Sunna, it certainly plays a crucial role. But, as most Muslims are not Arabs, do not speak Arabic, and generally lack knowledge of Arabic beyond the minimum needed to recite one's daily prayers, it is important that we find ways to listen to and read the thoughts and ideas of Muslims as they present them in their own vernaculars. Sadly, as Edward Curtis points out in his introduction to this volume, the academic study of Islam has for too long focused on Arabic as if it is the only language in which truly meaningful discourse about Islam has taken place. When colleges or universities make the decision to add an Islamicate language to their rosters, it is invariably Arabic—not Urdu, Swahili, Bahasa-Indonesian, or Turkish. Potential scholars of Islam almost always begin their study of language with Arabic. If they bother to learn a second language, it is generally Farsi, which, given its historical prominence as a literary language among premodern Muslims, makes eminent sense. However, as a result, relatively few scholars of Islam write about its expression in Turkish or Swahili or Gujarati or even Urdu, the literary language of Muslims in Islam's geographical and demographic center, South Asia. There remains an overarching belief that "the real Islam" is expressed in Arabic, and that expressions of it in other language can be diminished as mere vernacular.

This is a terrible mistake. The power of Sufi hagiography in vernacular language is not only profound but also important in the history of the evolution of the tradition. Sufi poetry in the vernacular is incredibly crucial for understanding the Islamic tradition. In a recent undergraduate seminar at Kenyon, I taught the twentieth-century Sufi intellectual and pir Kenan Rifai's annotation of the first book of the *Masnavi*: a Turkish commentary on a Farsi text. It was a remarkable introduction to the worldview of Sufism in the twentieth century, and I am glad that a scholar who works on Islam outside of the Arabic-speaking world took the time to translate it.[13] How much do we miss if we focus on Arabic alone as the language of Islam?

It is therefore gratifying to note the number of essays in this collection that write about Islam outside of the context of the Arabic-speaking world. Tess Waggoner and Henry Brill have written powerful essays based on Turkic sources. Holly Donahue Singh has similarly authored an exceptional piece allowing her readers powerful insights into the lives of Urdu-speaking South Asian women. Edward Curtis, a student of Arabic, has nevertheless chosen to write about English-speaking African American Muslims. Max Johnson Dugan gives us a global view into tattooing as a Muslim practice that nowhere presumes the centrality of Arabic.

In terms of binaries central to the study of religion, the tendency has long been to privilege those religious traditions and phenomenon that most resemble modern Protestantism (discursive in tone, rooted in textual analysis, dismissive of images, magic and ritual) over other versions of religion that more resemble Catholicism (affective in tone, rooted in tradition, embracing images and ritual performance). We prefer religion in the form of textual inquiry into philosophical questions and social ethics over issues that touch on the magical, the miraculous, and the ineffable. Thus, there is a tendency to privilege Zen Buddhism over Pure Land, Advaita nondualist Vedanta over the theistic monotheism of Madhvacarya. In terms of Islam, we privilege Sunnism in its most discursive forms over Shi'ism and Sufism. This attitude helps explain the calls from so many people for a "reformation" in Islam and the ongoing fascination with figures like Sayyid Qutb and Jamal al-Din Afghani, modernists whose criticism of popular religious practices such as tomb visitation echo Protestant dismissals of Catholic saint veneration and ritual.

In line with this mode of thought in recent years, Talal Asad's definition of Islam as "a discursive tradition that includes and relates to itself the Qur'an and *hadith*" that is engaged in a search for prescriptive orthodoxy has become increasingly popular.[14] This may well be true if we see Islam as somehow identical with sharia, but I would argue that Islam is much more than a discursive tradition, and it is certainly concerned with much more than defining orthodoxy. Among other things, for many Muslims Islam has been primarily about the mysteries of love— love between God and humanity, love between Muslims and their Prophet, love between *pir* (teacher) and *murid* (student). It is also, as Shahab Ahmad points out in his brilliant posthumous work *What Is Islam?*, an exploratory tradition through which

Muslims seek to experience and understand ineffable truths. While the rational discourses of *kalam* and *fiqh* are clearly important, they represent only one aspect of the tradition.[15]

Within the study of Islam, the tendency has been to treat the discursive traditions of fiqh and kalam as the core of Islam, its true center, its "straight path," and thus to marginalize other equally important components of the Islamic tradition: hagiography, pilgrimage to the tombs of the *awliya*, and the pir-murid relationship. The affective and exploratory aspects of Islam are too often treated as peripheral or marginal. Shi'i Islam becomes the Other, as does much of the Sufi tradition, although the more Sufism embraces sobriety in its mystical outlook the more it is seen as genuinely Islamic. Throughout, there remains a tendency to describe Islamic diversity by imagining a "real Islam" and defining other aspects of Islam in comparison to it.

The solution to his dilemma seems obvious. We need to let the voices of those who identify with communities and ideas that others see as peripheral speak for themselves and define themselves in their own terms. We need Shi'i Muslims and Alevis to describe themselves rather than describe them in comparison to Sunni Muslims. Let people associated with the Nation of Islam and the Five-Percent Nation of Gods and Earths define their own identities, as Edward Curtis and Michael Muhammad Knight have long done in their work, rather than start from the premise that these communities are somehow distortions of a real Islam.

Without a center, there is no Other. Without a center, there are no margins. Marginality is an illusion. To restate Pink Floyd's famous insight: "There is no dark side of the moon, really." As a matter of fact, it's all equally light, because it all reflects the light of humanity—and there is only one humanity, with one shared human history.

OUR SHARED GLOBAL HUMAN HERITAGE

A primary corollary to the aforementioned principle that there is no center is the rather straightforward idea that, as human beings, we are all the inheritors of a shared global human heritage—that is to say, we are not merely shaped and formed by the persons and events of the cultures and civilizations with which we primarily identify but by all of human history. This may seem obvious, but I still regularly encounter people teaching at prestigious institutions who insist that we should teach Plato and Aristotle as "us" because they are Europeans and crucial to the textual and philosophical traditions of "the West," but that we should teach non-European luminaries, such as Rumi, Ibn 'Arabi, Mencius or Shankara, as "the Other."

This opinion is often rooted in the mistaken belief that Asia and the Islamicate world had no serious impact on the history of Europe and North America until the emergence of the colonial dominance of Europe over the rest of the world. Of course, the reality is that Europe did not develop in isolation. If there were no Muhammad, no Genghis Khan, no Confucius, no Siddhartha Gautama, the entire world—and not just the Asian and Islamicate worlds—would look very different, including Europe and North America.

An example I frequently use in my classes to make this point is the likely connection between the Islamicate world and the creation of the most American of musical forms, the blues and rock and roll. At first this may sound farfetched, but there is significant evidence to support such a thesis. The various stringed (*tar*) instruments that evolved from the two-stringed *dutar* of Central Asia—which was used by nomadic peoples to accompany songs of love, loss, and longing—traveled across Eurasia facilitated both by Mongol expansion and the emergence of Turco-Mongol Muslim empires. Over time it morphed into the Iranian *setar*, the South Asian sitar, and other instruments. In Islamicate Spain it became the guitar, the engine of Flamenco, an artistic form deeply influenced by Sufi music traditions. When the guitar made its way into the hands of enslaved Africans in the Americas, many of them Muslims who had their own stringed instrument traditions, it provided the primary tool for the creation of both the blues and what was to become rock and roll.

This view of history, one that strives to decenter the world and treats Islam a part of a commonly shared human legacy, has reached many more people than those I have been able to teach directly through the work of a talented and charismatic former student who has helped carry it out into the larger world. While at Kenyon, the novelist John Green, the author of *The Fault in Our Stars* and *Paper Towns*, took many of my courses dealing with Islam and the Islamicate world. Several years ago, I became aware of John's extremely popular YouTube video series on World History, *Crash Course*, through my son who was then in middle school, and who like millions of other kids his age watched episodes of it frequently to learn about the world. When I watched the episode on Islam, I was pleased to see that it presented the early history of Islam in a manner very similar to the way I did in my introductory course. At one point in the video, "John Green from the Past" asks "John Green from the Present" why we know so little about Islamic history. "John Green from the Present" replies that we don't know about Islamic history because "we don't learn about it, because we are taught that our history is the history of Christianity in Europe when in fact our history is story of people on the planet."[6] It is because we erroneously do not recognize that the civilization of Islam is part of our shared human legacy, but instead treat it as the Other. Through that video, thousands have kids have been exposed to the idea that, even if we are not ourselves Muslim, it is important to study the civilization and cultures associated with Islam because it is part of our shared past.

Muslims may have a unique spiritual relationship with Muhammad, but in a very real sense Muhammad belongs to all of humanity—as do Plato and Shankaracharya, Jesus and the Buddha, Sinan and Frank Lloyd Wright, Hafiz and Shakespeare, Umm Kulthum, and the Beatles. We are all the product of a shared global human heritage, and it is imperative that we study the history and humanities of the entire globe as our own.

This idea, which is at the core of my pedagogy—that we are all the product of a shared global human history—may seem rather obvious. I freely admit is not unique to me. One of the major reasons that the academy too often treats the non-Western world as the Other is the notion that many of the positive attributes frequently associated with it—the equality of all human beings, the necessity of religious tolerance, the primacy of reason—are somehow unique to the West and, even more specifically, the Enlightenment. Thus, modern figures like Nehru, Tagore, Jinnah, Iqbal, or the Turkish Sufi Kenan Rifai must have learned and adopted such ideas primarily from their exposure to Western education. This idea is linked to the notion of civilizational seminal traits that are often used to explain Western supremacy in terms of the unique connection of the West with the rational philosophical traditions of Ancient Greece. How better to defend the concept of the "rational West" versus the "mystical Orient?"

This notion is seriously flawed. First of all, it ignores the fact that some of the most insightful readers of the ancient Greeks' philosophical tradition were Muslims. More importantly, as Marshall Hodgson argues so effectively in *The Venture of Islam*, the concept of "seminal traits," which, in order to be more inclusive, are better described as germinal or generative traits, is deeply problematic as well.[17] All civilizations have their mystics and their rationalists. Furthermore, anyone with even a cursory knowledge of Asian intellectual and religious history should be able to see that such ideas as the equality of all human beings, religious tolerance, or the primacy of reason had their proponents in premodern Asia. The fact that modern and contemporary Asians and Muslims see resonances between those ideas as expressed in their own cultures and in the West should come as no surprise. The West is not special. There are no civilizational germinal traits that define particular civilizations. We are all human and capable of seeing things from multiple perspectives.

NEITHER CARETAKER, NOR CRITIC

I recently shared the manuscript for my forthcoming book, *Teaching Humanity: An Alternative Introduction to Islam*, with a younger scholar who suggested that, because of the generally positive tone of my writing about Islam, I might be perceived as coming down on the caretaker side of the Russell McCutcheon's binary between "caretakers" and "critics" in the study of religion. While I freely admit that I write enthusiastically about what I see as the inherent beauty and elegance apparent in aspects of Islamic piety and spirituality, I would deny that that makes me a caretaker—or, worse yet, an apologist, unwilling or unable to critique the Islamic tradition in any meaningful way. First if all, I do not find McCutcheon's binary particularly useful. Much of the debate about critics or caretakers seems to me to be rooted in an essentialist understanding of religion that ignores its inherent multivalence. As Michael Muhammad Knight notes in his chapter on multivalence in the hadith corpus in this volume, there is no single univocal Islamic tradition. In the face of Islam's diversity and multivalence I find it difficult to understand exactly what it means to be a caretaker or a critic.

I am continually perplexed by what it means to be a critic of Islam. I can understand being a critic of Ibn Sina, or Al-Ghazali, or Ibn Taymiyyah, or Ibn 'Arabi, but to be a critic of Islam? The multivalence of the tradition seems to make that notion almost incomprehensible. If being a critic means using theory and method from the history of religions as an analytical tool, I am indeed a critical thinker when it comes to both Islam and religions. But if being a critic means challenging basic Muslim assumptions such as the existence of God, or that the Qur'an is a revealed text, I am not. As a historian of religion, I find such questions fundamentally unanswerable within the context of academic study of religion and thus not particularly profitable as paths of inquiry. There are so many things one can write about Islam and Muslims without attempting to answer the question "Is Islam true?"—a question that seems to me to be an intellectual rabbit hole. It is better asked in a *dergah*, or a *khanqah*, or perhaps a *madrasah*, but is out of place in a secular classroom.

I should note at this junction that because I identify as a Muslim, for some this makes my opinion on these matters suspect. I should also point out that for most of my career as a professor I did not identify as such. And, as I tell my students, I don't teach my courses in any appreciably different way now than I did before I became a Muslim, except that I have many more interesting anecdotes. I may be an insider who teaches about religion, but I do not teach as an insider. Furthermore, I am not engaged in *dawa* or proselytization. The central focus of my courses on religious traditions is not to teach people how be religious, but, as Kathryn Blanchard demonstrates in her chapter in this volume, it is almost impossible as a believer taking an academic course on religion to not be impacted by learning about the religions of others in ways that may cause one to examine one's own religious beliefs. This is something we all learn as we go both as students and as teachers.

Blanchard was one of the first students I taught at Kenyon College. She went on to become a professor at Alma College in Michigan, a short drive from Central Michigan University, where I had my first tenure-track position. In her chapter, "Journey to the Teaching of Islam," she comments on my article "Thoughts on Dissecting an Octopus: Aaron Hughes, Marshall Hodgson, and Navigating the Normative/Descriptive Divide in the Study of Islam." In it, I entered the ongoing debate between Orsi and McCutcheon about critics and caretakers that had spilled over into the study of Islam because of a similar debate between Aaron Hughes and Omid Safi.[18] Blanchard bravely puts her positionality front and center, describing the way her understanding of religion changed as she went from someone who was interested in religion primarily as an insider to someone engaged in the academic study of religion. She describes how my classes and those she took with my colleagues at Kenyon caused her to think about her faith in new and challenging ways. I have always told students that as a teacher I am not trying to teach them how to be religious—how to be Christians or Jews or Muslims or agnostics, for that matter. However, it is almost inevitable that studying religion, especially other peoples' religions, might lead them to question things that they might otherwise take for granted. I had not realized until reading her chapter the impact of my Islam course on her both as a Christian and a scholar of Christianity. Her description of the ways in which she has grappled with the question of how one balances the dilemma of being simultaneously an insider and outsider in the classroom is both insightful and thought provoking.

I must insist that seeing beauty or eloquence in a worldview does not make one its caretaker. It does not it even imply that one accepts that worldview as true. For example, I see tremendous beauty in Buddhist thought although I am not a Buddhist. Nor does my appreciation of Buddhism lead me to refuse to criticize those within the Buddhist community who, for example, tolerate or encourage the suffering of the Rohingya in the name of Buddhist nationalism. Similarly, I seriously doubt anyone would seriously accuse philosophers who see the elegance of the Aquinas philosophy as necessarily serving as caretakers of the Catholic tradition, or as necessarily even Catholic.

I freely admit to emphasizing aspects of Islam and the Islamicate world in my teaching and writing that I find compelling. I tend to write and teach about elements of Islam that I believe add something meaningful to our shared global human heritage: the poetic genius of Maulana Jalaluddin Rumi; the remarkable spiritual intellect of Ibn 'Arabi; the dramatic power of both the narrative of Imam Husayn's martyrdom at Karbala and ways in which those who love him commemorate it through ritual and poetry; the magnificent architecture of Isfahan and the Taj Mahal; the musical genius of Arıf Sağ and Nusrat Fateh Ali Khan. That should not be surprising. After all, scholars tend to write and teach about things that they appreciate. On the other hand, I certainly do not ignore beliefs and practices that I reject or aspects of early Islamic history that might be discomforting or controversial to many of my students. The civilization and cultures associated with Islam certainly have their share of intolerant puritan exclusivists, misogynists, and tyrants, as do all civilizations and culture, but they no more define the entirety of Islam as a human and historical phenomenon than the Holocaust, the North Atlantic slave trade, and manifest destiny define the entirety of European civilization.

Interestingly, these kinds of questions seem to arise more within the study of religion than other aspects of culture. Scholars who specialize in the study of particular authors or thinkers in other fields are not generally criticized because they find beauty and worth in the focus of their inquiry; most of us are drawn to study this or that particular thinker or writer or historical movement or phenomenon precisely because we find it fascinating. One can recognize the power and beauty of Bach's music without being an apologist for European culture. One can recognize the genius of Shakespeare while simultaneously being aware of troubling aspects of his work, especially in terms of his portrayal of gender, race, and religion. To do so does not make one a caretaker of Western civilization. Scholars of romantic poetry or Elizabethan drama seldom find themselves having to defend themselves against accusations that they are acting as caretakers of a tradition. Similarly, there is surprisingly little criticism of people who teach Kant or Heidegger, despite their sometimes troubling ideas. But, when it comes to religious traditions, and especially Islam, suddenly finding beauty within them brings the risk of accusations of apologism. I find this unfortunate. As scholars who write about Islam, we seldom write about Islam or Islamicate civilization in its entirety but, rather, particular aspects of it. Revealing beauty and wisdom within the traditions of Islam is not a violation of scholarly objectivity.

WE ARE ALL HUMAN, WE ALL HAVE BODIES

As much as it is true that the central idea of Islam is *tawhid*—the Unity of God—the corollary idea of *insaniyya*, or humanity, is in many ways equally important, as for Muslims it is the existence of humanity that makes Islam as a revealed religion a theological and logical necessity. This is perhaps best reflected in the famous *hadith qudsi* where God states that "I was a hidden treasure and I would be known." Accordingly, God creates the universe so that human beings can have a place to come into existence and become knowers of God. For me, a key narrative for unlocking the meaning of the Qur'an is the creation of Adam, a story told multiple times in the Qur'an that affirms the uniqueness of humanity—the knower of "the Names," the symbiosis of matter and spirit, the receptacle of the *ruh* of the creator, the *qibla* of the Angels, the bearer of God's Trust (*amana*). Within Islam, humanity plays a crucial role within the cosmos and, not surprisingly, Islam addresses itself to humanity as something unique and special within the cosmos.

As a college professor, I try to teach and study Islam not as a transcendent reality but instead as a human and historical phenomenon. I could never claim to speak for the mind or intention of God, or even the Prophet Muhammad. I am not trying to teach the "Truth with a Capital 'T.'" That is the provenance of *pir*s, *shaykh*s, and *murshid*s, a status I would never presume to claim. As a scholar, I am interested in the ways that human beings behave—in the things that they do and say as windows into their inner experiences, not the experiences themselves.

I believe that there is a pervasive and largely invisible and often unconscious Neoplatonist bias in the academy that privileges "the mind" over "the body." It assumes that the mind or spirit is eternal and lives forever, while the flesh fades. It takes as a given that the life of the mind is more important than that of the body, as if the former could somehow exist without the latter. By this I don't mean to imply the need for "physical culture" as part of the liberal arts in some Victorian or Edwardian veneration of the ideal human form, but, rather, that we must never forget that we are physical beings who live in history. As human beings we are by definition embodied creatures, in large part defined by the limitations and possibilities of the flesh. By virtue of our physical existence, we exist not only as minds and souls but also as members of classes, ethnic groups, cultural communities. We are gendered, in a variety of ways, with all of the repercussions entailed by that reality. We exist within history and are impacted by it on a daily basis. It is, thus, always important to root our understanding of the transcendent in the historical.

Colleges and universities are by definition places where people go to cultivate the life of the mind, to think, to read and to write; to prepare for careers largely divorced from physical labor. They are also communities that give off a certain illusion of eternal youth, if not immortality, as the core population remains forever between the ages of eighteen and twenty- two, as if no one ages (except, of course, for the faculty and staff).[19] As a result, I frequently—only half-jokingly—tell my students that I understand that part of my job at Kenyon is to provide a much needed anti-Platonic voice, to counter the argument that the life of the mind is somehow superior to that of the body by asking them if they would choose immortality as "severed heads" over mortal lives within bodies that allow them to experience the simple pleasures of physical intimacy, romantic love, childbirth, and parenting, even though the inevitable price of the physical body that allows for those experiences is mortality and death. Perhaps this attitude has fueled my interest in those manifestations of Islam that maintain a mystical understanding of a spiritual reality rooted in creation itself: in *wahdat al-wujud*, and in the Alevi dictum that "My *qiblah* is a man" and their corollary notion, shared with the larger Sufi tradition, that the ultimate end of religion is the perfection of humanity.

I am gratified to see the way that the authors in this collection have foregrounded the body. Max Johnson Dugan's chapter on tattooing lets us see how the body becomes a way of expressing various sometimes contradictory notions of Islam and Islamic identity, and how tattoos that are sometimes seen as *haram* in Islam become ways in which some Muslims negotiate and present their own understandings of Islamic identity. In her chapter, Holly Donahue Singh foregrounds the complex issues of childbirth and pregnancy—the most intimately physical aspects of South Asian Muslim women's lives. Edward Curtis's chapter on the Nation of Islam spends considerable time discussing the role of food and diet, not to mention clothing, in the teachings of The Honorable Elijah Muhammad, who stressed not only the necessity for maintaining the body but also the economic implications of those teachings for members of the Nation.

THERE IS A REASON WE CALL IT FOLK WISDOM

For me, one of the great flaws of a liberal arts education is its overemphasis on the textual. Defining the humanities in terms of the written seems to me rather problematic, as most human beings throughout our history on the planet have been nonliterate. It is as if we are claiming that our humanity is somehow dependent upon our literacy. In point of fact, I know many people who are well versed in both classical and modern literature but are not particularly humane in their outlook or behavior. Similarly, some of the most remarkable and humane people I have ever known have not had formal educations. Many of the most important things I have learned about Islam have come from speaking to people, and not necessarily religious experts or specialists, but ordinary believers. When I was doing research on the resurgence of the Sufi tradition in Central Asia, some of my colleagues were astonished that I spent so much time talking to *kababchis* and taxi drivers. But, the fact is, I learned a great deal from them. Ordinary people are frequently repositories of tremendous knowledge passed on through a vibrant living oral tradition.

Again, it is heartening to see how many essays in this volume write take seriously the voices of ordinary people. Holly Donahue Singh writes elegantly of the experience of ethnography "grounded in participant observation" described evocatively as "deep hanging out" and what she refers to as the "practice of immersion and paying attention." Max Johnson Dugan addresses the issues of tattoos in contemporary Islam by presenting studies of actual people in ways that "reveal the complex perspective of those tattooed Muslims" and keep them from being drowned out by the "familiar, harmful cacophony of Orientalism." The volume presents Islam as a lived religion rather than something imprisoned in texts.

LOVING THE MARGINS, LOVING THE ALIEN

As I have noted throughout this chapter, when writing about religion, and especially about Islam, the problem with centers is that if they become understood as the Truth, or orthodoxy, inevitably that which is described in a peripheral relationship to them becomes the Other. This prevents us from truly appreciating the marginal and peripheral on their own terms, from seeing their intrinsic beauty and elegance. For example, there are classic works in the field that dismiss devotion to the Sufi *awliyah* as alien "saint worship" by comparing it to an idealized legalistic version of Sunni Islam. There are other works more sympathetic to Sufism that seek to isolate it from Islam proper by locating its origins outside of the tradition, pointing to possible Hindu, Christian, or Neoplatonic influences, rather than listening to the voices of the Sufi tradition that treat it as central to Islamic piety. Either way this important affective dimension of Islam is presented as something defective or heretical rather than an authentically Islamic way of responding to belief in *tawhid, nubuwwat,* and *qiyamat*.

In her contribution to this volume, Farah Bakaari makes a compelling argument in this regard. She notes that Islam is often described in terms of its prohibitions, and she describes how we are too often presented with a tragic vision of an Islam that is inherently closed to the modern sensibility of secularism and the possibility of reform. This results in a stereotyped image of "melancholy Muslims" forever caught between the unchanging prohibitive nature of Islam and the world of modernity. From this perspective the margins of Islam are often seen as attempts to break free from the supposed "repressive spirit of mainstream Islam."[20]

One characteristic shared by the contributors to this volume is that they refuse to speak of Islam primarily through "the lens of its prohibitions" or "deny the elasticity of its traditions."[21] In fact, the chapters in this volume point to an Islam that is full of both elasticity and contestation. For example, whatever the discursive tradition of Islam may or may not say about tattooing, Max Johnson Dugan shows us that, nonetheless, Muslims find their own way to navigate the contested question of tattoos. Similarly, Tess Waggoner shows us how Alevis continue to define themselves through their musical traditions despite government and cultural repression. In the pages of this volume no one is presented as living in a timeless sharia world. Even in the chapter in this volume that deals with hadith—something one might ordinarily think of as one of the least marginal elements of Islam—Michael Muhammad Knight's analysis points to the existence of diverse and contradictory voices in the canonical sources.

The chapters in this volume deal with Muslims whom some might see as marginal or peripheral, but none of them describes such people as "the Other," either in relation to the West or to mainstream Islam. They speak for themselves. Though the purpose of this volume is to highlight the margins of Islam, we first need to cease seeing them on the margins if we hope to know them. When I first started studying Islam at Oklahoma State University, I remember eavesdropping on a conversation between two members of the Humanities and Religious Studies faculty who were upset at the way in which the Nation of Islam was regularly portrayed as a heresy or a cult rather than as truly Islamic. I freely admit that from my limited understanding at the time I did not fully comprehend the legitimacy of their complaint. After all, I thought, Islam is about tawhid. If Master Fard is Allah, isn't that *shirk*? The famous Hajj narrative in *The Autobiography of Malcolm X* seemed to draw a bright line in the sand once and for all between "Orthodox Islam" and the weird world of motherships, Yaqub the mad scientist, and white devils presented by the Nation. How could the Nation of Islam be Islamic?

Unfortunately, nowhere is the tendency to reject that which is perceived as alien and marginal as non-Islamic more evident than in discussions of African American iterations of Islam such as the Nation of Islam, the Moorish Science Temple, and Five Percenters. Instead of being presented as coherent worldviews, they are frequently dismissed as heresy by comparing them to an essentialist version of Islam. Thankfully, in their body of work, both Edward Curtis and Michael Muhammad Knight have time and again demonstrated the eloquence of these traditions by presenting them on their own terms rather than comparing them to an idealized Sunni tradition. In his chapter in this volume, Edward Curtis convincingly argues, referencing Devon DeWeese's similar defense of the Islam of Central Asian nomads, that the very fact that it is called the Nation of *Islam* is incredibly significant. By identifying itself with global Islam and presenting Islam as a religion in opposition to white supremacy the Nation of Islam did something profound. As Curtis writes:

> The mythologies of Elijah Muhammad no longer seem stranger to me than other religious myths. Over time, I have understood the feelings of love that many of Elijah Muhammad's followers have for him. I have also come to understand the foundation of my own deep interest in the Nation of Islam and its long-time leader. . . . For me, the key to understanding the lives of those who appreciate their membership in the Nation of Islam—as they also surely questioned or resisted various elements of it—is the creation of an Islam that that loved Black people and that was synonymous with their freedom.[22]

"Loving the margins"—or, as David Bowie has put it "loving the alien"—first requires "believing the strangest things," or at least learning to appreciate things that on first acquaintance may seem strange and disorienting. To come to love and appreciate the alien as Edward Curtis has done, we first need to stop seeing it as alien, to see it on its own terms and to comprehend how people can believe what initially may seem bizarre or impossible.

My own work has emphasized that necessity of understanding Shi'i, Sufi, and especially Alevi voices on their own terms. I learned from listening to Shi'i voices that, for them, the conflicts in early Islamic history that led to the creation of Shi'i and Sunni Islam were not primarily about a political struggle over the Caliphate but, rather, about the rejection of Ali and his sons' inherent spiritual station of *imamat*. And by actually listening to the voices of Alevi Muslims, who refer to their tradition as "real Islam" (*gerçek Islam*) and to their rituals as *ibadet*, I was able to understand them as part of the larger world of Islamic mysticism rather than as a disguised from of shamanism, a syncretistic heresy, or some form of *ghulluw*. Tess Waggoner's chapter in this book comes to a similar conclusion.

One can only recognize the logic and the beauty of a system of belief by viewing it on its own terms. One cannot love the alien until one first sees how the people who believe in it do not see it as alien at all. Loving the alien and the marginal first of all requires seeing it as normal. Loving the alien because it is exotic, simply because it is alien, is not so much love as it is a fetish, the kind that lies at the heart of Orientalism. In her contribution, Farah Bakaari describes her understanding of the purpose of this volume as follows: "To render a deeper and more encompassing view of what Islam and Muslims do by centering those who occupy the geographic, pedagogical, social, political, queered, embodied, reproductive and doctrinal margins of the world of Islam."[23] As I look back at the book's chapters, it's clear to me that it does so without ever treating its subjects as Other, either in relationship to some imagined West or to some essentialized vision of Islam. Each of the chapters in this book recognizes that we cannot treat the human beings we write about as specimens on a dissecting table. In order to truly appreciate that which seems initially Other, one must first get beyond that fetish of Otherness and see the humanity that underlies it.

NOTES

1. I am grateful to historian of South Asia Wendy Singer, my Kenyon College colleague, for this insight and this line.
2. I should note that I have never stopped playing and writing music, both as a solo performer and as a guitarist in local blues and rock bands. It has remained an essential part of my identity, one that likely accounts for my lifelong interest in the more performative aspects of religion.
3. Vernon Schubel, "Muharram Majlis: Ritual and the Preservation of Religious Identity," in *Muslim Family of North America* (Alberta: University of Alberta Press, 1991), 118–31.
4. Vernon Schubel, *Religious Performance in Contemporary Islam: Shi'i Devotional Rituals in South Asia* (Columbia: University of South Carolina Press, 1993).
5. Marshall G. S. Hodgson, *The Venture of Islam*, vol. 1 (Chicago: University of Chicago Press, 1974), 39–45.
6. If life on the road as a musician is in many ways a liminal experience, so is life at a rural liberal arts college. College students exist in the marginal space between adolescence and adulthood, no longer children but not yet fully recognized as men and women. Kenyon College is also geographically and demographically liminal; it sits at the farthest edge of Appalachia, in a clearly working-class area, where many people have never left the state of Ohio, but the campus is simultaneously plugged into the most cosmopolitan aspects of the contemporary world. In fact, I have noticed over the years that some of my colleagues never make any real connection with the local world around them, which remains somehow forever alien.
7. Hodgson, *Venture of Islam*, 26–30.
8. Edmund Burke III, "Islamic History as World History: Marshall Hodgson, *The Venture of Islam*," *International Journal of Middle East Studies* 10, no. 2 (May 1979): 241–64.
9. Victor Turner, *Dramas, Fields and Metaphors: Symbolic Action in Human Society* (Ithaca, NY: Cornell University Press, 1974), 64–68.

10. I once attended a public talk by Turner at the University of Virginia. A very conservative-looking academic wearing a blue blazer and khakis, clearly exasperated with Turner's embrace of the marginal, asked him if he was actually saying that nothing creative ever really emerged from out of institutions. He replied (and I am paraphrasing), "Absolutely. Creativity always comes from the margins."
11. See Vernon Schubel, "When the Prophet Went on the *Mirac* He Saw a Lion on the Road: The *Mirac* in the Alevi-Bektaşi Tradition," in *The Prophet Muhammad's Ascension: New Cross-Cultural Encounters*, ed. Frederick Colby and Christiane Gruber (Bloomington: Indiana University Press, 2010), 330–43.
12. Thankfully, this current generation of undergraduates seems more open to these concepts than previous ones. Many of them see positionality and intersectionality as givens. They have come of age in the wake of Black Lives Matters. They are far more willing than their parents and grandparents to accept the fact that gender needs to be understood more as spectrum than a simple binary.
13. Kenan Rifai and Jalaluddin Rumi, *Listen: Commentary on the Spiritual Couplets of Mevlana Rumi*, trans. Victoria Holbrook (Louisville: Fons Vitae, 2011).
14. Talal Asad, quoted in Shahab Ahmed, *What Is Islam? The Importance of Being Islamic* (Princeton, NJ: Princeton University Press. 2016), 271–72.
15. Ahmed, *What Is Islam?*, 271–86.
16. John Green, "Islam, the Quran, and the Five Pillars All Without a Flamewar: Crash Course World History #13," YouTube Video, 12:52, https://www.youtube.com/watch?v=TpcbfxtdoI8 (accessed November 4, 2022).
17. Hodgson, *Venture of Islam*, 30–39.
18. Vernon Schubel, "Thoughts on Dissecting an Octopus: Aaron Hughes, Marshall Hodgson, and Navigating the Normative Descriptive Divide," *Bulletin for the Study of Religion* 42, no. 4 (2014): 15–21.
19. In the case of Kenyon College, this situation is exacerbated by the fact that we sit upon a hill overlooking a valley filled with "townies" who work with their bodies in farms and factories, as we engage the world of ideas (and also by the presence of a popular Political Science

department populated by disciples of Hodgson's former colleague at the University of Chicago, Leo Strauss, who envisioned "Western civilization" as largely an ongoing dialogue with Plato and Aristotle).
20. See Farah Bakaari, "Islam and Its Others" (in this volume).
21. Bakaari, "Islam and Its Others."
22. Edward Curtis, "On the Margins of Islamic Doctrine" (in this volume).
23. Bakaari, "Islam and Its Others."

CONTRIBUTORS

Farah Bakaari is a PhD student in the Department in Literatures of English at Cornell University. Her publicly engaged writing on African, postcolonial, and diasporic fiction, poetry, and politics has appeared in *History News Network, Africa Is a Country*, and *LSE Africa*.

Kathryn D. Blanchard is the Charles A. Dana Professor of Religious Studies, emerita at Alma College. She is the author of multiple articles and books about Christian ethics and the environment, including *The Protestant Ethic or the Spirit of Capitalism: Christians, Freedom, and Free Markets*.

Henry D. Brill studies early modern Islamic history and is senior associate at Breakwater Strategy, a strategic communications and insights firm based in Washington, D.C. He previously worked at the Berkley Center for Religion, Peace, and World Affairs at Georgetown University.

Edward E. Curtis IV is William M. and Gail M. Plater Chair of the Liberal Arts and professor of religious studies at Indiana University, Indianapolis. He is the author or editor of over a dozen books about Black, Muslim, and Arab American history and life, including *The Call of Bilal: Islam in the African Diaspora*.

Max Johnson Dugan is a doctoral candidate in the Department of Religious Studies at the University of Pennsylvania, where he studies Islamic material and visual culture, embodiment, and emotions. He is also the designer of several projects in the digital humanities.

Michael Muhammad Knight is assistant professor of religion and cultural studies at the University of Central Florida. Knight has authored over a dozen books about Islam, including *Muhammad's Body: Baraka Networks and the Prophetic Assemblage* and *Metaphysical Africa*.

Vernon James Schubel is professor of religious studies, Asian and Middle East studies, and Islamic civilization and cultures at Kenyon College. He is author of *Teaching Humanity: An Alternative Introduction to Islam* and *Religious Performance in Contemporary Islam*.

Holly Donahue Singh is associate professor of instruction at the Judy Genshaft Honors College at the University of South Florida. A sociocultural and medical anthropologist focusing on South Asia, she is the author of several articles and the book *Infertility in a Crowded Country: Hiding Reproduction in India*.

Tess M. Waggoner is a writer, producer, translator, and researcher who has focused much of their professional life on cultural exchange and understanding between the Middle East and the United States. Waggoner has studied at New York University and Middle East Technical University in Ankara.

ACKNOWLEDGMENTS

The making of this volume is a testament, first and foremost, to the contributors' willingness to work together during the COVID-19 pandemic, using both email and videoconferencing to conceptualize and produce it. Most of us who ended up writing for the volume began meeting in early 2021 to brainstorm possible foci. Max Johnson Dugan was particularly helpful in our collective efforts to gather a large group of potential contributors. Not everyone who first met together had the time to complete a chapter, and, once I had refined the overall purpose and tenor of the book, I reached out to additional writers. Each contributor submitted an abstract by end of March 2021, at which time I gave everyone some initial feedback. We then drafted our chapters and met in October 2021, via videoconference, to share our questions and comments on our work. I have found this step essential to making edited volumes cohere. Once every contributor knows what the other is arguing, they can make both explicit and implicit allusions to one another's chapters, as we do in this book. But there was another benefit of meeting, even if, at that moment, it had to be over Zoom. Still deep in the pandemic, we were able to connect with one another—some of us old friends, some meeting for the time, some of us knowing one another only through our publications—for a half day spent talking about meaningful questions in our scholarly and, in many cases, personal lives. The urgency of our topic, the diversity of Islam and Muslim communities, intensified the connections that day, but we also enjoyed one another's company; it was a chance to be in community in an atomistic era.

Contributors then finished their final drafts by the end of 2021, and I made some editorial changes here and there in preparing the volume for anonymous peer review. The reviewers were largely supportive, but they also offered several helpful suggestions for improvement, which I then implemented in the version submitted for copyediting. I thank Wendy Lochner, my editor at Columbia University Press, for giving me sound advice and support throughout this process, and especially for working through the difficulties of the pandemic to obtain reviews of the book and guide it through the approval process at the press. I am grateful, as well, to the book's copyeditor, Emily Shelton, and to its production editor, Susan Pensak.

As readers will note, there are many other people who deserve credit for whatever contribution this book makes to the body of scholarly knowledge, and a lot of them are thanked, either explicitly or anonymously, in the volume's chapters. Every author in this volume is committed to the idea that scholars should be accountable, in some way, to the communities with whom we collaborate in order to teach and write. We hope that we have played at least a small role in encouraging an inclusive, accurate, and just vision for the study of Islam, one that makes room for all those with whom we work.

INDEX

AAR. *See* American Academy of Religion
abbuttu (slavery mark), 78
Abdal, Kaygusuz, 99
Abdal, Kul, 116
Abingdon v. Schempp, 244n6
Abrahamic religions, 21–22, 30–31. *See also specific religions*
activism: by Black women, 177; for children, 181; kinship and, 179–80; by Muslims, 20–21, 24, p1; political, 258–60; religion and, 21–22; social, 255, 258–60; against stereotypes, 32–33; for women, 183–85, 187
Advaita nondualism, 263
advertising, 20
aesthetics, 10–12, 26–27, 81, 84–86, 148–57, 271–72
Afghani, Jamal al-Din, 263
Afghanistan, 67–68, 74
African Americans. *See specific topics*

African Times and Orient Review (D. M. Ali), 137
Agha, Ali, 116
Ahmad, Mawlana Khwaja, 210–11
Ahmad, Sara, 42n30
Ahmadiyya Muslim Youth Association, 20
Ahmed, Shahab, 8, 220n50, 263–64
Ahmet, Karaca, 115
Ahrar, Khwaja, p9
Aisha, 51–52, 56, 61–63
Akarsu, Muhlis, 125
Aksoy, Ozan, 110
Alawite Muslims, 131n7
alcohol, 57–58
Alevi Muslims: Alawite Muslims and, 131n7; Anatolian, 131n8; as ashiks, 115–19; belief of, p10; culture of, 127–30; in Europe, 103; Haci Bektas to, 132n15; history of, 101–8; identity of, 119–20, 126–27, 274, 277–78; marginalization of, 11;

Alevi Muslims (*continued*)
  oppression of, 129–30; Othering of, 105; poetry of, 108–14, 119–27, 131n13, p5; scholarship on, 105–6; Sunni Islam and, 110, 264; syncretism and, 131n14; tradition of, 280; in Turkey, 9, 99–101, 251, 259–60; violence against, 118–19
Algeria, 86–88, 96n62
"Algeria's Tattoos" (Bendaas), 88
Ali, Ayaan Hirsi, 28–29
Ali, Dusé Mohamed, 137
Ali, Kecia, 26, 36–39
Ali, Muhammad, 149, p6
Ali, Noble Drew, 137
Ali, Sunni, 145
'Ali, 51–52, 56, 61, 104–5
Allah. *See* God
Alma College, 270
alms (*zakka*), 30
American Academy of Religion (AAR), 8
Anatolian Alevi Muslims, 131n8
anthropology, 169–70, 177–86, 252–53, 257–58
anti-Black racism, 85–86
anti-Muslim sentiments, 22–24, 26
anti-Muslim violence, p1
Arabic, 90n4, 96n63; Arabic texts, 6; hegemony of, 262; in Iraq, 104; 9/11 and, 7; Orientalism and, 6–7; Qur'an and, 8, 261–62; scholars of, 7–8; as tradition, 47–48; Turkish and, 5

Armstrong, Lyall R., 54
Arshaduddin, Mawlana, 210–13
Asad, Talal, 6, 30–31, 263
ashiks: Alevi Muslims as, 115–19; language to, 118–19; Mahzuni Serif as, 115, 117–27; poetry and, 108, 127–30; tradition of, 101, 128–29; Veysel as, 115–18, 126–27, p5; zikr by, 110–11
Asians. *See specific topics*
"Asiklarin Sozu Kalir" (Zula), 127–28
Aurora, Kendyl Noor, 73–74, 83–84
Autobiography of Malcolm X, The (Malcolm X), 278
Azwar, Khawlah Bint al-, 145

Baba, Kemter, 116
Bağcan, Selda, 127, p5
Bahasa-Indonesian, 261
Balbay, Mustafa, 115–18, 126
Baqrah, Surat al-, 85
Bara Imambara complex, p8
baraka, 60–63
bards. *See* ashiks
Barlas, Asma, 26
Barlas, Muhammadi, 201
Barnett, Richard, 170
Bayhaqi, 62
Bektash, Haji, 121, 125
Bektashi order, 103–4, 106–8, 111, 115–16, 121
belief: of Alevi Muslims, p10; in bible, 226–27; in concepts, 256–57; in God, 3, 140–41;

identity and, 168–69, 227–28;
  reproduction and, 184–85;
  tawhid, 256, 272–73
Bendaas, Yasmin, 86–88
Benegal, Shyam, 166
Bhagavad Gita, 224
Bible, 140–41, 157, 224, 226–27,
  229–30, 244n6
Black consciousness movement,
  153–54
Black liberation, 11–12, 135–39,
  148–58
Black Muslims: communities of,
  140; hegemony to, 278–79;
  identity of, 11–12; Islamization
  and, 14n6; F. Muhammad and,
  137, 140–41, 143, 145–47, 157–58,
  278; Nation of Islam to, 45,
  155–56, p6; Prophet Muhammad
  to, 140–41; in United States,
  157–58
Black Muslims in America, The
  (Lincoln), 143
Black people: Asians and, 73; Black
  Muslims, 89–90; Blackness and,
  144–45; communities of, 18;
  culture and, 146, 156–57; history
  of, 142; identity of, 15–16; Islamic
  doctrine to, 138–48; Nation of
  Islam to, 148–57; religion and,
  26–27; slavery of, 150; Sunni
  Islam and, 26–27; in United
  States, 136–37, 142, 146, 151
Black Shriners, 139–40
Black Skin, White Masks (Fanon),
  15–16

Black women, 76, 177
Blyden, Edward Wilmot, 137, 140
Boas, Franz, 169
bodies, 60–63, 81–83, 148–57, 272–75
Bora, Amir Ortu, 198
Bowie, David, 279
Brown Girl Magazine, 83–84,
  96n54
Buddhism, 174, 263, 271
Bush, George W., 74–75

Campbell, Joseph, 228
Carter, Jimmy, 228
Catholicism, 75, 263, 271
Central Asia, 12, 111–14, 216n9, 251,
  265–66, 276, 279. *See also*
  Mongols
Chaghatayid-Moghul network. *See*
  Mongols
children. *See* reproduction
China, 26
Chishti, Muʻinuddin, 253–54
Christianity: Bible in, 140–41, 157,
  224, 244n6; culture of, 185;
  education and, 13, 231–35; ethics
  of, 226–31, 242–43; in Europe,
  265–66; God in, 85; identity in,
  235–36; Judaism and, 94n41,
  225–26, 229, 232–33, 270; prayer
  in, 226–27; Quakers in, 254–55;
  in Qur'an, 20; in religious
  studies, 224–26; religious
  studies and, 246n33
Chughtai, Ismat, 172–73
Çimen, Nesimi, 125
Clinton, George, 147

colonialism, 10, 72–73, 163–65
communities, 94n41, 217n27; of Black Muslims, 140; of Black people, 18; heresy in, 11; language in, 103; leadership in, 70–71; marginalization in, 3–4, 9–10, 28–29, 71–72; in modernity, 102–3; of Muslims, 1, 17, 45, 53, 55–56, 157–58; political marginalization in, 12; of Salafism, 59; scholarship and, 129; of Sunni Islam, 4–5
Companions of Muhammad, 7, 49–56, 58, 60–65, 77
comrades (*dost*), 126–27
concubines, 95n50
Converse, Hyla, 253–54
conversion, 212–14, 269–70
Crash Course (YouTube series), 266
culture: Abrahamic religions in, 21–22; of Alevi Muslims, 127–30; anti-Muslim sentiments in, 22–23; Black people and, 146, 156–57; of Christianity, 185; of Europe, 261, 272; folk Islam in, 63–64; of Germany, 29–30; globalization of, 32; of higher education, 281n6, 282n19; human heritage and, 267; of India, 167–68; marginalization in, 45–46; Mongols in, 265–66; of Muslims, 176, 181, 269–71; Muslim women in, 168–77; after 9/11, 234; Othering in, 15, 265; pamphlet Islam in, 2; political, 199, 207–8, 219n42; popular, 31–32, 114; Qur'an in, 5; religion and, 17, 87, p10; reproduction and, 161–62; of South Asia, 162–68; of Sufism, 100; tradition and, 32–35, 95n52; of Turkey, 42n25, 101–8; of United States, 72–73, 238–39, 282n12; from Western civilization, 273–74
customary practices (*'urf*), 35

Dakake, Maria, 240–41
Dawkins, Richard, 257
Deanar, Tynetta, 144, 153
dedes (religious leaders), 103–4, 110
deen (*dīn*), 70–71, 90n4
DeWeese, Devin, 139
Divani, Dertli, 111
Divine Reality (Haqiqat), 256
divorce, 36
dost (comrade), 126–27
dower (*mahr*), 37–38
Dressler, Markus, 105–6
du'a (supplicatory prayer), 110
Dughlat, Mirza Muhammad Haydar ("Mirza Haydar"): history from, 193–97; for Mongols, 197–207; reputation of, 12, 216n9, p9
dystopia, 58–59

education, 281n6; Bible in, 244n6; Christianity and, 13, 231–35; ethics and, 224–25, 268–72; at Kenyon College, 249, 262, 266, 270, 274, 282n19; from Mapping Islamophobia Project, 22–23;

marginalization and, 18–19, 249–53; Muslims and, 13–14, 235–39; poetry and, 115–16; religion and, 2, 28, 30–31, 42n25, 226–31, 239–43; of stereotypes, 19–20; in Sufism, 203–4, 209–10; teaching and, 235–39. *See also specific topics*
Egyptian Americans, 32
Elfenbein, Caleb, 19, 22–25
embodied marginalization, 12
embodied rituals, 149–50
embodiment, 69, 259. *See also* tattooing
emotional communities, 217n27
Encyclopaedia of Islam, 104, 109
Epic of Köroğlu, The, 112–13
Erdogan, Recep Tayyip, 104–5
Ernst, Carl, 7
Ertel, Murat, 128
Essien-Udom, E. U., 156
ethics: of Christianity, 226–31, 242–43; education and, 224–25, 268–72; from history, 141–42; humanistic values, 9; identity and, 34; of Islamic doctrine, 135–38, 157–58; of Nation of Islam, 27; philosophy of, 153–54; of progressive values, 36; religion and, 7; rituals and, 154–55; theology and, 75
ethnic cleansing, 26
ethnography, 26–27, 168–77, 252–53
Europe: Alevi Muslims in, 103; Christianity in, 265–66; culture of, 261, 272; Eurocentrism, 71–72, 260; history of, 72; Turkey and, 111
Evans-Pritchard, E. E., 169

Fadlallah, Muhammad Hussein, 93n32
faith. *See* belief
Fanon, Frantz, 15–16, 18
Farrakhan, Louis, 144
Farsi, 262
fasting, 2, 21, 30, 57, 114, 151, 229
Fatima, 51
Federal Bureau of Investigation (FBI), 138, 143–44, 148
feminism, 26, 31–32, 37, 245n16, 258–59
Feminist Theory (hooks), 76
Fertility (film), 166–67
fiqh (jurisprudence), 35–36, 39, 251, 264
Five Pillars of Islam, 2, 228
folk Islam, 63–64
folklore, 129–30
folk music, 99–101, 126, p5. *See also* poetry
folk wisdom, 275–76
food, 150–53, p7
Foster, Craig, 223
Foundation for Ethnic Understanding, 20
France, 26, 109
Frazer, James George, 231
Fruit of Islam, 153–55, 157, p6

Gandhi, Mahatma, 162–63
Garvey, Marcus, 137, 140

Geertz, Clifford, 6
Germany, 29–30
Ghazali, Al-, 269
globalization: Central Asia in, 279; of culture, 32; of Eurocentrism, 71–72; of human heritage, 265–68; of Islamophobia, 25–26; Muslim women in, 162–68; tradition in, 268–69; transnational media, 46–47; Turkey in, 127–28
God: belief in, 3, 140–41; in Christianity, 85; consciousness, 21, 30; humanity and, 263; in Judaism, 30; jurisprudence and, 37; to Muslims, 256–57; in poetry, 119–25; praying to, 21; Prophet Muhammad and, 10, 62, p10; Qur'an and, 2, 120, 269, 273, p10; relationship with, 82; in religion, 4, 110–11; in scholarship, 35–36; slavery and, 153; *taqwa*, 21, 30; *tawhid*, 256, 272–73
Golden Bough, The (Frazer), 231
Golden Horde, 139
governmental law (*qanun*), 35
Green, John, 266
Green, Todd, 22
Grinnell College, 23
Gültekin, Hasret, 125

Haci Bektas, 121, 132n15
hadith: bodies in, 60–63; in Islamic studies, 45–49; prayer in, 59; Qur'an and, 7, 64; scholarship on, 10, 49–60, 63–65; Sunan Abu Dawud, p3; tattooing in, 79–80, 95n51; theology, 8
hajj (pilgrimage), 57, 92n19, 278
El Hajj Malik El Shabazz. *See* Malcolm X
Hak. *See* God
Hallaj, Mansur Al-, 86
Haqiqat (Divine Reality), 256
Hari Bhari (film), 166–67
Hasan, 51
Hassan, Shakeela, 157
Hauser, Walter, 170
Hayat al- Anbiya' fi Quburihim (Bayhaqi), 62
Hazrat Abbas Dargah, p8
healing bodies, 81–83
Heaven (*jannat*), 256–57
hegemony, 10, 49, 102, 119, 262, 278–79
helal (permitted), 125
Hell (*jahannam*), 256–57
heresy, 8, 11
higher education, 281n6; at Kenyon College, 249, 262, 266, 270, 274, 282n19; at Oklahoma State University, 250, 278; religion in, 231–39; at University of Virginia, 252–53, 258
hijabs, 16, 26
Hindi, 171, 174
Hindus, 30–31, 173, 224
Hisham, 52
history. *See specific topics*
Hodgson, Marshall, 7, 253–55, 254, 261, 267–68
homosexuality, 58
hooks, bell, 67, 76

How to Eat to Live
 (Muhammad, E.), 150–51
human heritage, 264–68
humanistic values, 9
humanities, 13–14, 275–76
humanity (insaniyya), 259, 263, 267, 272–75, 276–81
human sacrifice, 125
Huntington, Samuel P., 74–75
Hurston, Zora Neale, 169
Husayn (Imam), 51, 111, 271
Hüseyin of Akkaşlar, 116

"I Am on a Long Thin Path" (poem), 99–100
'ibada (act of worship), 20–21
Ibn 'Abbas, 54–63
ibn Anas, Malik, 48, 61–62
Ibn 'Arabi, 256, 265, 269, 271
ibn Da'ima, Qatada, 55
Ibn Hanbal, 56
Ibn Manẓūr, 78
Ibn Mas'ud, 54–60, 62
ibn Rabah, Bilal, 140, 145
Ibn Sa'd, 62–63
Ibn Shumayl, 78
Ibn Sina, 269
Ibn Taymiyya, 256, 269
ibn 'Uqba, al-Walid, 59
ibn al-Zubayr, 'Abd Allah, 52
ibn al-Zubayr, Hisham, 52
ibn al-Zubayr, 'Urwa, 52
identity: aesthetics and, 10–11, 26–27; of Alevi Muslims, 119–20, 126–27, 274, 277–78; in anthropology, 185–86; belief and, 168–69, 227–28; of Black Muslims, 11–12; of Black people, 15–16; in Christianity, 235–36; after conversion, 269–70; Dughlat, 198; ethics and, 34; of Muslims, 4–5, 250–51; from Orientalism, 35; from Othering, 21, 32; politics, 270; public, 119; from religion, 175–76, 183–84, 235–39; scholarship on, 185–87; sexuality in, 168–69; stereotypes of, 17–18; in Sufism, 207; of women, 39–40
ijtihad, 21, 37
'Ikrima, 58
immigrants, 23, 25, 29–30, 144
inclusion, 13–14
India: Bara Imambara complex in, p8; culture of, 167–68; Hazrat Abbas Dargah in, p8; Muslims in, 162–63, 173; Pakistan and, 164–65; religion in, 173; reproduction in, 166–67; United States and, 165–66, 172, 177; women in, 12, 179–80, p8. *See also* South Asia
Infidel (Ali, A. H.), 28–29, 31–32
insaniyya (humanity), 259, 263, 267, 272–75, 276–81
Instagram, 90
intellectual tradition, 50–51, 64
Iraq, 104, 111
Islam. *See specific topics*
Islamic Awareness Week, 23
Islamic Circle of North America, 20
Islamic doctrine: to Black people, 138–48; ethics of, 135–38, 157–58

Islamic embodiment, 69
Islamic revivalist forces, 46–47, 46–48
Islamic studies, 220n50; hadith in, 45–49; history of, 6–7; in humanities, 13–14; Muslims in, 64–65; philosophy of, 168–77; scholarship from, 105; stereotypes before, 6; in Western civilization, 102
Islamization, 14n6
Islamophobia: after colonialism, 164–65; globalization of, 25–26; Mapping Islamophobia Project, 19–20, 19–25; marginalization and, 1; Othering and, 17; prejudice and, 9

Jafri, Iqbal, 20
Jahan, Rashid, 172–73
jahannam (Hell), 256–57
Jaikaran, Elizabeth, 83–84
Jamaluddin, Shaykh, 209–10
jannat (Heaven), 256–57
jinns, 59–60
Judaism, 30, 78–79, 94n41, 225–26, 229, 232–33, 270
jurisprudence (*fiqh*), 35–37, 39, 45, 89, 251, 264

Kapila, Shuchi, 169
Karababa, Gülsüm, 125
Kehl-Bodrogi, Kristina, 107–8
Kenyon College, 249, 262, 266, 270, 274, 282n19
Khabeer, Abdul, 26–27
khalq (creation), 62–63
khamr (wine), 57

Khan, Abdul-Rashid, 199–202
Khan, Chagatay, 197
Khan, Chinggis, 194, 197–98. *See also* Mongols
Khan, Ira, 74
Khan, Nusrat Fateh Ali, 271
Khan, Sultan-Sa'id, 199, 201–5
Khan, Tughlugh-Temür, 208–14
Khandelwal, Meena, 169
Khanim, Muhibb-Sultan, 199
Khanish, Habiba-Sultan, 202
Khare, R. S., 170
Khomeini (Ayatollah), 228
kinship, 216n6; anthropology and, 177–80; philosophy of, 196, 198–99; Sufism and, 197–207
"Kizilbas" (Mahzuni Serif), 119–21
Kizilbash. *See* Alevi Muslims
Kılıç-Schubel, Nurten, 206, 250
Kool and the Gang, 152
Köprülü, Fuat, 105–7, 114
Köroğlu (Su), 111–12, 115, 128
"Köroğlu-Türküler- Şir," (song), 112
Kugle, Scott, 58

language: to ashiks, 118–19; in Central Asia, 251; in communities, 103; fluency in, 174–75; marginalization with, 107; of Muslims, 5; of non-Arab Muslims, 6; in poetry, 124; politics and, 126–27, 261–62; reputations of, 163–64; in South Asia, 262. *See also specific languages*
law. *See specific topics*
Lawrence, Bruce, 7

Lebanon, 90
liminality, 257–58
Lincoln, C. Eric, 143
Lombroso, Cesare, 72
Lowe, Ermine X, 153

Madhvacarya, 263
Mahmoud, Saba, 6
Mahmud, Khwaja, 203–6
mahr (dower), 37–38
Mahzuni Serif, Ashik, 115, 117–27
Majied, Eugene, 144
Malcolm X, 135–36, 144, 146–48, 156–57, 278
Maldonado-Estrada, Alyssa, 75, 87–88
Malinowski, Bronislaw, 169
Mapping Islamophobia Project, 19–25
marginalization, 282n10; of Alevi Muslims, 11; in communities, 3–4, 9–10, 28–29, 71–72; concepts of, 89; in culture, 45–46; education and, 18–19, 249–53; embodied, 12; experience of, 178–79; in higher education, 252–53; Islamophobia and, 1; with language, 107; of Mongols, 207–15; of Muslims, 9–10, 25–31, 73, 185–86; of Muslim women, 161–62, 185–87; oppression and, 3–4; from Orientalism, 76; Othering and, 39, 260–64, 276–81; poetry and, 99–101; political, 9–10, 12, 18, 24–25, 29–30; rebellion against, 32–34; from religion, 13; scholarship on, 27–28; of Shi'a Islam, 47; social, 12; of tattooing, 73–76; of tradition, 46; in United States, 17, 164–65; of women, 186–87, 259. *See also specific topics*

marriage, 33, 36–39, 95n49
Marshall, Wende, 171
McCutcheon, Russell, 239–40, 268–69, 270
McKinnon, Susan, 171
Mead, Margaret, 169
Mecca, 2, 38, 57, 92n19, 136
media, 46–47, 67–70, 73–76, 90, 111–12, 225
mediating tradition, 70, 83–86, 88–89
melancholic Muslims, 31–40, 42n30, 277
Melchert, Christopher, 54
Mencius, 265
menstruation, 58
Message to the Blackman (Muhammad, E.), 141
Middle Ages, 35
Middle East, 54, 194–95, 253
minorities, 12, 15–16, 71–72, 162–63. *See also specific minorities*
Mirza, Sayyid-Muhammad, 199–200
Mirza Haydar. *See* Dughlat
modernity: communities in, 102–3; dystopia in, 58–59; to Islamic revivalist forces, 48; modern affectivity, 197–207; Muslims and, 31–40, 262–63; Othering in, 27; religion in, 29–30; secularism in, 31, 39; Sufism in, 218n29

Mongols: in culture, 265–66; Dughlat for, 197–207; history of, 193–97, 215n3; marginalization of, 207–15; Turkey and, 12
Moorish Science Temple of America, 137
al-muʻallaqāt, 77–78
Muʻawiyya, 56
Muhammad. *See* Prophet Muhammad
Muhammad, Clara, 146, 158
Muhammad, Elijah: leadership of, 148–57, 157–58, p6; Nation of Islam and, 11–12, 135–38, 140–47, 157–58; teachings of, 275, 279
Muhammad, Fard, 137, 140–41, 143, 145–47, 157–58, 278
Muhammad, Wesley, 63
music, 99–101, 108–12, 115, 126–29, 260–61, p5, p10. *See also specific topics*
Muslims, 216n6; activism by, 20–21, 24, p1; alcohol to, 57–58; in anthropology, 257; Asians and, 268; Bektashi order of, 103–4, 106–8, 111, 115–16, 121; Black, 89–90; communities of, 1, 17, 45, 53, 55–56, 157–58; conversion and, 212–13; culture of, 176, 181, 269–71; education and, 13–14, 235–39; embodied marginalization of, 12; ethnography of, 26–27; five pillars of Islam to, 2; God to, 256–57; Hazrat Abbas Dargah to, p8; heresy to, 8; history of, 50–51, 207–15; human heritage to, 265–68; *ʻibada* to, 20–21; identity of, 4–5, 250–51; as immigrants, 144; in India, 162–63, 173; in Iraq, 111; in Islamic studies, 64–65; Islamophobia to, 19–25; language of, 5; marginalization of, 9–10, 25–31, 73, 185–86; in media, 67–68, 73–76; modernity and, 31–40, 262–63; Muslims Against Hunger Project, 19–20; mysticism and, 230–31; non-Arab, 6, 253; non-Muslims and, 1, 13, 30, 48, 89, 224–25, 249; oppression of, 31–32; Orientalism for, 254; Othering of, 265–66; philosophy of, 162–68; Prophet Muhammad to, 263–64; queer, 26; reputation of, 135–36; ritual purity to, 57, 60–61; Rohingya, 26; scholarship on, 5–9, 258–60, 268–72; slavery and, 78–80, 271; in South Asia, 251–52; stereotypes of, 228–29; Sufism and, 195–97; tattooing by, 10–11, 67–70, 80–90, p4; taxonomies on, 101–2; terrorism and, 22–23; tradition to, 77–80, 90n3, 277–78; in Turkey, 102–3; Twelver Shiʻa, 9, 51, 65n4, 85–86, 90, 93n32; in United States, 21, p6; violence against, 23–25. *See also specific topics*
Muslim studies. *See* Islamic studies

Muslim women, 245n16; in culture, 168–77; in globalization, 162–68; marginalization of, 161–62, 185–87; reproduction to, 177–85
Musnad (al-Tayalisi), 54–56, 58–60
My Octopus Teacher (documentary), 223

nabidh (fermented beverage), 57–58
Naeem, Abdul Basit, 144
Nanji, Azim, 253
Naqshbandi-Ahrariyya, 203–4, 209–10, 220n59, p9
Naqshbandi Sufi Muslim network, p9
narratives, 68, 72–73
Nation of Islam: to Black Muslims, 45, 155–56, p6; to Black people, 148–57; ethics of, 27; food in, 150–53, p7; history of, 138–47; Malcolm X and, 148–49, 278; E. Muhammad and, 11–12, 135–38, 140–47, 157–58; stereotypes of, 264; women in, 153–54. *See also* Black Muslims
Nation Salafism, 63
Native Americans, 71–72
Nawas, John, 54
Negro World (Garvey), 137
neocolonialism, 10
New Zealand, 74
9/11, 5–6, 7, 22–25, 234, 236–37
non-Arab Muslims, 6, 253
non-Muslims, 1, 13, 30, 48, 89, 224–25, 249
nubuwwat (belief in Prophets), 256

Ocak, Ahmet Yasar, 104
Oklahoma State University, 250, 278
Omar, Ilhan, p2
Operation Desert Storm, 229
oppression: of Alevi Muslims, 129–30; marginalization and, 3–4; of Muslims, 31–32; from Othering, 19, 29; in patriarchy, 83; scholarship on, 23–24; from stereotypes, 25; by Sunni Islam, 11; from violence, 39–40; of women, 37–38, 53–54
Orientalism: Arabic and, 6–7; identity from, 35; marginalization from, 76; for minorities, 15–16; for Muslims, 254; narratives from, 68; Othering and, 280; renaissance for, 7–8; in scholarship, 251; stereotypes from, 34, 74–75, 276; Sunni Islam and, 47; tropes of, 70; Western civilization and, 73
Orientalism (Said), 16, 74, 254, 261
Othering: of Alevi Muslims, 105; in culture, 15, 265; in humanity, 259; identity from, 21, 32; Islamophobia and, 17; marginalization and, 39, 260–64, 276–81; in modernity, 27; of Muslims, 265–66; oppression from, 19, 29; of Shi'a Islam, 264
Ottoman Empire, 103–4
Ozdemir, Ulas, 125, 133n25

Pakistan, 164–65, 251, 258–59, p10.
    See also South Asia
Pakistani Twelver Muslims, 9, 51, 65, 83–86, 90, 93
pamphlet Islam, 2, 21–22
Papua New Guinea, 229–30
patriarchy, 83, 125
pedagogy, 13–14
Persian language, 5
philosophy: of Black liberation, 138–39, 157–58; of ethics, 153–54; of higher education, 274; of Islamic studies, 168–77; of kinship, 196, 198–99; after Mecca, 57; of mediating tradition, 83–86; of Muslims, 162–68; of prayer, 154–55; of sharia law, 30, 124–25; of Sufism, 204–5; Truth, 260–61, 273; in Western civilization, 272
physiognomy, 72
pilgrimage (hajj), 56–57, 92n19, 278
Pink Floyd, 264
Pir Sultan Abdul, 109, 117–18, 121–22, 126–27, 259–60
poetry: of Alevi Muslims, 108–14, 119–27, 131n13, p5; anthologies of, 109–10; ashiks and, 108, 127–30; ecology in, 114; education and, 115–16; God in, 119–25; language in, 124; marginalization and, 99–101; Naqshbandi-Ahrariyya in, 203–4; religion and, 111–12; as resistance, 11, 119–27; Schubel on, 109; Sufi, 100, 116, 203–5, 214, 219n40

police violence, 144
political activism, 258–60
political culture, 199, 207–8, 219n42
political liberation, p7
political marginalization, 9–10, 12, 18, 24–25, 29–30
politics, 126–27, 261–62
Poole, Elijah. *See* Muhammad, Elijah
popular culture, 31–32, 114
prayer: bodies and, 62–63; in Christianity, 226–27; daily, 2, 32, 261, 273; fasting and, 21, 229; in hadith, 59; at nighttime, 57; prayer-callers, 140; space for, 16, 154–55, p8; for Sunni Islam, 122; tradition for, 71–72, 110–11
pre-commitment scholarship, 253–58
prejudice, 9, 33
Presumed Guilty (Green, T.), 22
progressive values, 36
Promise of Happiness, The (Ahmad, Sara), 42n30
Prophet Muhammad, 220n50; accounts of, 60–63; to Black Muslims, 140–41; Companions of Muhammad, 7, 49–56, 58, 60–65, 77; death of, 56; family of, 252; God and, 10, 62, p10; for humanity, 267; interpretations of, 7, 49, 58, 77, 79; Mecca and, 2; to Muslims, 263–64; in Qur'an, 49–53, 256; reputation of, 35, 60; scholarship on, p3; in Shi'a Islam, 64, 118–19; Truth and, 273
public identity, 119

qanun (governmental law), 35
Qawwali musicians, p10
qiyamat (day of judgment), 256
Qizilbash-Alevi tradition, 109–10
Quakers, 254–55
queer Muslims, 26
Quilt and Other Stories, The (Chughtai), 172–73
Quraishi-Landes, Asifa, 37–39
Qur'an: Arabic and, 8, 261–62; Bible and, 140–41, 157, 224; Christianity in, 20; in culture, 5; God and, 2, 120, 269, 273, p10; hadith and, 7, 64; jinns in, 59–60; Prophet Muhammad in, 49–53, 256; to Sunni Islam, 35; tafsir, 28; women and, 26–28, 31–32
Qur'an and Woman (wadud), 27–28, 31–32
Qureshi, Jawad Anwar, 240
Qutb, Sayyid, 263

racism, 42n30, 72, 85–86, 158, 261
radical humanism, 102
Ramadan, 30, 151
Ramy (TV show), 32
Rauf, Muhammad Abdul, 144
rebellion, 32–34
reclamation, 148–57
reform, 22, 31, 36–37, 40, 150, 177, 263, 277
relationships, 86–88, 180–81, 201–2, 205
religion: AAR, 8; activism and, 21–22; aesthetics of, 11–12; Black people and, 26–27; culture and, 17, 87, p10; diversity of, 270; education and, 2, 28, 30–31, 42n25, 226–31, 239–43; ethics and, 7; in feminism, 258–59; God in, 4, 110–11; in higher education, 231–39; history and, 254–55; identity from, 175–76, 183–84, 235–39; in India, 173; law and, 90n4; marginalization from, 13; in modernity, 29–30; poetry and, 111–12; political culture and, 207–8, 219n42; prejudice in, 33; religious performance, 170–71; religious studies, 223–26, 235–39, 235–43, 244n9, 246n33, 270; reproduction and, 182–83; roots of, 256–57; scholarship on, 47–48, 245n12; sex in, 33–34; in South Asia, 253–54; spirituality and, 40; stigma from, 12; theology, 8, 75, 251, 264; tradition in, 107–8; in Turkey, p5; in United States, 154–55, p7; women in, 38–39
Religious Performance in Contemporary Islam (Schubel), 47
Renard, John, 110–11
reproduction: in anthropology, 177–84; belief and, 184–85; culture and, 161–62; in India, 166–67; minorities and, 162–63; to Muslim women, 177–85; religion and, 182–83; scholarship on, 176–77; women and, 167–68
resistance, 11, 119–27

Rifai, Kenan, 262
ritual purity, 57, 60–61
Robinson, Marilyn Waldman, 7
Rohingya Muslims, 26
Róisín, Fariha, 68–69, 81–83, 87
roots, of religion (*usul al-din*), 256–57
Rosenwein, Barbara, 217n27
Rumi, Maulana Jalaluddin, 265, 271
Russia, 228
Rutgers Shalom-Salaam, 20

Sachedina, Abdulaziz, 170, 253–56, 254
Sadiq, Ja'far as-, 51, 63
Sadiq, Muhammad, 137
Safi, Omid, 270
Sağ, Arif, 271
Saglam, Hande, 126
Said, Edward, 6–7, 15–16, 74, 254–55, 261. *See also* Orientalism
Salafism, 42n25, 46–47, 59, 63
salah (prayer), p8
Santibañez, Tamara, 75–76
Saudi Arabia, 42n25
Sayeed, Asma, 53–54
"Saying Allah Allah Comrade'" (Mahzuni Serif), 121–25
saz (lute music), p10
scholarship, 133n25, 216n9; aesthetics and, 271–72; on Alevi Muslims, 105–6; anthropology, 169–70, 177–78, 177–84, 177–86, 252–53, 257–58; communities and, 129; on Companions of Muhammad, 7, 49–56, 58, 60–65, 77; ethnography and, 168–77; feminism in, 26, 31–32; God in, 35–36; on hadith, 10, 49–60, 63–65; history of, 53–54; from humanities, 275–76; for humanity, 276–81; on identity, 185–87; from Islamic studies, 105; on marginalization, 27–28; on Muslims, 5–9, 258–60, 268–72; Muslim studies, 6; by non-Muslims, 13; on oppression, 23–24; Orientalism in, 251; political marginalization in, 9–10; pre-commitment, 253–58; on Prophet Muhammad, p3; on religion, 47–48, 245n12; religious studies, 223–26, 235–39, 235–43, 244n9, 246n33, 270; on reproduction, 176–77; from Schubel, 9, 47–49, 89, 169; from Shi'a Islam, 35; on slavery, 78–79; social activism and, 255; on South Asia, 257–58; from Sunni Islam, 50–51; tattooing in, 78; taxonomies in, 109; Truth in, 260–61; women in, 23. *See also* Islamic studies
Schubel, Vernon: on poetry, 109; on religious performance, 170–71; on religious studies, 241–42; scholarship from, 9, 47–49, 89, 169; teaching by, 229, 231
secularism, 31, 39
semah (dance), p10

seminal traits, 268
Seneviratne, H. L., 170
sex, 33–34, 36, 79
sexism, 95n49
sexuality, 168–69
Shabazz, Abdul, 156
Shaheedi, Suraya, 68, 74
Shankara, 265
Shankland, David, 105
sharia: law, 7, 30, 124–25, 253–55; stereotypes of, 35–36, 263–64, 278
Shi'a Islam (Shi'ism): in colonialism, 163; marginalization of, 47; for non-Arab Muslims, 253; Othering of, 264; in Pakistan, 258–59; Pakistani Twelver Muslims, 9, 51, 65, 83–86, 90, 93; Prophet Muhammad in, 64, 118–19; representation of, 63; scholarship from, 35; Sufism and, 86, 252, 255–57, 280; Sunni Islam and, 8–9, 30–31, 35–36, 48–49, 52, 93n32, 263; tradition in, 170–71; Twelver Shi'a Muslims, 9, 51, 65n4, 85–86, 90, 93n32
Sikhs, 173
Singer, Wendy, 169
Sistani, Ali al-Husseini al-, 93n32
Sıtkı of Tarsus, 116
slavery, 78–80, 145, 150, 153, 271
social activism, 255, 258–60
social marginalization, 12
social media, 90

Somalia, 18–19, 23, 25, 42n25
"Some would damn me, some would hang me" (Mahzuni Serif), 119–21
South Asia, 162–68, 251–54, 257–58, 262. *See also specific topics*
South Pacific Islanders, 71–72, 91n11
Spellberg, Denise, 26
spirituality, 40
Spivak, Gayatri, 249
stereotypes, 91n11; activism against, 32–33; education of, 19–20; fasting and, 21; of identity, 17–18; of melancholic Muslims, 31–40, 42n30, 277; of minorities, 71–72; of Muslims, 228–29; before Muslim studies, 6; of Nation of Islam, 264; after 9/11, 22–23; oppression from, 25; from Orientalism, 34, 74–75, 276; of sharia, 35–36, 263–64, 278; of Sunni Islam, 253; of terrorism, 236–37; in United States, 231; of violence, 28–29; of women, 15–16
stigma, 12, 107
students. *See* education
Su, Ruhi, 111–12, 118–19, 128
Sufism: affectivity in, 206; authority in, 205–6, 213; in Central Asia, 220n59, 276; culture of, 100; dedes in, 103–4; education in, 203–4, 209–10; history of, 6, 115–17, 262, p9; identity in, 207; kinship and, 197–207; in modernity, 218n29;

Sufism (*continued*)
  Muslims and, 195–97; networks in, 202–3, 213–14; in Pakistan, 251; philosophy of, 204–5; Shi'a Islam and, 86, 252, 255–57, 280; Sufi hagiography, 218n33; Sufi poetry, 100, 116, 203–5, 214, 219n40; Sunni Islam and, 277; tradition in, 212, 264, 266, 274; Turko-Mongols and, 12; virtues of, 258. *See also* Alevi Muslims
Sunan Abu Dawud, p3
Sunni Islam: Alevi Muslims and, 110, 264; Black people and, 26–27; communities of, 4–5; in media, 69–70; Nation of Islam and, 136; normativity, 9, 105; oppression by, 11; Orientalism and, 47; prayer for, 122; Qur'an to, 35; Salafism in, 46–47; scholarship from, 50–51; Shi'a Islam and, 8–9, 30–31, 35–36, 48–49, 52, 93n32, 263; stereotypes of, 253; Sufism and, 277; tattooing in, 77–80; tradition in, 80–81, p4. *See also* hadith
supplicatory prayer, 110
Supreme Wisdom, The (Muhammad, E.), 141
Suspended Odes, 77–78
Swahili, 261
syncretism, 107, 131n14
Syria, 104, 131n7

Tabaqat (Ibn Sa'd), 62–63
tafsir (Qur'anic commentary), 28

Taliban, 74
taqwa (God consciousness), 21, 30
Tarikh-i Rashidi (Dughlat). *See* Dughlat; Mongols
tattooing: aesthetics of, 81, 84–86; in Algeria, 96n62; Arabic literacy and, 96n63; in hadith, 79–80, 95n51; history of, 70–73; in Judaism, 78–79; marginalization of, 73–76; Mecca and, 92n19; by Muslims, 10–11, 67–70, 80–90, p4; relationships from, 86–88; in Sunni Islam, 77–80; women and, 69–70, 93n33
tawhid (belief in the unity of God), 256, 272–73
taxonomies, 101–2, 109
Tayalisi, Sulayman Abu Dawud al-, 54–55
teaching: education and, 235–39; in higher education, 235–39; of Islam, 223–26, 239–43; religious studies, 270; by Schubel, 229, 231
teleology, 254
Temple of Islam. *See* Nation of Islam
Temür, Amir, 194
terrorism, 5–6, 7, 22–25, 234, 236–37
"That I be the ink of the pen in your hands" (Pir Abdul Sultan), 126
theology, 8, 75, 251, 264
Thompson, Hunter S., 45

"Those Who March with Song" (radio show), 112
Timurid dynasties, 194–95, 217n22
tradition: of Alevi Muslims, 280; Arabic as, 47–48; of ashiks, 101, 128–29; in Catholicism, 271; culture and, 32–35, 95n52; in France, 109; in globalization, 268–69; intellectual, 50–51, 64; marginalization of, 46; of marriage, 33, 36, 38–39; of Mecca, 38; mediating, 70, 83–86, 88–89; to Muslims, 77–80, 90n3, 277–78; pilgrimage, 56–57; for prayer, 71–72, 110–11; Qizilbash-Alevi, 109–10; in religion, 107–8; ritual purity, 57, 60–61; in Shi'a Islam, 170–71; in Sufism, 212, 264, 266, 274; in Sunni Islam, 80–81, p4; in Wahhabism, 46–47
transnational media, 46–47
trauma, 75–76
Truth, 260–61, 273
Tüläk, Amir, 212–14
Turkey, 133n25; Alevi Muslims in, 9, 99–101, 251, 259–60; Central Asia and, 113–14; culture of, 42n25, 101–8; Europe and, 111; in globalization, 127–28; history of, 105–6; Mongols and, 12; Muslims in, 102–3; religion in, p5; Syria and, 104; Timurid dynasties in, 194–95; Turkish, 5, 126, 261. *See also* Mongols
Turko-Mongols. *See* Mongols

Turner, Edith, 169
Turner, Victor, 169, 252–53, 257–58
Tuskegee syphilis experiment, 142
Twelver Shi'a Muslims, 9, 51, 65n4, 85–86, 90, 93n32. *See also* tattooing
Twitter, 90

Umm 'Abd Allah, 51–52
umra, 57
UNIA. *See* Universal Negro Improvement Association
United States, 244n6; AAR in, 8; advertising in, 20; Afghanistan and, 68; anti-Muslim sentiments in, 23–24; anti-Muslim violence in, p1; Black liberation in, 11–12; Black Muslims in, 157–58; Black people in, 136–37, 142, 146, 151; culture of, 72–73, 238–39, 282n12; discrimination in, p2; FBI in, 138, 143–44, 148; hijabs in, 16; history of, 85–86; India and, 165–66, 172, 177; Islam in, 228–29; marginalization in, 17, 164–65; media in, 225; Muslims Against Hunger Project in, 19–20; Muslims in, 21, p6; Nation of Islam to, 147–48; after 9/11, 5–6; popular culture in, 31–32; religion in, 154–55, p7; stereotypes in, 231; violence in, 148
Universal Negro Improvement Association (UNIA), 140

University of Virginia, 252–53, 258
Urdu, 5, 163–64, 171–72, 174, 254, 261
'urf (customary practices), 35
usul al-din (roots of religion), 256–57
Uyghurs, 26
Uzbek, 251
"Uzun Ince Bir Yoldayim" (Veysel), 127

Veli, Haji Bektash, 121
Veli of İğdecik, 116
Venture of Islam, The (Hodgson), 254–55, 267–68
Veysel, Ashik, 115–18, 126–27, p5
violence: against Alevi Muslims, 118–19; anti-Muslim, p1; ethnic cleansing, 26; by Islamic revivalist forces, 46–47; Islamophobia and, 22–23; against Muslims, 23–25; oppression from, 39–40; police, 144; stereotypes of, 28–29; trauma from, 75–76; in United States, 148

wadud, amina, 27–28
Wahhabism, 46–47
War of the Worlds (Wells), 147
al-washm, 77–79
Wells, H. G., 147
Western civilization: culture from, 273–74; hegemony of, 10, 49, 102, 119, 262, 278–79; history to, 267–68; humanity and, 280–81;
Islamic studies in, 102; media in, 73–75; Othering in, 260–61; philosophy in, 272. *See also specific topics*
What Is Islam? (Ahmed), 8, 263–64
white gaze, 15–16, 18, 89
"Whiting H & G" (song), 152
Williams, Sonny Bill, 74, 92n19
Wittgenstein, Ludwig, 30
Woman (Jahan), 172–73
women: activism for, 183–85, 187; in Afghanistan, 67–68; Black, 76, 177; of color, 68–69; feminism, 26, 31–32, 37, 245n16, 258–59; identity of, 39–40; in India, 12, 179–80, p8; marginalization of, 186–87, 259; menstruation, 58; in Nation of Islam, 153–54; oppression of, 37–38, 53–54; in patriarchy, 83; political marginalization of, 18; Qur'an and, 26–28, 27–28, 31–32; in religion, 38–39; reproduction and, 167–68; in scholarship, 23; stereotypes of, 15–16; tattooing and, 69–70, 93n33. *See also* Muslim women
Wortham, Jenna, 81–82, 87

Youssef, Ramy, 32–34

zakka (alms), 30
Zawzanī, al-, 78
Zen Buddhism, 263
zikr, 110–11
Zula, Baba, 127–28

GPSR Authorized Representative: Easy Access System Europe, Mustamäe tee
50, 10621 Tallinn, Estonia, gpsr.requests@easproject.com

www.ingramcontent.com/pod-product-compliance
Lightning Source LLC
Chambersburg PA
CBHW022033290426
44109CB00014B/843